BRITAIN
AGAINST ITSELF

By Samuel H. Beer

BRITAIN AGAINST ITSELF

MODERN BRITISH POLITICS

BRITAIN
AGAINST
ITSELF

THE POLITICAL
CONTRADICTIONS
OF COLLECTIVISM

BY

SAMUEL H. BEER

faber and faber

First published in Great Britain in 1982
by Faber and Faber Limited
3 Queen Square London WC1N 3AU
First published in the United States of America 1982
Printed in the United States of America

British Library Cataloguing in Publication Data
Beer, Samuel H.
Britain against itself.
1. Great Britain—Politics and government—1964–
I. Title
320.941   JN234
ISBN 0-571-11918-2

Contents

Part Two: Class Decomposition

Part Three: The Collapse of Deference

Tables

Preface

When I asked a student recently why she was taking my course, she replied, "It was my father's advice. He said, 'Study England, a country on its knees. That is where America is going.' "

Not too long ago the usual reason for studying British politics would have been very different, but no less persuasive. Writing shortly before World War I, A. Lawrence Lowell of Harvard introduced his classic work on the British system with these words:

Measured by the standards of duration, absence of violent commotions, maintenance of law and order, general prosperity and contentment of the people, and by the extent of its influence on the institutions and political thought of other lands, the English Government has been one of the most remarkable in the world.

Nor were these merits lost upon the governed. "The typical Englishman," observed Professor Lowell

believes that his government is incomparably the best in the world. It is the thing above all others that he is proud of. He does not, of course, always agree with the course of policy pursued . . . but he is certain that the general form of government is well-nigh perfect.[1]

Not all American and British observers were quite so blandly uncritical as these remarks suggest. Still, Britain was very rich and powerful. It had been first in the industrial revolution and had made itself the dominant power in the world. That was bound to attract attention and incite inquiry. Above all, as Professor Lowell emphasized, its political achievement was exemplary. In the rise of self-government in modern times, it had led the way. In Britain one found not only "the workshop of the world" and the home of the

---

1. *The Government of England.* 2 vols. (New York, 1908), Preface.

Fleet, but also "the Mother of Parliaments." From the early years of the modern era, champions of political liberty in many lands had admired the British system and tried to imitate its ways. Bertrand de Jouvenel has remarked how in the early eighteenth century "my compatriots suddenly came to admire the governance of England and its praise was carried throughout Europe in the French language."[2] In France, Voltaire and Montesquieu were succeeded by Tocqueville, Taine, and Halévy in their admiration, not to say envy, of British institutions.

Other countries and later generations continued to provide admirers and imitators. Not least, among the Americans. The Fathers had adapted British representative institutions to their new foundation. Scholars studied British institutions, often declared them superior to American analogues and sometimes sought to import into this country features of the British legislature, administration, party system, and public policy.

Even as Britain's economy weakened and its position in the world was challenged by other nations, its political performance at home continued to win respect. During the interwar years, while much of Europe was swept by violent ideological conflict and in many countries self-government succumbed to dictatorship, Britain maintained the fundamental decencies, further democratized its institutions, and made substantial economic and social reforms. During the war with Hitler, British democracy, although slower to get under way, achieved a far higher level of mobilization than the Nazi dictatorship. "You defeated us," said Albert Speer, Hitler's minister for armaments, "because you made total war and we did not."

When peace had been won, Britain turned its attention to domestic affairs and, building on the advances of earlier years, began to create a social and economic order that promised to cope with many of the disorders and deprivations of industrial society. In those early postwar years, it might well have seemed that as Britain had led the way out of the age of absolutism, creating classic protections for the rights of individuals and extending the power of the people toward a democratic standard, so now it was setting an example to advanced industrial societies in its managed economy and welfare state.

2. *Government and Opposition* 1 (October, 1965): 135–136.

The evaluations of foreign observers reflected this view of Britain's achievements and promise. From the end of the war to the mid-sixties, judgments of American scholars were without exception highly favorable.[3] "Just as Alexis de Tocqueville travelled to America in 1831 to seek the secrets of democracy," wrote Richard Rose in 1965 on the opening page of his *Politics in England* "so today we might travel to England in search of the secrets of stable democracy." A book of my own published in the same year concluded on the same note of praise: "Happy the country in which consensus and conflict are ordered in a dialectic that makes of the political arena at once a market of interests and a forum for debate of fundamental moral concerns."[4]

This long course of favorable evaluation was abruptly and harshly reversed. From the mid-sixties to the present, a flood of criticism by British, American, and other foreign observers launched wave after wave of attack on British institutions. Some of the titles suggest the prevailing tone: "Suicide of a Nation?" "Can Britain Survive?" "The Future That Does Not Work," "Is Britain Dying?" These critiques have ranged widely over British society and into British history.[5] In virtually all, the political system has been a major target of attack. The rise of this massive dissatisfaction with the British polity is an intellectual puzzle that must excite the curiosity of any student of politics. How could it happen that a country which had governed itself so well for so long should suddenly do so poorly?

That question is surely a problem for me, as the author of a book in which I found that Britain, although no longer rich and powerful on the old scale, still excelled in self-government. This present work, therefore, is in the nature of a second volume of the book which first appeared in 1965 and which is being reprinted simultaneously. The

3. See Leon D. Epstein, "What Happened to the British Party Model?" *American Political Science Review*, 84, no. 1:9–22 and Dennis Kavanagh, "An American Science of British Politics," *British Journal of Political Science*, 22, no. 3:251–270.

4. *British Politics in the Collectivist Age* 2nd ed. (New York, 1965, 1969), p. 390. This book was published in London under the title of *Modern British Politics: A Study in Parties and Pressure Groups.* Henceforth I will refer to it as *Modern British Politics*, since that is the title that will be used in a new edition to be published simultaneously with this present volume.

5. They have been cogently summarized and classified in William B. Gwyn, "Jeremiahs and Pragmatists: Perceptions of British Decline," in William B. Gwyn and Richard Rose, *Britain: Progress and Decline* (New Orleans, 1980).

model of the "collectivist polity" that I set forth there still seems to me to give a good account of how the British system worked at that time. Moreover, I find in the political system, as sketched in that model, the source of the political failures of later years. My explanation of the sudden discontinuity in political performance does not repudiate the earlier analysis. Instead, I start from it to argue that the collectivist polity, that culminating success of political development in the postwar years, itself engendered the processes which converted success into failure and today seem to point toward a radically different system.

In contrast with various other accounts, I do not find the source of the trouble in the ignorant multitude, oppressive capitalists, selfish trade unionists, arrogant bureaucrats, egotistical politicians, misguided ministers, fuzzy traditionalists, or isolated élites. Indeed, in my version of the story there are no villains. Britain, I say, has been turned against itself by "the political contradictions of collectivism."

This self-contradictory course of recent British political development is the theme of the book. Although I have qualified my concern with Britain by occasional references to the United States, I have not tried to make a comparative study. At the same time, I should expect that, after allowing for the unique traits of different countries, one could find "the political contradictions of collectivism" at work in other modern democratic welfare states. In any case, I have stated my analysis in sufficiently general terms to make the test possible.

At first, as Britain's troubles mounted in the mid-sixties, it did seem as if Britain were alone in its discontents—in contrast with prosperous, stable, and efficient Germany, France, Sweden, and America. With the passage of time, troubled Britain has been getting more and more company. Even where the democratic welfare state has not become fully collectivist, it has often developed traits of politics and policy similar to those found in Britain. The consequent problems and efforts to deal with them find suggestive, if not exact, parallels in the British experience. As I write, for example, the dire consequences of Mrs. Thatcher's prodigious efforts to revive the British economy find ominous echoes among the policies and proposals of the Reagan regime.

In an ironic sense, Britain is maintaining its leadership. As it once showed the way toward democratic success, today it blazes the trail toward democratic failure. My analysis, however, does not dwell exclusively upon these gloomy inferences. The political contradictions of collectivism, as I shall try to show, also have a potential for democratic renewal. This possibility—I would claim no more for it—obliges anyone interested in the future of modern democracy to consult the British experience.

My debts are so many and so great that I can only begin to acknowledge them. Over the two decades with which this book is concerned I have continued to visit Britain periodically. During these visits, since I have a weakness for political rhetoric, I have probably spent an inordinate amount of time at political meetings and party conferences and in the gallery of the House of Commons. I have also tried to get into the detail, as well as to catch the flavor, of British political life from newspapers, periodicals, and watching television. But the main source of what I have to say in this book is a vast number of conversations, ranging from formal interviews with politicians and civil servants, to long talks with old friends at dinner, or brief exchanges with strangers on a bus. Their contribution can be only partially acknowledged in the text and footnotes.

I can in some degree make up for this failing by mentioning a few who were particularly helpful during my most recent visit of some months in the spring of 1979: Rodney Barker, Vernon Bogdanor, John Cole, Ivor Crewe, Bernard Crick, Bernard Donoghue, Michael Fraser, Jo Grimond, Barney Hayhoe, Denis Healey, Edward Heath, Hugh Jenkins, George W. Jones, William Keegan, Anthony King, Donald MacRae, Ben Roberts, Richard Rose, Peter Self, William Waldegrave, Shirley Williams, and Bob Worcester.

During this same visit the London School of Economics graciously made me an Academic Visitor with Library and Senior Common Room privileges and the governors of Birkbeck College appointed me an Honorary Research Fellow. I appreciated the good company as well as the facilities thus made available.

Given the scope of the book I have been obliged to rely heavily upon what other people have written. Since it is in essence an essay, I have kept down the number of footnotes, but trust that the references I do cite will express my thanks to the writers on whom I have mainly relied. I am astounded at the number of people who at one or another stage of its composition have read all or part of the manuscript and given me helpful comment. I must acknowledge a special debt to Douglas Ashford, Dennis Kavanagh, and Anthony King for their thorough and searching criticism. I also benefited from comment by Lawrence D. Brown, Henry M. Drucker, Leon D. Epstein, Vivien Hart, Hugh Heclo, Stephen Holmes, Joel Krieger, Janet Morgan, Philip Norton, Jorgen Rasmussen, and Robert Taylor. Howard Margolis and Jerome Rothenberg tutored me in some of the elementary notions of public choice theory. Although nominally my assistant, Peter Hall (of Harvard) was more a colleague, calling on his own wide knowledge of British affairs to challenge my assumptions and my inferences and to set straight and strengthen my assertions of fact. In the later stages of preparation, Ian Marsh was a great help. My thanks also go out to Yvonne Quinlan for her rapid typing and unfailing cooperation.

SAMUEL H. BEER

October 1981

BRITAIN
AGAINST ITSELF

INTRODUCTION

The Penalty of Success

From the end of the war until the mid-1960s, the record of British politics was a story of solid democratic success. Building on prewar foundations, successive governments created a welfare state and managed economy which provided proximate solutions to some of the worst problems of industrialism and the class system. These accomplishments in policy, moreover, were achieved by a political process that was a model of successful public choice, as the sharp partisan differences of the 1940s were converted by mutual adjustment into the consensus of the 1950s. And to cap it all, this story of success in policy and politics was crowned with a record of economic growth and full employment surpassing that of any previous period in British history.

The mood was euphoric. In 1959 Harold Macmillan returned the Tories to power under the slogan "You're Having It Good. Have It Better. Vote Conservative." and the data was gathered for the happy conclusions of Almond and Verba's classic study of the "civic culture."[1] In achievement and attitudes, the contrast could hardly be greater with the discontented, quarrelsome, unsteady, ineffective, self-defeating seventies.

It has been a curious sight: Britain, that exemplar of "stable democracy," where order and change have for so long flourished in a sane and civilized balance, unable to make up its mind. The figure of speech may be a bit too anthropomorphic. But it brings out the main problem of British politics: not ideological extremism, class war, unwillingness to change, selfishness, power-seeking, or ignorance, but a fragmentation of political life that has prevented the

1. Gabriel A. Almond and Sidney Verba, *The Civic Culture: Political Attitudes and Democracy in Five Nations* (Princeton, 1963).

1

abundant good sense available at all levels of the polity from being reflected in the process of public choice. Repeatedly, because of this sheer numerical pluralism—if I may be permitted the pleonasm—the dictates of collective rationality have been disregarded and the self-defeating logic of short-run self-interest has won out. In this sense the failure has been not that the public mind chose wrongly, but that it did not choose at all. The outcome has been incoherence and immobilism; drift not mastery. It is not hyperbole to call it a paralysis of public choice. That indeed was a transformation of British politics.

This transformation was abrupt and unexpected. No social scientist, Marxist or bourgeois, predicted its occurrence. In the 1950s the left wing of the Labour party still looked forward to a centrally planned, bureaucratic socialist society governed by a mass party of "workers by hand and brain" and supported by a cohesive trade union movement. In 1963 liberal optimism suffused Almond and Verba's assessment of the prospects of the civic culture in Britain. In 1965, in my *Modern British Politics,* I certainly saw no further into the future. Yet today in hindsight one can detect the sources of transformation in the political system of those years. That eminently successful "collectivist polity" produced out of itself the conditions that caused its later failure.

My concern, I must emphasize, is political and in two senses. In the first place I am interested in the failures of the British political system as a mechanism by which the British public decide how to concert their behavior and dispose of their resources for public purposes—that is, the failures of public choice. I am not primarily interested in the merits of the policies that were decided on, but rather in the quality of the process by which decisions on policy were made, and, especially, failed to be made. I am not, for instance, concerned with showing that at times British Governments "spent too much money" and so contributed to inflation. That is for economists to say. The question I ask of any spending outcome is whether it was the result of choice, or of drift. Can we say that this outcome corresponded pretty well with the preferences of the British public, or was it rather something they did not want, but unintentionally brought about through defects of the system by which they expressed their wishes? Such a loss of control of decision-making has at times, I am confident, led to excessive spending and thus exacerbated Britain's inflationary problem. In this sense, I would say there have been political causes for some of Britain's economic difficulties. Such a connection, if established, is important but nevertheless incidental to my central concern with the political process itself. Whether or not a democratic people are getting what they want, and if not why not, is in itself an important question, quite apart from effects on their economic life.

Secondly, I am interested in tracing this kind of political failure to its sources in the political system. Needless to say, I fully recognize the impact of many other forces. How much easier life would have been for ministers if it had not been for the Organization of Petroleum Exporting Countries (OPEC)! If only the Phillips curve—that once popular theorem that there is a close inverse relationship between the rate of unemployment and the size of wage increases—had fulfilled its promise as the basis for fiscal policy! Surely, Britain's exposed position in the international economy has confronted her Governments with complex and difficult problems that have been less urgent in more self-contained economies. In stressing political analysis I do not mean to deny the influence of these and other nonpolitical conditions that tended to impede and disrupt decision making in the 1970s. So far as I say much about them, it is that their negative impact was enhanced by the other specifically political dysfunctions produced by the collectivist system.

I will conclude this introductory statement by sketching the order of the argument. The terms will be more fully explained as the argument is developed, but this preliminary look should help familiarize the reader with the main headings. As a further help I also have, at the risk of gross oversimplification, attempted a diagram showing, so to speak, the principal players and their positions:

The collectivist polity	The contradictions
1. The choice mechanism: party government and the new group politics	pluralistic stagnation

welfare state ——————→ consumer
party government ←parliamentary representation← groups
←functional representation←
managed economy ——————→ producer groups

2. The social foundations: the class system   class decomposition

3. The ideal foundations: the civic culture   the new populism

As described in *Modern British Politics,* the collectivist polity had three parts: its ideal foundations in the civic culture; its social foundations in the class system; and its choice mechanism in the system of party government and the new group politics. If one follows the fortunes of each of these over the past twenty years or so, one can identify a set of interrelated changes which, issuing from the collectivist system, have transformed it. After looking more closely at the nature of the problem—the paralysis of public choice—we will examine how it has been produced by these contradictions under the following headings: pluralistic stagnation, a dysfunction of the choice mechanism; class decomposition, a development of the social foundations; and the new populism, which impelled the transformation of the civic culture.

The essential political failure was a failure of the choice mechanism. Intrinsic to the collectivist polity was a heightened group politics. This rising pluralism so fragmented the decision-making system as to impair its power of acting for the long-run interests of its members. At the same time, collectivism in politics and policy contributed to the decomposition of the class basis of the two major parties. With its basis in social identification so weakened, party government increasingly failed to integrate the pluralism of the new group politics and to mobilize the consent of its members. Yet neither the decay of the social foundations of party nor the self-defeating tendency of pluralistic stagnation is comprehensible until one takes into account the way in which the new populism undermined traditional authority. And that crisis of authority itself was occasioned, if not provoked, by the centralized bureaucratic polity. In this way the collectivist polity, that culminating success of political development during the postwar years, engendered the processes which converted success into failure and today seem to point toward a radically different system.

The order of the argument, it will have been observed, is opposite to the logic of the analysis. Analytically, the fundamental change is the change in political culture. The rise of the new populism and the coincident decline of the civic culture constitute the main background conditions that precipitated the other dysfunctions. In giving this emphasis to ideal factors I continue the viewpoint of the original study which took political culture to be ''one of the main variables of a political system.''[2] This approach makes the third part of this book, "The Collapse of Deference," its most important part. The central event in that discussion is the broad cultural revolution which swept through Britain during the sixties and the seventies, profoundly affecting values in just about every sphere of life: dress, music, manners, sport, education, sex, marriage, crime, work, and race relations.

Politics was not, could not be, exempt. The principal thesis of those pages is that the romantic revolt that exploded in Britain in the early sixties also transformed political attitudes. The decline of deference, along with other archaic attitudes long associated with it in Britain's unique political culture, has been the effect most commonly reported. The assault on traditionalism also had a positive side. The decline of the civic culture was grounded in the rise of a new populism. In its negative aspect the new populism has produced failure and frustration by undermining the collectivist polity. In its positive aspect it embodies values of radical democracy which in the future—just conceivably—could constitute the ideal foundation for a new political order.

While I have, in this way, given primary emphasis to the role of cultural change, the other changes, structural in nature, must be fitted into the analysis. It will be convenient therefore to consider them first in order to make clear what the consequences of the cultural revolution have been.

THE COLLECTIVIST ACHIEVEMENT

Government is one of the least perfectible of human institutions. We will not understand what ails the British system today, however, until we recognize its very considerable achievements during the first postwar years—as measured by comparison with other countries and by what has been historically possible. As I have pointed out in the Preface, one index of political success is the evaluation of foreign observers, and from the end of the war in 1945 to the mid-1960s, the assessments by American political scientists were admiring. Mainstream political science, moreover, absorbed the lessons of the

2. *Modern British Politics,* p. xii.

British achievement and elaborated a theoretical model to explain it.[3] In the 1950s students of comparative politics commonly distinguished between the stable democracies motored by two party systems and the unstable regimes immobilized by multiparty systems. Nor was such self-defeating fragmentation confined to the continent of Europe with its multipartism. It was also seen as a failing of American politics where a nominally two-party system did not conceal or control a disorderly array of powerful pressure groups. The exemplar was Britain where a stable party dualism provided Governments with cohesive majorities supporting distinctive outlooks which enabled the democratic electorate to make an effective choice. Party government was the key concept of this model.

This evaluation was reversed abruptly—indeed, with "indecent haste," according to Dennis Kavanagh—between the early and the later 1960s.[4] Those years were precisely the hinge of time on which the door swung shut on the successful politics of the postwar period and opened on the self-defeating politics of the 1970s. We will more clearly perceive the nature of that political failure if we first characterize the earlier achievement and note the way its mechanisms began to turn against themselves.

Party Government

The general election of 1945 was one of those rare instances in which programmatic party government launched a transformation of the social and economic order by means of an electoral victory.[5] Enjoying a huge majority, Labour took power in the name of a manifesto which, proudly declaring the party's "ultimate purpose" to be "the establishment of the Socialist Commonwealth of Great Britain," set forth a series of detailed pledges generated by nearly half-a-century of pressure and argument within "the Movement." While in office from 1945 to 1951, the Attlee Government took its domestic legislative program faithfully and explicitly from the manifesto, so that for virtually every paragraph of pledges, a corresponding act can

3. Cogently set forth in Gabriel A. Almond, "Comparative Political Systems," *Journal of Politics,* 18:391–409.
4. *loc. cit.,* p. 265.
5. *Modern British Politics,* Chapter VI.

be found in the statute book. Seven acts of nationalization; the establishment of the National Health Service; a vast expansion of the social insurance system—this selection of major accomplishments will suggest the massive legislative record.

The origins of many social services can be traced to an earlier generation; precedents for nationalization can be found in the interwar years; and in originating or developing both sorts of reform, the Conservatives had played an important role. But Labour's actions, like its promises, were distinctively different from what the Conservatives offered in 1945, or what they would have done if they had won that election. Symbolizing the difference, and in a sense quantifying it, was the question of the magnitude of public expenditure. When in the late 1940s the Conservatives did adapt to the widely popular social commitments of Labour, the prospect of huge continuing public spending was the most difficult issue for decision within the party.[6] Nor can one easily exaggerate the importance of the consequences, many unintended, which in time did flow from this decision by the Conservative party to assume the incalculable burdens of the welfare state then being constructed.

One immediate effect was to enable the party to enter into a competition for the votes of the emerging groups of beneficiaries of the developing social programs. In itself the prior financial commitment was not an effort to woo the votes of some particular clientele. It was a decision of a more basic kind: a shift in the rationale of party policy as a whole, moving it toward premises from which more particular appeals could be launched. These appeals were made with imagination and success in later elections, beginning with the many specific pledges of the 1950 manifesto regarding the health service, pensions, education, housing, the farm program, and, above all, "full employment as the first aim of a Conservative Government."[7] The new assurances were in pronounced contrast with the restrained prospects held out by the party five years earlier in *Mr Churchill's Declaration of Policy to the Electors*.

During the two decades after the war, major new policy changes were made from time to time by British Governments. Usually, how-

6. *Modern British Politics*, pp. 304, 306.
7. *This is the Road: The Conservative and Unionist Party's Policy*, General Election 1950, p. 8.

ever, these innovations took place, not as in 1945, after and because a general election had turned one party out of office and put another in. They occurred rather between elections as the parties adapted to the realities of governing and of winning votes. A process of mutual adjustment brought the parties closer together in what they said they would do and, even more, in what they actually did in office. Their nearly equal electoral strength sharpened their rivalry and heightened their readiness to make such adjustments. Thanks to these adjustments, when the Opposition did take power in 1951 and 1964, continuity in basic policy outlook was maintained.

Although general elections, therefore, did not mark the major shifts in policy, party government still operated to effectuate public choice, as the two main rivals for power sought to anticipate the drift of public favor. With awkward leads and lags, the two parties wheeled in unison to Left and to Right. Throughout the 1950s Conservative Governments maintained very much the same priorities in social policy as had been established by Labour.[8] The ways the two parties approached management of the economy were so much alike that they could be playfully characterized by one term, "Butskellism," created by joining parts of the names of two chancellors of the exchequer, the Conservatives' R. A. Butler and Labour's Hugh Gaitskell. Toward the end of the decade Labour, after repeated defeats, sought to broaden its appeal regardless of class and explicitly to woo the many beneficiary groups of the welfare state.[9] About the same time, the Macmillan Government, departing from mere economic management, adopted a new *dirigiste* strategy. It was followed with some variations by the successor Government under Harold Wilson.

This convergence of goals and methods between the two parties corresponded to a wide acceptance among voters of the new patterns of government and policy. Observers spoke of "the end of ideology." That was correct, not in the sense that people and parties no longer entertained ideas about the desirable social and political order, but in the sense that they came to share an agreement on that order amounting to a consensus. This consensus, the creation of no single party, was nonetheless the work of party government in that it had

8. *Modern British Politics*, pp. 352–358.
9. *ibid.*, pp. 240–242.

been produced by the interactions of the party system. The partisan choice of 1945, elaborated and modified by that interaction, had been converted into the general assent of the late 1950s. Over the years, party government had given rise to an agreement on the common good which, to be sure, fell far short of unanimity, but which did accomplish the aggregation of the preferences of a large majority of the electorate.

This was no small achievement, especially when viewed against the background of democratic failure in many European countries during the interwar period. In the 1920s and 1930s it had often seemed as if democratic choice was condemned to be paralyzed, or overwhelmed by ideological strife, or both. Even in Britain, some had feared that in an age of competition between "socialist" and "capitalist" parties, gross reversals of policy at each swing of the political pendulum would threaten the democratic order. Instead when the test came after the war, Britain went from strength to strength, demonstrating the hopeful possibilities of "stable democracy."

As the principal moving force in this development, party government performed three functions often attributed to it by political scientists: the functions of choice, aggregation, and consensus. In the first place, the party system gave the voters a chance to impress their preferences upon the course of government. In 1945 the parties were sufficiently polarized to enable the voters by choosing Labour to alter the economic and social order in a quite fundamental way. Secondly, each party was a coalition, aggregating the preferences of a wide spectrum of groups. This aggregation, moreover, was not a mere summation of particularistic interests, but was oriented by a distinctive outlook on the common good. In preferring one party to another, therefore, the voter could express not only his interests, but also his aspirations. In this respect the parties met Giovanni Sartori's specification that although a party can only be a part of the whole, it performs a function of the whole if and because it is moved by a conception of the "general interest."[10]

Finally, the functions of choice and aggregation were, so to speak, perfected insofar as the interactions of the party system moved the

10. Giovanni Sartori, *Parties and Party Systems: A Framework for Analysis* (Cambridge, Eng., 1976) 1:25.

preferences of the public toward a consensus.[11] In this way Britain's parties served the country well, enabling a democratic public to refashion its economic and social order in such a way that the end product was general assent. In political history, of course, there is no such thing as an "end product," but at most only brief culminations. Yet the substantial consensus achieved by the late 1950s in Britain was durable. A generation later in 1979 an election survey revealed that when given the alternative of lower taxes along with corresponding cuts in service, 70 percent of respondents preferred to keep the services.

I have called the political system that emerged from this historical process "collectivist."[12] Two aspects of my usage of that term should be emphasized. First, I use it to refer not only to a pattern of policy, but also to a pattern of politics. As the diagram on p. 3 indicates, the collectivist polity consists of the programs of the managed economy and the welfare state and also the political parties and pressure groups which have shaped those programs and in turn have been shaped by them. Policies and politics continually interact in the choice mechanism.

Secondly, when I use the term collectivism, I am thinking of a phase of political development that supervened upon the more individualist phase of the nineteenth century. That is conventional enough. I do not, however, call collectivist any degree or kind of intervention in the economy. I am concerned rather to identify that thrust of policy, emerging in this century, toward control over the economic and social order as a whole. The agents of such intervention may be socialist or Tory and their social inclinations accordingly more or less egalitarian. They have in common, however, a readiness to assume overall responsibility. The political formations through which they act, likewise, stand in contrast to those of the individualist phase. A comparison with the policies and politics that have typified British liberalism will illustrate my meaning.

In the early years of this century, Liberal governments were responsible for pioneering measures of social reform. Later, although

---

11. Sartori observes: ". . . the centripetal mechanics of twopartism *creates* consensus," *op. cit.,* p. 191.
12. For an elaboration of the concept of collectivism as I use it, see *Modern British Politics,* Chapter III, "Collectivist Politics: Socialist and Tory Democracy."

their electoral fortunes declined, the Liberals remained the party of
ideas as John Maynard Keynes and William Beveridge developed
the intellectual basis for an advanced liberalism that would cope with
the economic and social problems of an industrial society. During the
postwar years, these ideas were utilized by the people who framed
the programs of the collectivist polity. But Keynesian and Beveridgean thought did not itself require or imply the centralized, planned,
corporatistic state which was produced in the late 1940s and 1950s
and which was accepted by both Gaitskell and Macmillan.

In policy the thrust of collectivism was toward government intervention in and responsibility for the economic and social order as a
whole. We have seen the Conservative party make this "collectivist
commitment" in the late 1940s by accepting the incalculable financial burdens of the emerging welfare state. We shall have occasion
to examine its consequences in the proliferation of programs legitimated by this ideal premise of public policy. Moreover, and this is
the crucial point for our concern, the political instruments by which
these patterns of policy were sustained were also themselves collectivist and departed from the liberal model. Even in the era of advanced
liberalism, the Liberals remained strongly individualist in the way
they thought about political organization and in the way they actually
conducted their party and political affairs. In theory they were hostile
to class-based politics and in practice drew their adherents (though
not their activists) from all strata. While their Radicals tried to develop
a mass membership and give it a voice in party policy, Liberal
behavior outside Parliament as within it normally fell far short of the
heights of cohesion reached by Labour and the Conservatives.[13]

The Labour party's image of itself sprang from its conception of
the class nature of society. In this view political divisions derive
from economic class divisions which, in an industrialized economy,
are essentially two—workers and owners. Such fundamental duality
aggregates on each side the complex pluralisms of occupational and
other economic groups. Moreover, it roots the solidarity of the party
not merely in a meeting of individual minds, but in objective membership in a class with an overriding common interest. Here are firm

13. These passages summarize the discussion in *Modern British Politics,* Chapter
II, "Liberal and Radical Politics," and Chapter III, "Collectivist Politics: Socialist
and Tory Democracy."

grounds for joining and sticking with the party of your class and for cooperating with the demands which a Government representing that class may impose upon "the workers by hand and brain" and upon their organizations in the trade union movement.

The Conservative party, descending from the Tories of the seventeenth century, had a more complex tradition, with origins in the premodern Tory ideal of the hierarchic, corporate, Christian society. Old traditions of strong government, paternalism, and the organic society eased the Conservative acceptance of the massive reassertion of state power and helped justify a role for Conservative leadership in bringing it about. Old ideals of authority and deference were also adapted to political organization in the era of mass suffrage. Tories too entertained a theory of class politics in which the need for leadership at all levels and spheres of activity justified multiple gradations of inequality. In this view class did not divide, but united the polity. The demonstrated ability of Conservative candidates of the upper and middle classes to win millions of votes from the working class suggested that these preconceptions were widely shared by their countrymen. By a quite different route, the Tory theory of politics, like that of Labour, legitimized the collectivist polity's massive concentration of political power. Supported by such ideal and social foundations, party government was greatly strengthened in performing its functions of choice, aggregation, and consensus.

The New Group Politics

One other feature of the collectivist polity needs to be mentioned: the new group politics.[14] In the late nineteenth and early twentieth centuries, the economic groups produced by a highly industrialized economy began to exert influence in British politics. They were especially important in the formation of the Labour party which in its earliest days was little more than "a coalition of pressure groups."[15] From this "old" group politics, the "new" group politics was distinguished by its close and continuing connection with government and especially by the extent to which the groups owed

14. *Modern British Politics,* Chapter XII, "The New Group Politics."
15. *ibid.,* Chapter IV, "A Coalition of Pressure Groups."

their origin and expansion to programs initiated by government itself. In the welfare state and managed economy, while the lobby still sometimes created the program, the program also often created the lobby. Government intervention itself redefined the interests of participants and mobilized different clienteles.

Before the war, for instance, farmers like landowners voted almost exclusively for the Conservatives from whom alone they could expect favor toward their hopes for protectionism and controlled markets. When, however, the Attlee Government continued the new and heavily subsidized scheme of "guaranteed prices and assured markets" set up for wartime purposes, Labour developed warm relations with farmers and acquired a respectable following in rural areas. Since the new policy, moreover, required the cooperation in an organized way of the actual managers, the National Farmers Union, once a small and struggling organization, vastly expanded its membership and made the farmers rather than the landowners the dominant political force in agriculture.

In the collectivist polity, government undertook not only to lay down the rules under which individuals and groups would pursue their own purposes, but also increasingly to act for the sake of certain specific outcomes, economic and social, which had been adopted as public purposes. In order to achieve these outcomes, government could hardly do without the cooperation of the groups being so used, as in the case of the farmers with whom the agriculture ministry was obliged to negotiate if it was to secure the desired level of food output. In pursuit of specific objectives, such as an export drive for motorcars to improve the balance of payments, or of broad goals, such as restraint of inflationary wage demands, Governments had to win something more than the sullen acquiescence of the critical producer groups in command of the vital sectors of the economy. In this way the managed economy multiplied the syndicalist power of producer groups far beyond what it had been in the liberal economy.[16]

As we have seen, the consumer groups that enjoyed the benefits and bore the burdens of the welfare state loomed large in the electoral calculations of competing parties.[17] These groups too had a

16. *Modern British Politics,* Chapter XII, "The New Group Politics," 'Producer Groups and the Managed Economy.'

17. *ibid.,* 'Consumer groups and the Welfare State.'

kind of power over government beyond the votes they could command. Coercive law alone, for instance, would not suffice to make taxpayers bear their immense burdens in the welfare state. Consumer groups, such as those being educated or healed or helped to overcome some disadvantage, also had to cooperate willingly with the services provided, if those services were to realize their public purpose.

A civil servant with long and wide experience has summed up this paradox of power:

. . . as the scope of the Government's involvement in the life of the country gets wider and wider, the more the Government has to rely on the willingness of people who are not its employees to do what it wants done. There is a sense in which, contrary to the general belief, as Government intervention expands, the power of the Government (Ministers and civil servants together) actually diminishes; that is to say the ratio between the responsibilities the Government has taken on and its power to discharge those responsibilities becomes less favourable. Certainly my own feeling, and I suspect that of many of my colleagues, is not a consciousness of growing Government power over the last 10 or 15 years, but of diminishing power—and I think that is one reason for it.[18]

In a free country, the enormous new powers that government exercises over producer and consumer groups at the same time puts these groups in a position to frustrate those powers by refusing their cooperation and consent. Since action by the collectivist polity ramifies so widely and intricately through the whole society, the polity cannot make an effective choice unless it can mobilize consent on a no less wide and complex scale.

This concern with the problem of consent is shared by two political leaders who criticize British politics from opposite perspectives. "It is of course the breakdown of consent," writes Sir Ian Gilmour,

18. Richard Wilding (Deputy Secretary of the Civil Service Department), "The Civil Servant as Policy Adviser and Manager," *Public Administration Bulletin* (London). Special issue: Pressure Groups, Ministers, and Civil Servants. no. 32 (April, 1980):36. In what I like to call "Herring's law," E. P. Herring made the same point in his classic study of government regulation in the United States. "The greater the degree of detailed and technical control the government seeks to exert over industrial and commercial interests," he wrote, "the greater must be their degree of consent and active participation." *Public Administration and the Public Interest* (New York, 1936) p. 192.

the High Tory intellectual and former Conservative minister, "that is the root of our troubles. . . . Because the state lacks authority (by which I mean the ability to gain consent), it is not able to control the most powerful corporations in the state—the trade unions. Indeed to some extent they control the state." From that diagnosis he goes on to suggest how "the forces of legitimacy" may be strengthened and "the constitution . . . properly designed to mobilize popular consent."[19] The leader of Labour's left wing, Anthony Wedgwood (Tony) Benn, likewise holds that changes—rather different ones—must be made, or "the consent necessary to run our society will not be available." "Authoritarianism in politics or industry," he finds, "just doesn't work any more. Governments can no longer control either the organizations or the people by using the old methods." So deep and serious is that loss, he feels, that "the social contract" on which "parliamentary democracy by universal suffrage" was founded must be renegotiated on a new basis "before it can win general assent again."[20]

THE PARALYSIS OF PUBLIC CHOICE

Party government operating in the context of the new group politics created the collectivist polity and gave rise to the consensus of the late 1950s. It is not immediately evident why such an outcome should be the source of trouble. A moving equilibrium between two parties in basic agreement, but accommodating policy to the demands of groups of consumers and producers, may seem a bit dull. It may also have considerable appeal to those who live in more exciting times. There is much to be said for the politics of the Ins versus the Outs and of Tweedledum and Tweedledee.

The rest of this book will be devoted to showing how the collectivist polity did in fact undermine itself so as to produce the frustrations of the 1970s and 1980s. I will conclude this chapter with a brief sketch of the analysis and the narrative.

The danger arises from the consensus. Insofar as the alternatives championed by the parties come to be much the same, the electorate

19. *Inside Right: A Study of Conservatism* (London, 1977) pp. 198–199.
20. Tony Benn, *Arguments for Socialism,* Chris Mullin, ed. (London, 1979) pp. 49, 110–111.

is deprived of a choice between different views of the common good. Choice remains regarding those particular interests legitimated by the new consensus. Group politics therefore will flourish. Indeed it is likely to take on new life as groups, formerly attached to one or the other party, because of their position in its ordering of preferences, now become detachable. The competing party is able to detach them because it has adopted a rationale of policy legitimizing a broader electoral appeal and can now desert the battle of opposing social philosophies in favor of small raids on interest groups. The most striking instance of this tendency, it has seemed to me, was that glossy product of Gaitskellite revisionism put out in 1958 and entitled *Your Personal Guide to the Future Labour Offers You.* Conveniently thumb-indexed with references to "Your Home," "Your Job," "Education," "Health," "Age Without Fear," it enabled tenants, workers, patients, pensioners, and other prospective beneficiaries of Labour's largesse to turn directly to the promises beamed to them in accordance with the findings of the new science of survey research.[21]

Given the consensus, the danger arises insofar as the two parties may compete for group support with no other object than winning office. The logic is to promise anything which you think will bring you votes without regard for the mutual compatibility of your promises or their long-run consequences for the country. In such a process the parties may merely register group demands or they may manufacture them. In either case, they do not restrain or order or direct those demands. The upshot is that immobilism and incoherence in public choice against which party government was supposed to be the safeguard. Indeed, if the rivals are "strong" parties in the sense of being organizationally efficient (as well as normatively unrestrained) the results will be even worse, since the winners can attempt to keep their promises and so will probably make even more emphatic their self-defeating consequences.

Needless to say cynicism in such a degree did not arise among British politicians in the hey-day of collectivism. Yet the tendencies were present. The competition of these two parties, exacerbated by their nearly even electoral strength, was intense. The normative

21. *Modern British Politics,* pp. 241–2 and below p. 32.

premises of the collectivist polity, moreover, by lifting the restraints on government responsibility of the precollectivist liberal state, legitimated a much greater scope for expansive competition.

The 1960s was the time of transition. It was in those years that the pressures generated within the collectivist polity substantially and visibly escaped from public control. By the later sixties what had previously appeared as the common ground of a new social and economic order began to look like a swamp of pluralistic stagnation.

In the face of this situation the political system was not inert. The parties did respond and with an identical reversal of tactics, each attempting to escape from the collectivist consensus by a militant assertion of basic partisan values. In the 1970s sharp ideological conflict at elections led to discontinuities in policy when the Opposition took power—only to be followed by a forced return to the policies of the consensus. The dominant motif in the development of policy changed from right turn and left turn to the U-turn.

The best known U-turn, which we shall later examine in detail, was that of Edward (Ted) Heath. It was he who in 1970 first gave general elections the sharp adversary character they had not had for many years. With painstaking care—at one time he had thirty-six committees at work on party policy—he prepared his new departures and set them forth in a manifesto with a detail and length reminiscent of the old Fabians. In office he persisted for a year-and-a-half with his neoliberal thrust proudly redeeming pledge after pledge. His U-turn began with the relaxation of budgetary restraint under the pressure of unemployment, and then curved back toward the consensus in a familiar pattern of state intervention.

The succeeding Labour Government also executed its dramatic U-turn. In preparing its program while in opposition and in carrying out its promises when first in power, the party made a sharply radical swing as trade unions and the left wing in a brief, unusual, and irresistible combination converged in their demands. The terrible year of 1975 when inflation reached an annual rate of 26 percent, however, obliged Labour to reverse direction and to resort to the old painful remedies of spending cuts, tight money, and wage restraint.

Neither effort to escape from the consensus succeeded. About this time Michael Stewart, an economist who had advised the first Wilson Government, summed up:

The Left regard as essential a drastic move towards far greater state control of the economy; the Right regard as essential a drastic move towards a free market economy. Such claims cannot be disproved; indeed, they may even be correct. But one thing that is conclusively demonstrated by the history of the last decade or so is the impossibility of achieving drastic change—in either direction—by democratic procedures: the resistance is too strong.[22]

His implication was that solutions would have to come from further effort within the political and policy bounds of the consensus. In the spring of 1978 one might well have agreed. It did appear as if the Labour Government (with help from the International Monetary Fund) had at last got a grip on how to make the collectivist polity work. In spite of its bogus rhetoric, the social contract between the unions and the Government had helped reduce wage pressures on the price level, while the astringent regime of Denis Healey at the Treasury had imposed severe restraints on the growth of public spending. And after falling during the first years of this Labour Government, the real living standards of working people began to rise in 1977 and 1978.[23] Then came the wage explosion of the following winter. Public expenditure also resumed its seemingly inexorable growth, as in the renewed trend upward of local authority spending and staff in 1978.[24] The pressures that for a decade had paralyzed the power of public choice had not yet been brought under control. Neither drastic nor consensual solutions seemed possible.

In the general election of 1979 Mrs. Thatcher won an opportunity for the Conservatives to make another escape attempt. Elected on an emphatically neoliberal program she made control of the money supply her principal instrument for conquering inflation. Otherwise, her program resembled Mr. Heath's: lower taxes, less government spending, a reduced budget deficit, and withdrawal from intervention in the economy. As a departure from the economic and social policies of the collectivist consensus, this strategy represented a "drastic move." After two years her chances for economic success seemed slight. But her political success in overcoming the "resis-

22. *The Jekyll and Hyde Years: Politics and Economic Policy since 1964* (London, 1977) p. 246.
23. Peter Townsend, "The Fall and Rise of Living Standards," *New Society,* 5 April 1979, p. 24.
24. *Local Authority Joint Manpower Watch: December 1978 Return* (Department of the Environment, London, 10 April 1979).

tances'' to her "drastic move" was hardly greater. Insisting that "the lady's not for turning," Mrs Thatcher persisted in the fight for her antiinflation policy despite the heavy economic, social, and political costs. Yet when we compare her performance with the main items of her original policy, we shall see that the Government had executed not one but several U-turns.[25] Pluralistic stagnation continued to paralyze public choice.

There is a puzzle here. A young friend of mine, who was doing some research in Britain, put it best: "I often ask myself how all these intelligent, decent people manage to make so many mistakes."

25. Below pp. 214–218.

PART ONE

Pluralistic Stagnation

CHAPTER I

The Benefits Scramble

I use the concept of pluralistic stagnation to characterize and to analyze the processes of self-defeating action that have constituted the political failure of the collectivist polity. The term is useful in part because it has an intellectual history which suggests the sorts of concrete situations to which it may be applied and which also places it in the developing thoughts of political scientists about party government and the problems of pluralism. Originally, the term "pluralistic stagnation" was used to describe the paralysis of public choice that resulted from the large number of political parties and the general fragmentation of political action in Germany during the interwar years.[1] The German term is *die pluralistische Stockung,* from the verb, *stocken,* "to stagnate, to cease to run or circulate, as when blood coagulates." Even more aptly it is used to refer to a traffic jam.

With regard to the Weimar Republic, pluralistic stagnation meant the tendency of the Reichstag to be immobilized because any majority was so divided that it could not agree on a policy, while no coherent policy had a sufficiently wide appeal to attract a majority. To put the matter starkly: if a Government had a majority, it had no policy; if it had a policy, it had no majority. All Governments were based on coalitions. Moreover, coalitions that added up to a majority were hard to put together and quick to fall apart. Thus in the decade 1920–30, there were twelve Governments with an average life of ten months. For almost half that time these Governments included only a minority in their parliamentary base, mustering a majority on cru-

1. I picked up the term and its usage in the early 1950s from Prof. Sigmund Neumann when working with him on his symposium, *Modern Political Parties: Approaches to Comparative Politics* (Chicago, 1956).

cial votes thanks to the "tolerance" of another party or parties. As Governments so weakly based failed to cope with rising economic and political disorder, the extremes of Left and Right gained until finally between them Communists and Nazis included so large a proportion of the Reichstag that no Government with majority support could be found. This "negative" majority brought about a complete stalemate of public choice.

Needless to say, the dictatorship that then arose was shaped by demonic forces that far transcend the terms of the present analysis. It would be a wild non sequitur to infer that political fragmentation today threatens to drive Britain toward the fate of Weimar. Yet abstracting from these catastrophic possibilities, the experience of the distracted German democracy of those years is suggestive. Pluralism is a blessed word in the liberal vocabulary. The immobility and incoherence of government under the Weimar Republic are a classic warning that there can be too much of this good thing.

PLURALISM AND PUBLIC CHOICE

The term, pluralistic stagnation, has not only a descriptive but also an analytic use since it suggests the causal sequence between pluralism and the failure of public choice. It is, however, ambiguous, and more precise meanings need to be extracted from it. First, the function respectively of large numbers and of conflicting purposes should be distinguished. In the case of the Weimar Republic, the large number of parties did contribute to the likelihood of paralysis by putting each party in a minority and so multiplying the number of alliances that had to be arranged in order to provide a parliamentary base for governing. Yet the harshness of conflict among these often ideological and class-based parties also meant that even if there had been only a few, it would still have been very hard to create the political base for sustained and effective choice. In Britain today some observers fear the rise of a new bitterness in political and social conflict. And in the 1970s the temper of ideological conflict between parties—and within them—did sharpen. But a pluralism of conflicting ideologies and interests, while real enough, was not the root of the problem.

In another form, pluralistic stagnation arises not from irreconcilable conflict but from the opposite, viz., defense of a quiescent status quo. The participants, many in number, defend a variety of interests. Individual groups may be so placed strategically in the managed economy as to be able to veto government action. Or perhaps several, which view some proposal or set of proposals as injurious, constitute an electoral threat strong enough to prevent change. The cumulative effect is to slow down or stop new departures. In a review of *Modern British Politics,* a British observer so viewed the political problem:

The interests have grown too strong. Try to introduce change into any British institution and the log jam piles up at once. . . . The interests are so faithfully represented and bring such pressure to bear indicating how far each is prepared to move—which is usually little distance at all—that the degree of movement is negligible.[2]

In a country like Britain where a small "c" conservatism pervades all parties, classes, and regions, such defensive pluralism can be readily illustrated. From the early 1960s the "stagnant traditionalism" of managers, unions, and bureaucrats has drawn the fire of critics who have held it responsible for economic failure. In his scholarly survey of pressure politics in Britain, Graham Wootton has identified a wide range of cases in which groups have successfully defended their interests by preventing or substantially slowing down innovation.[3]

To emphasize the negative consequences of the avoidance of change, however, may obscure the equally bad and, indeed, often similar consequences of excessive change. And an excessive proclivity to change may fairly be charged to British Governments over the past twenty years. In programs, policies, and institutions, this period has been an era of constant innovation. A list of new departures would range from major steps—such as joining the European Economic Community (EEC), the "new managerialism" in administration, reforms of local government, and attempts at devolution—to many variations in economic planning and management and a vast proliferation of new social programs. Reflecting on the record of the

2. Noel Annan, in *The New York Review of Books,* vol. 5, no. 7 (Nov. 11, 1965).
3. *Pressure Politics in Contemporary Britain* (Lexington, Mass., 1978) Chapter 10.

recently departed Wilson Government, the Heath Government proclaimed in a 1970 white paper that "government has been attempting too much."[4] Heath then set out to fulfill his own massive manifesto, which, as one associate has said, promised enough action to occupy not one but several parliaments, a conclusion in harmony with Douglas Hurd's wry title to his summing up, *An End to Promises.*[5] Far from bringing promises to an end, the Labour Opposition soon produced an extravaganza, running to 122 pages, as a sketch of its program,[6] which was the basis for the detailed and carefully numbered pledges of its 1974 manifesto and much of the furious activity of the first year or two of the second Wilson Government. To pile program on program and add action to action can lead to an overall incoherence of outcomes that is as self-defeating as the conservative refusal to act at all.

This reflection suggests a third sort of pluralistic stagnation which results not from the aggressiveness or the defensiveness of the interests involved, but simply from their large number.[7] To emphasize this distinction I will offer as a name the pleonasm, "numerical pluralism."

Let us suppose a society consisting of a large number of participants. We can think of them as individuals or as groups. Let us suppose further that there is some common rule which, if followed generally by participants, will bring considerable benefits to each.

4. *The Reorganisation of Central Government,* October 1970. Cmnd. 4506. par. 2.

5. Douglas Hurd, *An End to Promises: Sketch of a Government 1970–74* (London, 1979). Hurd was political secretary to Heath while Heath was prime minister.

6. *Labour's Programme for Britain* (London, 1973).

7. In developing this version of the concept of pluralistic stagnation I am drawing on ideas made current by game theory. The basic motivational structure is that of the "prisoner's dilemma" which brings out the logic of "a commonly occurring situation . . . in which two people hurt each other more than they help themselves in making self-serving choices and could both be better off if obliged to choose the opposite." Thomas C. Schelling, *Micromotives and Macrobehavior* (New York, 1978) p. 110. In "numerical pluralism" there are not two, but many participants, so the motivational structure is that analyzed by Garrett Hardin in his notable address, "The Tragedy of the Commons," [*Science,* 162, no. 3869 (Dec. 13, 1968)]. Schelling terms Hardin's "commons model" "a multi-person prisoner's dilemma" (pp. 110–111, 218). The difference from my model, of course, is that I am talking about the interaction of individuals in groups, not in isolation.

We suppose also that participants understand the consequences of complying or not complying. In this situation, although each member wants these benefits for himself, he will be reluctant to follow the rule unless he knows that the others will do the same. Otherwise, if he alone follows it, while the others do not, the benefits will not be realized, yet he will have borne the cost of complying, while they will get such advantages as their deviation may have brought them.

Presumably if there were so few participants that each could monitor the actions of the others, they could coordinate their actions. But in the situation we have supposed, the large number of participants: (1) will continually tempt each participant to refuse to take decisions which have immediate costs to him, even though he recognizes that it would benefit him if he along with others made this choice; and (2) for the same reason, will encourage each participant to take decisions which bring immediate benefits to him, even though he recognizes that it will harm him if he and the others make such a choice. The results respectively are immobility and incoherence—in brief, a paralysis of choice.

Pluralistic stagnation in this sense can be identified at various levels of decision-making. Recording his experience as a member of the Labour cabinet from 1964 to 1970, Richard Crossman continually returns to his lament that the cabinet rarely looked at government policy as a whole but instead made its decisions *seriatim* and in isolation with little regard for their effects on one another or on the economic or social whole. "We come briefed by our Departments to fight for our departmental budgets, not as Cabinet Ministers with a Cabinet view," he wrote in a comment typical of these reflections.[8] With regard to fiscal policy, for instance, individual ministers recognized the need for overall restraint, but the pursuit of departmental goals by more than a dozen spending ministers continually threatened to push the totals resulting from the respective cabinet decisions beyond the limits of prudence.

The logic of the process is revealed by the fate of a minister who did cooperate with the chancellor by accepting a cut in his department funds without putting up a fight. As a result, Wildavsky and Heclo report, "the man had crippled his reputation. Department offi-

8. Richard Crossman, *The Diaries of a Cabinet Minister*. 3 vols. vol. 1, *Minister of Housing 1964–66* (London, 1975–77) p. 275.

cials considered him weak. His cabinet colleagues believed that they could easily run over him."[9] Among ministers and officials the problem was widely recognized, and from the early 1960s a series of bold and imaginative reforms of central policy machinery attempted to strengthen the cabinet's capacity for collective choice.[10] Their success was limited as the centrifugal pluralism of ministers and departments was exacerbated by the penetration of Whitehall by the new group politics. As the unfortunate minister recalled: "So when I went to the Cabinet and did not fight, I looked bad. It made me very unpopular because word leaked out and some people informed journalists that I did not fight and this gets around to the . . . lobby." The groups affected no longer wanted him to deal with their subject. Other groups who wanted a strong minister to look after their affairs would have been upset if he had come into an office affecting them. Because of these ramifications, the problem could not be solved by reforms designed to elicit from central policy machinery acts of rational coordination which were then imposed upon the economy. The microcosm of departmental pluralism was integrated into the macrocosm of the new group politics and within that macrocosm the same self-defeating logic reigned.

Alan Peacock and Martin Ricketts illuminate the dual nature of the problem in some comment on ways in which central decisions on economic policy are affected by "backlash" from affected groups: "Firstly," they write,

the use of a policy model in which the public sector is delineated as a 'control system' with the 'government' in charge of efficient levers which will produce the desired trade-off between price stability and other objectives is misleading. So long as governments are voted into office, then, it seems more useful to accept that the correct analogy in these cybernetic terms is with a system in which the efficient operation of the levers is itself dependent on their effect on the actions of those whose actions the levers seek to control.

. . . Secondly, in employing this methodology one soon observes that the

9. Hugh Heclo and Aaron Wildavsky, *The Private Government of Public Money: Community and Policy inside British Politics* (London, 1974) pp. 136–137.

10. The "new managerialism," which "at its heart is an attempt to combat departmentalism," is surveyed by L. J. Sharpe in "Whitehall: Structures and People," in Dennis Kavanagh and Richard Rose, eds., *New Trends in British Politics: Issues for Research* (London and Beverly Hills, 1977).

control of inflation by fiscal means is beset by the 'isolation paradox.' Individual taxpayers (voters) will recognize the dangers of inflation and support fiscal action to mitigate these, at least in principle. However, the political process encourages taxpayers to adopt strategies that enable them to seek to minimize the sacrifices that the fiscal action is expected to impose on different taxpaying groups. However willing they may be to make some sacrifice, they will wish to protect their position because they cannot be certain that everyone will play the game.[11]

The term "isolation paradox," one may add, also aptly characterizes the position and behavior of the cabinet minister, who recognizes the need for fiscal restraint, but cannot be certain that if he acts on its dictates his cabinet colleagues "will also play the game."

Peacock and Ricketts rightly show how the choice mechanism is not confined to central policy machinery, but extends into the macrocosm of group politics. The link between ministers and the new group politics, moreover, is not only electoral. Central decision makers are affected not only by backlash, actual or anticipated, from groups of voters, such as taxpayers. In addition to facing the electorally transmitted influence of the consumer groups who bear the burdens and enjoy the benefits of the welfare state, they must also seek to win the consent and cooperation of producer groups in carrying out the programs of the managed economy. Among these groups too—trade unions, big companies, trade associations, professional organizations—the isolation paradox continually creates the temptation to refuse their consent for long-run common benefits in favor of the pursuit of short-run particular benefits.

Government may be affected by backlash from both the electoral power of consumer groups and the syndicalist power of producer groups. One may hope that the mobilization of consent will move the members of both sorts of groups out of their "isolation paradox" and so reduce backlash. Their consent is no mere matter of words. In the collectivist polity the dependence of governors on the governed means that "the efficient operation of the levers is dependent on their effect on the actions of those whose actions the levers seek

11. Alan Peacock and Martin Ricketts, "The Growth of the Public Sector and Inflation," in Fred Hirsch and John H. Goldthorpe, eds., *The Political Economy of Inflation* (Cambridge, Mass., 1978), p. 126.

to control.'' The mobilization of consent is the essential process of choice. Pluralistic stagnation defeats it at many levels and in many sectors of the polity.

The failures of British politics today no doubt owe a great deal to conflicts arising from such grounds as ideology, traditionalism, ignorance, and class struggle. The concept of pluralistic stagnation, however, depending on none of these, can be applied widely throughout the political system and does much to explain the self-defeating tendencies of what at first may appear to be a behavioral hodgepodge.[12] How it helps explain incoherence and immobility in the polity will appear if we try it out in relation to particular sectors of policymaking. Two are peopled by consumer groups and two by producer groups. We have already considered briefly the backlash resulting from the ''isolation paradox'' as it applies to taxpayers, a consumer group bearing some of the main burdens of the welfare state. More familiar is the ''benefits scramble'' among beneficiary groups. The most prominent example of pluralistic stagnation is the self-defeating competition for higher wages called the ''pay scramble.'' The corporatistic relations of government with business in its efforts to promote modernization display a similar sort of self-defeating pluralism in what may be called the ''subsidy scramble.''

THE BENEFITS SCRAMBLE

If applied directly to the benefits scramble, the logic of pluralistic stagnation is simple but lethal. The welfare state in Britain has produced a large and increasing number of social programs with corresponding beneficiary groups. The large number of groups—their numerical pluralism—has two effects. Because so many are making claims, the claim of no single group can make much difference to

12. The comment of Prof. Jorgen Rasmussen who read an earlier version of this book in manuscript is relevant:

It really had not occurred to me until I read [your account] how Britain's experience is a classic case of the prisoner's dilemma in game theory. Clearly individual rationality with a payoff matrix of this type results in group or collective irrationality. A game theory approach fits perfectly.

It is interesting how little Adam Smith applies to the pay and benefits scramble. In these cases perfect competition—a large number of relatively equal players—results in jam for everyone now and ultimate disaster for the collectivity. The unseen hand here has negative, rather than beneficial, impact.

the level of public expenditure. Self-restraint by a particular group, therefore, would bring no discernible benefit to it or to any other group, but on the contrary would penalize the self-denying group with a significant loss. Hence, even though the group may recognize the need for all participants to moderate their claims, it will be tempted to raise its own and indeed may feel forced to do so as it sees other groups leading the way. The situation, so to speak, presents each group with no budget restraint which would induce it to give the proper weight to the long-run costs of the action of all.

The source of the problem is not a lack of knowledge, but the structure of the situation, which continues to have compelling force even when participants recognize its tendencies. Their numerical pluralism makes it difficult, if not impossible, to make and enforce a bargain, tacit or explicit, that would achieve moderation. If there were only a few, each could know what the others were doing and all would be aware of being watched. But pluralism destroys the basis for such a self-enforcing social contract. "A political system that presents the individual voter with highly uncertain outcomes," write Peacock and Ricketts, "and that gives him no assurance that he will not become the victim of the strategic behavior of others, will be ill-equipped to provide a solution to the problems of inflation." For both reasons, then, the outcome is to defeat the moderation that all concede is needed and to produce the excess that all wish to avoid. The structure of the electorate itself tends to generate excessive demands upon government.

Party Competition

This stark portrait is close enough to reality to justify the sketch. But to be fully recognizable it must be fitted into the perspective of the choice mechanism of the collectivist polity. First, the benefits scramble also supposes for its operation the existence of two major parties so evenly balanced in electoral support and convergent in policy outlook that they compete sharply and widely for the support of consumer groups. The latter are notoriously weak in generating demands for government action on their own initiative and in fact usually do not take the aggressive role in policy making that our first sketch of the benefits scramble allotted to them. Competition disposes the parties to look with favor on programs that may enhance group support. As competition intensifies, so also will their search for "program material." Parties thus perform the catalytic function of converting latent group needs into overt group demands. The groups drawn into this competition may not initially be organized, existing simply as categorical groups defined by certain traits they have in common which provide the basis for the partisan appeal. That appeal, nevertheless, will normally be targeted to a group, for this process gives power to groups, not to individuals. As for the latter, in the huge modern electorate, the intelligent political competitor—unless propelled by habit, tradition, or sense of duty—will not find it worth his while to spend political resources on winning so insignificant an atom of support.

The rise of "bidding" between the parties is richly illustrated by the elections of 1959, 1964, and 1966. We have already taken note, for example, of the stress on group appeals in *The Future Labour Offers You,* put out in 1958. In the following years the party leadership turned to survey research to identify "target groups" toward which its promises and propaganda were directed.[13] This new tactic was strongly resisted by the fundamentalists, led by Aneurin Bevan, who felt that the party should stick to its socialist orthodoxy in program and to its traditional working class constituencies in electoral appeal. Surveys, however, showed that the uncommitted voters in marginal constituencies were nonideological in outlook and mainly interested in "issues that affected themselves—housing, consumer protection, town planning and roads, education, and care of the old." Propaganda was accordingly concentrated on "particular groups of uncommitted electors," some being "directed at parents of school children, some at old people, some at people with poor housing accommodation, some at motorists." During the period of this activity, Labour did improve its image among the "target voters" and in the 1964 general election was finally returned to power. While group appeals became particularly important in this period of political transition, they continued to flourish in later years, as we shall have occasion to note from time to time.

13. This account is based on David E. Butler and Anthony King, *The British General Election of 1964* (London, 1965) pp. 65–72.

Repercussions and Technocracy

If one asks, however, where the specific ideas came from for new and expanded programs, the main source must be not those generalists of social invention, party leaders and MPs, but people closer to the problems of modern society and to attempts to solve them. These were bureaucrats with managerial responsibilities but also increasingly experts of many kinds in and around government: for instance, members of the myriad advisory committees that clustered around departments. In the rising welfare state, once policy had been embodied in program, the way was opened not only for quantitative increase, but also for the transfer of the policy rationale of one program to the formulation of another. In the higher civil service, "repercussion" is the term for this process, which the official may try to halt if he seeks to save money, or which he may favor if he sees it as benefiting some group with whose welfare he is charged. "There is a close connection between this aspect of policy advice," writes Richard Wilding, deputy secretary of the Civil Service Department, "and the principle of evenhandedness—the principle that any Government must, within reasonable tolerances, treat all groups of citizens equitably." He continues:

Thus, for example after the Finer Committee on One-Parent Families had reported in favour of additional monetary benefits for single parents there was a long argument about whether this could be fenced off in such a way that it would not immediately give rise to demands on behalf of other poor families. The children of the sick and the children of the unemployed have the same needs, in physical terms, as the children of the single parent. Would it be just, and for how long would it be practicable, to provide extra money for the one without doing so for the others?[14]

Hugh Heclo has used his insight into this process to illuminate the development of social policy in Britain. "Policy invariably builds on policy," he concludes; indeed "the momentum and experiences generated by established policy" may be more influential in policy making than "the possession of political power."[15] The same idea and

14. Wilding, *loc. cit.*, p. 37.
15. *Modern Social Policies in Britain and Sweden: From Relief to Income Maintenance* (New Haven, 1974) pp. 315, 317–318.

some of the same words were used by Sir Richard Clarke, a high official, who became deeply disturbed by the threat of public expenditure to escape from control in the late 1950s and early 1960s. Although reforms reflecting his concern were adopted, he concluded some years later that they underestimated "the momentum of growth of public expenditure implicit in the policies which the Government was adopting."[16]

Given the broadening of the limits of government action by what I have called "the collectivist commitment," this process of bureaucratic "repercussion" could be expected to multiply programs. But in those years a further influence within the public sector also worked in the same direction. This was the role of increasingly specialized professionals in policy making. The background for this development was the rapid advances during and after World War II in the natural and social sciences and in the technology for applying such new knowledge to practical problems. The wider impact of these technocratic influences will be considered later.[17] They need to be mentioned here to suggest that further source of program proliferation arising from the tendency of scientific and technical knowledge to develop by specialization.

In the United States in the postwar years, new "professional specialisms" gave to technically and scientifically trained people in government service a growing influence in the initiation and formation of public policy. In Britain the technocratic influence was slower to arise and weaker in its effects. But there too a great surge of social spending took place in the 1960s, shaped by the *expertise* of central departments, heavily financed by the Treasury and leading to a great expansion of services delivered by the local authorities. Data on the growth of local manpower trace the process. From the 1950s to the early 1970s staff increased steadily, regardless of the party in power, the biggest increases taking place in education, health, and personal services, as professionals at the center and in the localities combined informally to support new services and higher standards. As programs multiplied, increasingly specific beneficiary groups were alerted to what government could do for them, and the numerical pluralism of the benefits scramble was heightened.

16. *Public Expenditure, Management and Control: The Development of the Public Expenditure Survey Committee* (PESC) (London, 1978) p. 31.
    17. Below pp. 120–126.

Proliferation

That the numbers are large and that they have increased is my contention. So far as I know, the exact quantitative analysis comparing numbers of programs and groups in the 1950s with their numbers in the 1960s and 1970s has not been made. It seems clear, however, that the growth in the number of pressure groups in general during the past twenty years has been "spectacular."[18] In 1980 the *Guardian Directory of Pressure Groups and Representative Associations* listed 350. Of the groups giving their dates of formation, more than half were formed in the 1960s and 1970s. As Ian Bradley has observed, the proliferation of such groups started in the mid–1950s. It was about this time that the welfare state with its "individualized benefits"[19] for separate categories of recipients became established and simultaneously academic observers first took notice of pressure groups.[20] The increase in the rate of new formations in the 1960s parallels a sharp rise in the growth of professional, scientific, and technical members of the civil service[21] and, as we shall see, a similar increase in the rate of increase of the proportion of public expenditure to total national product.[22]

The *Guardian Directory* does suggest a growth in the numbers and influence of pressure groups. One thinks of organizations included in it, such as the European Movement, Child Action Poverty Group, Friends of the Earth, the Consumers Association, or the Campaign for Nuclear Disarmament. Yet the mere 350 entries in the directory make it a misleading guide to the actual number of groups that take an interest in and try to influence what the public sector does. A quick probe of one of the main areas of expansion of the welfare state, the National Health Service, will suggest the real order of magnitude. In 1979 the Royal Commission on the Health Service (the

18. Ian Bradley in a series of four articles on pressure groups, *Times* (London) 7–10 April 1980.

19. On the importance of this aspect of the social programs, see Peter Self, "Public Expenditure and Welfare," in Maurice Wright, ed., *Public Spending Decisions* (London, 1980) p. 138.

20. Alan Potter, in his *Organized Groups in British National Politics* (London, 1961) p. 14, lists these first publications.

21. See *The Civil Service*. vol. 1. *Report of the Committee 1966–68* (Fulton Committee). Cmnd. 3638, par. 294.

22. Below, p. 37.

Merrison Commission) submitted its report.[23] In an appendix it listed the organizations that had submitted evidence. The total was 1,224.

"Associations" alone numbered seventy-three and ranged from the Association of Anaesthetists of Great Britain and Ireland to the Association of Welsh Health Authorities. "British Association" added another eighteen, ranging from British Association for Behavioural Psychotherapy to British Association of Teachers of the Deaf. There were many "Institutes" and "Royal Colleges" and "Societies." One must look at that series of names in its plentitude if one wishes to get a true sense of the proliferation of pressure groups in the collectivist polity. I will hazard an attempt to give the reader a feel for the variety, functional and territorial, private and governmental, with a sample of one name from each alphabetical grouping:

Ayrshire and Arran Health Board Nursing and Midwifery Commission, Back Pain Association Ltd., Cambridgeshire Area Dental Advisory Committee, Doncaster Area Chemists Contractors Committee, East Birmingham Hospital Social Work Department, Federation of Associations of Clinical Professors, Gwynedd Health Authority, Health Service Social Workers' Group, Institute of Operating Theatre Technicians, Junior Hospital Doctors' Association, King Edward's Hospital Fund for London, London Postgraduate Teaching Hospitals' Matrons, Medical Womens' Federation, Nurses and Midwives Whitley Council (Staff Side), Overseas Doctors' Association in the UK, Pharmaceutical Society of Great Britain, Royal College of General Practitioners, Society of Chiropodists, Tayside Health Board, University of Aberdeen Faculty of Medicine, Victoria Hospital Blackpool Medical Staff Committee, Worthing District Consultants and Specialists, Yorkshire Regional Council of the Association of Community Health Councils.

Needless to say it would take an enormous amount of work to find out how much and what sort of influence, if any, each and all of these organizations had on the Health Service. They surely complicate any simple distinction between public and private sectors; much of the "pressure," if that is the right word, which they represent is exerted by one level and sector of the public sector upon others. Moreover, this listing suggests that syndicalist and electoral influ-

23. Cmnd. 7615.

ence may often be combined. Most of the organizations consist of providers of services. That makes them producer groups in my classification. Yet the groups of patients who are the beneficiaries of these services may also gain a voice for their needs and wishes through these channels, even though they are not formally represented. Above all, however, the point driven home by a glance at this list is that when one speaks of the pluralism of groups in the collectivist polity one is speaking of very large numbers indeed.

Hubristic Keynesianism

The concept of pluralistic stagnation helps us understand some curious passages in British politics in the 1960s. The first is the explosion in public spending as the 1950s changed into the 1960s; the second is more interesting, viz., why was it so difficult for Governments to get control of this spending? One answer is bad policy decisions; another is political irresponsibility. In my view the trouble was not so much ignorance or immorality as the structure of the situation.

From the late 1950s to the late 1960s public expenditure surged upward in an unprecedented and unexpected movement. The period extended roughly from 1957 when Harold Macmillan became prime minister of a Conservative Government and launched a wave of social spending, to 1967 when Roy Jenkins took over the Treasury under a Labour Government and imposed a new regime of austerity on public finance. This surge in public expenditure presents a discontinuity that requires explanation.[24] The interesting fact is that spending not only increased substantially in real terms, but also rose sharply as a fraction of the national product, so much so that there was a significant rise in the rate of increase of the public expenditure/gross national product ratio (PE/GNP)—an upward bow in Wagner's famous curve. That ratio, to be sure, had risen over the previous generation—from 20.1 percent in 1938 to 36.5 percent in 1958—but the leading authorities on that historical trend did not expect it to increase noticeably on the basis of what was happening in the 1950s.[25] Actually,

24. Rudolf Klein, "The Politics of Public Expenditure: American Theory and British Practice," *British Journal of Political Science*, 6:401–432.
25. Alan Peacock and Jack Wiseman, quoted in Klein, *loc. cit.*, p. 411.

however, the PE/GNP ratio rose steeply, though fitfully, peaking for a while at 50.6 percent in 1968 before moving up again.

When one looks at the economic theory on which ministers in the 1960s were basing their actions, one may well conclude that their troubles arose from bad policy decisions. The foundation of the reigning outlook on economic matters had been laid in the optimism—indeed the hubris—that arose in the 1950s. I have heard it called "growthmanship." "Hubristic Keynesianism" might be more descriptive. Among civil servants, politicians, and the public, attitudes toward public spending differed enormously from what they had been during the interwar years when Keynesian thoughts were heretical, if not unknown, and the PE/GNP ratio had actually declined. The new rationale for spending that had been accepted by all parties in the postwar years legitimated increases for social programs and for economic management. This acceptance of spending, however, was given a sharp favorable twist by the unprecedented and unexpected economic growth that accompanied the longest boom in the history of capitalism.

On the Labour side one can date the emergence of the new doctrine somewhere between the *New Fabian Essays* of 1952 and Anthony Crosland's *Future of Socialism* published in 1956. In the former, even Crosland could only cautiously hope that national income would "rise annually by more than the 1½ percent which was the norm before the war."[26] Four years later in the work that became the bible of revisionism, he set forth the full doctrine of growth-oriented social democracy. The Conservatives did not lag in perceiving the possibilities. In 1954 R. A. Butler, who as chancellor of the exchequer had carried out the new commitments to social spending and Keynesian fiscal policy, foresaw that with proper management the British economy could double the standard of living in twenty-five years—a goal that would require an annual per capita growth of about 3 percent.[27] By 1963 the forecast in the Conservative exercise in indicative planning was 4 percent, raised by the next year by Labour to 4¾ percent.[28] As the optimistic outlook of the new doctrine was incorporated into the ambitious growth targets

26. p. 41.
27. Michael Stewart, *op. cit.,* p. 8.
28. Heclo and Wildavsky, *op. cit.,* p. 210.

of government planners, "the Treasury found it difficult to control public spending. What was the point? Everyone argued that the alchemist's magic of economic growth could accommodate their spending plans and dissolve the hard choices of the past."[29]

A similar optimism spread among the general public, reaching its peak in 1964. In their perceptions of being better off than in the past and their expectations of a further increase in well-being, public responses were more positive than at any time before or after.[30] One cannot understand the overexertions of the following years without appreciating this foundation in ideas. But if these beliefs were unrealistic, they did not arise from the stupidity or ignorance of the masses. They were fervently embraced by leaders and followers alike.

The Spending Explosion

Conditioned by this climate of opinion, party competition and the new group politics shaped the choices of the next critical years. Inaugurated under Macmillan and reaching its highest point under the first Wilson Government, a new phase of promises of social spending supervened. The process of escalation was circular, party promises exciting voter expectations and voter expectations heightening party promises. Some commitments were general, pledging more growth, less inflation, and better times for everyone: the appeal to valence issues on which voters generally agreed. Others were beamed to particular groups: the appeal to position issues, which had been emphasized by the revisionist approach of Labour and fully met by the Conservative response.

The upshot was a loss of control. The brilliant procedural reforms associated with the Public Expenditure Survey Committee (PESC) could not cope. They "got swamped in the manifesto commitments of the Labour government of 1964, anticipation of which had itself swollen the growth and public expenditure plans of the Macmillan/Maudling years, 1963–4." Nor did taking office bring surcease. "Ministers and their departments were urged on by a veritable proliferation of pressure groups with bright ideas for parting taxpayers

29. *ibid.*
30. James E. Alt, *The Politics of Economic Decline: Economic Management and Political Behavior in Britain since 1964* (London, 1974) pp. 91, 259.

from their money.'' In sum, ''the controllers found themselves supervising plans which, when added together, were, in a real sense, out of control from the start.''[31]

The result of this loss of control was massive public expenditure. Between 1964 and 1968, public spending as a proportion of national income surged to new heights, rising from 43 to 50.6 percent. But this is not to say that the Wilson Government cynically increased spending without regard for the consequences. Ministers agonized over cuts, and taxes, already heavy, were raised. Indeed the budgets of the fall of 1964 and spring of 1965 were mildly deflationary, although the deflationary tax actions of the early years were offset by later expansive policies, especially in the climactic year of 1967– 68.[32] But even when balanced by taxes, soaring spending meant that domestic uses were absorbing resources that should have gone into exports. For when Labour took office, the economy, already over-burdened by recent big increases in Conservative spending, was running a severe external deficit. An early devaluation would have helped, but only if protected by an effective incomes policy, which, although attempted, was not forthcoming. Ministers succeeded in reducing only investment, public and private, and defense, while social spending continued to mount. By 1968 the annual increase in public expenditure was absorbing virtually the entire annual increment in national product.[33]

Labour's National Plan had had three prongs: an industrial policy to boost investment and productivity; an incomes policy to hold wages in line; and an array of new and increased social programs financed from the ensuing increase in national product. Growth was the key to success and planners projected an annual rate of around 4 percent, although the average during the dawn of affluence under the Conservatives had been less than 3 percent. The plan was never put into effect, because of the pressures of the external crisis. But the pledges of social spending were honored. In February 1965 the Government promised to raise public spending in real terms by 4 percent per year;

31. William Keegan and Rupert Pennant-Rea, *Who Runs the Economy: Control and Influence in British Economic Policy* (London, 1979) pp. 195–196.
32. *ibid.*, p. 197.
33. Heclo and Wildavsky, *op. cit.*, p. 210.

and in actual fact over the next three years the average annual increase reached just about that figure.[34]

The elections of 1959, 1964, and 1966 best illustrated how "bidding" between the parties pushed up social spending. But a closer view of the political context is provided by Harold Wilson's recollections of 1967. The hoped for growth had not materialized, the foreign deficit was deepening and unemployment was rising. As the time for the party conference approached, relations between the Government and "the Movement" had begun to sour and opinion in the country was turning against Labour, as shown in the loss of by-elections and low ratings in the opinion polls. With no valence issues on which he could appeal to the party, the press, and the voters, the Leader found in the record of social spending an abundance of position issues on which he could take his stand. "I decided," he recalls, "to give a detailed account of our achievements in the social services."[35]

It was indeed "detailed" and long even by the standards of political oratory, running to some 10,000 words and probably taking more than an hour to deliver. The headings under which Wilson reports the speech indicate the detail: provision for the old, the sick, the disabled, the young; provision for health and welfare services, housing and slum clearance, education, scientific and technological research, technology in industry; and provision for the humanizing of the technological revolution. Under each heading, programs were matched with beneficiary groups—sometimes personalized as "an old age pensioner" or "a newly bereaved widow"—and Labour's achievement measured by the increase in spending and by scoffing comparisons with Conservative stinginess. "The speech," reports Wilson, "secured a standing ovation."[36]

A few weeks later the Government finally devalued. After some months delay, the new chancellor, Roy Jenkins, mustered the support of the Government for a drastic regime of increased taxation and real cuts in spending. Consumption, public and private, was held

34. Michael Stewart, *op. cit.,* p. 52.

35. Harold Wilson, *The Labour Government: A Personal Record* (London, 1971) p. 432.

36. *ibid.,* p. 436.

down to less than demand, thereby releasing resources for export. In crucial respects the new policy achieved remarkable success. By the spring of 1970 for the first time in many years, Britain had a healthy foreign surplus against the background of moderate home demand. Other things being equal, the country was poised to embark on a sustained, export-led, reasonably rapid growth.[37] Other things were not equal, however. In 1968 a wage explosion erupted which sustained and heightened the cost-push inflation which continued to rage through the following years. In 1970 Labour lost the election.

The Frustration of Social Learning

Looking back on events of the 1957–1967 decade, their lesson may seem obvious. The excesses of the Wilson Government resulted from bad policy choices. The Government was acting on the basis of faulty economic theory, hubristic Keynesianism, which led it to try to do too much. Once ministers had learned from hard experience that growth could not be so easily and abundantly achieved, they reestablished control over the nation's economic fortunes by switching to the right line of policy.

There are two things wrong with that summary. First, the Jenkins regime did not reestablish control over the economy; it merely displaced the lack of control from one sector to another. No sooner had the benefits scramble been moderated than the pay scramble erupted. (See Chapter II.) Second, social learning does take place and in the 1960s ministers did learn and did act on their lesson. But why did it take them so long to learn? Or is the problem rather that they did learn quickly enough, but shrank from facing the political costs of acting on what they had learned? Or were they in the grip of a dilemma?

The failure of growth to come up to expectations was evident from each year's outturn. Looking at these events, Rudolf Klein puts the question precisely: "Why did governments not act to correct their errors by cutting the planned expansion rate of public expenditure to take account of the failure to reach the hoped-for economic growth target?" After considering some possibly perverse side-effects of

37. Michael Stewart, *op. cit.*, p. 91.

administrative procedures, his explanation is essentially political: "... most governments seem to have decided that the political costs of trying to keep down the economic costs of public services are too great."[38] The same explanation is implicit in Keegan and Pennant-Rea's analysis of these events when they emphasize "the sheer political will" that led to the assertion of control over spending during the years that Roy Jenkins was chancellor.[39] The political calculations of ministers likewise are a main variable in the model that Samuel Brittan elaborates in his analysis of "the economic contradictions of democracy." The lack of a budget constraint among voters leads them to expect too much from government at too little cost. "The temptation to encourage false expectations among the electorate becomes overwhelming to politicians. The opposition parties are bound to promise to do better and the government party must join in the auction—explaining away the past and outbidding its rivals for the future, whether by general hints or detailed promises."[40]

The implication is that the pursuit of power by the politician leads him to avoid the restraint which he has learned is necessary for the common good, and moreover, that the problem could be solved and such excesses of public policy avoided, if he had the "political will" to put the known needs of the common good above his pursuit of power. But as Brittan's summary of the politician's calculation indicates—and surely that summary rings true in the light of the party competition of the decade we have reviewed—for one leader to adopt the path of restraint does not at all solve the problem. For the promises he has refused to make will quite possibly be made by the opposition, which, moreover, with the help of these promises may win the power to carry them out.

The choice confronting the first politician is not either to win power at the cost of the common good or to protect the common good at the cost of losing power. It is rather whether to have his crowd in power doing the wrong thing or to have the other crowd in power doing the wrong thing—no doubt even more stupidly. The question of whether or not he has the will to confront personal political loss

38. *loc. cit.,* pp. 416, 418.
39. *op. cit.,* p. 197.
40. "The Economic Contradictions of Democracy" *British Journal of Political Science,* 5:139–140.

is not relevant. No matter how strong his will may be to pursue the known needs of the common good, his intelligence tells him that whichever alternative he chooses, the common good will be put at risk. What may look like lack of political will or selfish pursuit of power is merely his anticipation of the objective logic of the situation.

Anyone with first-hand experience in politics will recognize this dilemma.[41] Its recurrence may have tragic echoes. Edward Heath confronted such a dilemma in the months before the general election of 1974, according to the account of events given by his personal secretary, Douglas Hurd. When that election did come it was, in Hurd's words, "a bleak honorable affair, an exercise in presenting reality." In Heath's view the oil crisis threatened Britain with catastrophe, and certainly with a severe cut in the standard of living. Not the miners' dispute, not the need for incomes policy, but the duty of explaining these grim facts clearly to the people and the hope of winning a new mandate were Heath's reason for calling the election when he did. As he approached the decision, he saw that his policy of economic growth was in ruins. "We were entering a period of lean years"—so Hurd reconstructs Heath's deliberations— ". . . People would have to understand, because only with that understanding could their Government do what was needed."

High praise for Heath's courage and responsibility. Yet within the context of that praise, Hurd conveys a quiet but severe criticism. In communicating with the public, he says, Heath failed like other Governments which, "having run out of skill or luck . . . tried to put the most favourable interpretation on increasingly unfavourable events." The economic news had been getting worse all year. But "it was not until too late that the Prime Minister put into full practice his belief that bad news was best presented bleakly, that it was possible to reach behind the interest groups to a national interest, and that on a political as well as a patriotic calculation, there should be an end to promises." And even more bluntly: "The few weeks of an election campaign were not enough. It was a mistake not to make the break in style and content before there was any question of an election."[42]

The echo reverberates from the 1930s when another Conservative

41. For those interested in game theory the dilemma is a version of the prisoner's dilemma. See above, footnote 7 Chapter I.
42. *An End to Promises,* pp. 152, 135–136, 142.

Government failed, in Hurd's words, "to insist on . . . a policy requiring much effort by the British people," the need to rearm against the Nazi threat. During the election of 1935 a pacifistic mood to which the Labour party appealed was strong among the voters. Prime Minister Stanley Baldwin accordingly spoke only vaguely of the need to remedy "deficiencies" in British defenses, letting the emphasis fall rather on his promise to the Peace Society that "I give you my word that there will be no great armaments." "A singular promise," observed Winston Churchill later, "in light of the knowledge which the Government had of strenuous German preparations."[43] But politically the tactic was successful and the Conservatives came back with a big majority. Moreover, there is no doubt that they decided to rearm more quickly and more substantially than Labour would have done. From a patriotic as well as a political angle, Baldwin's deceptive tactic was successful. Yet it became commonplace to condemn Baldwin for failing the requirements of "democratic leadership." So wrote the London *Times* years later after rearmament had been accomplished and the war had been won, presuming with hindsight that if Baldwin had told the "inconvenient truth" he still would have succeeded in educating "public opinion" and winning the election.[44] A presumption no less singular than Baldwin's promise.

The Schumpeterian Critique

The dilemma that tempts leaders to promise too much also tempts followers to demand too much. The objective logic of a pluralistic politics may lead voters also to act against their better knowledge and their better instincts. Peacock and Ricketts' taxpayer, for instance, may know full well that an increase in public burdens, which he would share, is needed to avoid certain excesses. But he has "no assurance that he will not become the victim of the strategic behavior of others." Fearing that other tax groups may, so to speak, sell their support for the promise of relief, he and his peers take time by the forelock and strike their bargain first.

Similarly with the various beneficiary groups of the welfare state. Any one of them may come to recognize the need for a fiscal restraint which will frustrate its present expectations if those expectations are

43. *The Gathering Storm* (London, 1948) p. 180.
44. Editorial, 15 December 1947.

not to be even more cruelly dashed in the future. But for one group to refrain from urging its needs on politicians and governments will do no good to it or society unless it can be sure that other groups generally will practice a similar self-restraint. And their fragmentation makes assurance on that score dubious. When voters reacted to this sort of situation in recent years by making excessive demands, the reason was much less their stupidity or their selfishness, than their intelligent appreciation of the situation. Among the masses, as among the élite, it was the structure of the situation, not the motivation of the actors that was at fault.

Brittan's study of the "economic contradictions of democracy," however, premises excesses of the welfare state on the low capacities of the voters, holding them to be poorly informed, easily manipulated, and at best capable only of judgments of short-run self-interest. A principal source of this political sociology is Joseph Schumpeter's powerful vision of democracy as the competition of two teams of power-seeking politicians for the favor of voters who, typically, are moved by "an indeterminate bundle of vague impulses loosely playing about given slogans and mistaken impressions."[45] In Britain as in the United States, while earlier studies of public opinion seemed to support this depreciatory view of the ordinary voter, recent works have come to quite different conclusions. Indeed, these studies have shown that as party identification has declined in recent years, voters have become more rational in their perceptions and conclusions. James Alt has traced among the general public in Britain the growing appreciation of economic realities and an increasing skepticism of politicians' promises. In 1966 perhaps two-thirds of the population had some conception of the roots of inflation and of the connection between rising wages and rising prices. In the following years, the number rose, reaching nine-tenths by the end of the 1970s.[46]

By the mid 1970s after the bitter frustration of the pursuit of economic growth under two quite different sorts of leadership, hubristic Keynesianism had been gravely weakened among both the élite and the masses. Yet the promises and the pressures continued to support

45. Joseph A. Schumpeter, *Capitalism, Socialism and Democracy*. 2nd ed. (New York, 1947) p. 253.
46. Alt, *op. cit.*, p. 59.

public expenditure. A 1973 survey reported that 67 percent of respondents felt that their standard of living was below the one to which they were entitled, the average respondent feeling that he was entitled to 20 percent more than he actually had.[47] And the behavior of politicians in the election year subsequent to the survey, according to Brittan, showed that they were still very sensitive to such aspirations and prone to play upon them.

That voters should feel such desires or make such demands, however, did not mean that, contrary to the other survey evidence, they were still enthralled by dreams of affluence or afflicted with Schumpeterian stupidity. Alt nicely identifies the source of their feeling. The demand for a considerably higher standard of living, he notes, "may not be an irrational demand, for irrationality in this circumstance depends on what everyone else is doing. If everyone else is going to demand 20 percent, only a fool would not, and a rational person would moderate his demands (though not his desires) only if guarantees were forthcoming about the behavior of others."[48] In short, evidence of increasing individual rationality among voters is entirely compatible with their increasing rejection of the dictates of collective rationality. If voters or politicians seemed slow to learn the lesson of the failure of hubristic Keynesianism, the fragmentation of political life suggests a likely explanation. This explanation becomes even more credible when we observe the continuation of the excessive demands after the beliefs on which they were presumably founded have disappeared. Social learning is a fact, but as a control on actual choice, it can be offset by pluralistic stagnation.

Hubristic Keynesianism did spawn bad policy choices. It would have been better to make choices based on less extravagant expectations. But what the analysis of these events shows is that it is not enough to have learned what is the better choice. The choice mechanism must have the capacity to adopt and put into effect that better choice. No doubt economists can identify quite a few policy choices in the 1960s and 1970s that would probably have had better results than those actually made. The political scientist should continually raise the political question: suppose people had known what to choose, would they have been able to choose it?

47. Brittan, *loc. cit.*, p. 142.
48. Alt, *op. cit.*, p. 265.

CHAPTER II

The Pay Scramble and the Subsidy Scramble

Lester Thurow has observed that for the purposes of stopping inflation, the American economy is both "too competitive and too
monopolistic." When productivity falls or oil prices rise, therefore,
since the economy is not perfectly atomistic, it cannot respond with
the necessary wage reductions, in the manner prescribed by the text-
book models of the free market. But also since the economy is not
perfectly concentrated, with all workers belonging to one union
working for one company, it cannot make the required adjustments
in the manner of rational planning. He concludes:

Each of the major groups understands the economy's inflationary dilemma,
but each thinks that it can avoid the necessary cuts by shifting its share of
the burden onto someone else. While only too rational for each group, this
leads to irrational aggregate economic behavior. The result is an ever accel-
erating wage spiral with each group trying to avoid the consequences of the
unavoidable inflationary shocks that are now buffetting us.[1]

THE PAY SCRAMBLE

Pluralistic stagnation afflicts economies other than the British. The
American case is less serious for various reasons, such as its lower
degree of concentration and higher degree of free market flexibility.
On the other hand, in contrast with Thurow's portrait, the economic

1. *New York Times,* 11 January 1981, Business Section.

48

actors in Britain, including its trade unionists, while attempting to escape the immediate costs of wage restraint by putting the burden on others, have increasingly recognized the long-run costs of this choice.

Translating from the general concept of pluralistic stagnation, I would describe the logic of the pay scramble as follows:

The pay scramble in the market place displays much the same logic as the uncoordinated competition of consumer groups in the electoral arena. The collectivist polity promoted a decentralization of wage bargaining which put power into the hands of a large number of groups, some quite small, but each with some degree of market power. A wage gain for any such group is not likely in itself to have a significant effect upon the overall level of wages and any consequent price rise. Yet such a gain is pure benefit for the group. Hence, even if the group does recognize the need for overall wage-price stability, it will be greatly tempted to refuse the immediate burden and try for the immediate gain. If it does not do this and forgoes the immediate gain, it confronts the probability of a double loss from not only its self-denial, but also the general price rise brought about as other unions yield to the very rational temptation to do what it has not done. Such calculations throughout the fragmented world of organized labor will tend to reflect rising prices in rising wages, and to prevent downward adjustments and so to perpetuate and often to exacerbate the inflation from which everyone suffers.

As unionists learn from experience that results of this sort may flow from uncoordinated wage bargaining, they should become—as in fact they have become—receptive to government efforts to moderate wage-push inflation by an incomes policy. But such efforts, whether or not they have a statutory basis, in fact depend largely upon the voluntary cooperation of very large numbers of groups with market power. Given any such agreement, therefore, that cooperation will continually and increasingly be menaced by the same logic which precipitated the pay scramble in the first place and which now encourages participants to fudge their compliance or withdraw it altogether in anticipation of others doing the same. What was in the first instance a flaw in the economy now appears as a failure of the polity. By refusing their cooperation with the managed economy, unions are preventing it from controlling crucial aspects of economic activity and from carrying out its responsibility for economic stability.

The pluralism that accounts for these tendencies is of an intermediate degree. If the economy were wholly atomized, as in some laissez faire model, participants, who would be individual workingmen, would not be able to push the price of their services above market value. For numerical pluralism to have its immobilizing effects, there must be a level of organization among individuals giving them some degree of market power. On the other hand, if the level of organization were to become "highly encompassing," to use Mancur Olson's term,[2] the chances would be greatly increased that the recognized common interest of the labor movement in an orderly determination of wages would prevail. Insofar as such a level of organization would firmly assure each participant that all others would "play the game" it would be safe for each voluntarily to abide by a coordinated wage bargain. The British labor scene displays its self-defeating features because its degree of numerical pluralism is intermediate: too highly organized for market forces to prevail but not organized enough to yield overall sensible and lasting bargains with employers and governments.

The "New Unionism"

In his comprehensive study of wage politics in Britain since the war, Gerald Dorfman has skillfully deployed the concept of pluralistic stagnation to show how trade union behavior has immobilized a crucial aspect of government policy.[3] Weakness at the center, going back to the failure of interwar attempts to strengthen the authority of the Trades Union Congress (TUC), has made it impossible for the movement to make and keep bargains that would have moderated wage demands. Tracing this story of frustration and failure from the

2. Mancur Olson, *The Rise and Decline of Nations* (New Haven, 1982). Like me, Olson is concerned with the way in which an intermediate degree of pluralism results in self-defeating behavior. His focus, however, is on the failure of unions to strive for efficiency because, as in Britain, they are in fact not sufficiently "encompassing" to bear the costs of any growth-repressing policies on their part.

3. *Wage Politics in Britain 1945–1967: Government vs. the TUC* (Ames, Iowa, 1973); *Government versus Trade Unionism in British Politics Since 1968* (London, 1979).

1940s through the 1970s, Dorfman ends his account on the eve of the disastrous breakdown of 1978–79 (to which we will turn at a later point). Since it is not my intention to write a history of government-trade union relations, but to bring out the underlying conditions that determine them, I will focus attention on the crucial period of transition.

The new group politics had two sides. The proliferation of consumer groups provided a material basis for the benefits scramble. The fragmentation of a growing union movement provided a material basis for the pay scramble. This "new unionism" goes far to explain a major discontinuity in the role of organized labor in the collectivist polity dating from the late 1960s—a discontinuity as marked as the earlier discontinuity in the trend of public expenditure and likewise contributing to the blight of inflation that continued and deepened through the 1970s.

As we have observed, the Jenkins regime at the Treasury did not reestablish control over the economy; it merely displaced the lack of control from the consumer group to the producer group sector. If the fruits of devaluation were to be gathered, wage demands had to be moderate. The instrument by which the Government sought such moderation was an incomes policy whose essential component was the effort to secure agreement on wage restraint among the unions. Through its many variations this effort had never been as effective as the Wilson Government had hoped it would be. Mounting hostility among the unions was voiced at the TUC and Labour party conference. The surge of average earnings to a new level in 1968 recorded the growing futility of the effort, which was abandoned the next year.

"It is tragic," writes Frank Paish, "that just as this policy [the Jenkins regime at the Treasury] had been successful and it was becoming possible to allow consumption to resume its rise, the trade unions felt obliged to adopt a more militant policy in order to raise the real disposable income of their members."[4] In a despairing comment, Thomas Balogh, a leading economic adviser to the Wilson Government, put this adoption of "a more militant policy" in a dramatic and revealing light. Full employment, he said, had shifted the

4. *Lloyd's Bank Review,* January 1976, p. 2.

balance of power away from employers and toward workers, thereby accomplishing "the most outstanding social gain made since before the war." The resulting wage-push pressure on prices could be contained only through the cooperation of the unions. By refusing this cooperation to the Wilson Government the unions had "smashed the most hopeful social experiment of our time."[5]

The chaotic world of the "new unionism" contrasts radically with the stable patterns of the previous generation. After the failure of the General Strike in 1926, the strike almost ceased to be a weapon of industrial conflict in Britain. The end of mass unemployment led to some rise in strike activity; but even with achievement of full employment during and after the war, the level remained moderate as compared with the record of other countries or with the new phase inaugurated by the late 1960s. At one point President Truman sent over a team of American trade unionists to learn the secret of Britain's exemplary industrial relations! In harmony with the long-run strategy of Ernest Bevin and other outstanding national labor leaders, the trade unions, which had been brought into close cooperation with central departments during the war, continued as a partner of government in the new relations of functional representation.[6] The early postwar years were a time of unprecedented social reform; hence, as James E. Cronin observes, the workers heeded the government plea not to strike.[7] This tacit agreement was given explicit form when the unions mobilized, with remarkable success, the consent of their members to the wage restraint bargain of 1948–50. Although the Conservatives could not repeat that success, the unions remained cooperative and responsible partners in the managed economy. During the 1950s, for instance, outside the coal industry, the number of strikes actually declined. A rise in unofficial strikes from the late 1950s was sufficiently troublesome to lead to the Government's setting up the Donovan Commission, which reported in the fateful year 1968.[8] But, as Michael Moran observes, "at the very time the Com-

5. *New Statesman and Nation*, 11 December 1970, pp. 789–790.
6. See discussion of "The New Social Contract" in *Modern British Politics* pp. 212–216.
7. *Industrial Conflict in Modern Britain* (London, 1979) p. 139.
8. Royal Commission on Trade Unions and Employers' Associations 1965–1968 (Donovan Commission). *Report* (London, 1968). Cmnd. 3623.

mission was carrying out its investigations conditions were changing in such a way as to render its description a historical record. ''[9]

The Wage-Price Explosion

In its unexpectedness the wage-price explosion of the late 1960s reminds one of the spending explosion of a decade before. Looking at the record of the following years, Cronin found that "recent increases in the levels of strikes and strikers have been on a scale and of a magnitude which no serious student of strikes considered possible before 1965.''[10] Nor do the equations developed in his own detailed statistical analysis of the waves of strike action over the previous eighty years account for the great wave that inundated the British economy in 1968. In addition to these quantitative discontinuities organized labor's new behavior differed from earlier patterns in three respects. Shop stewards and militant local leaders played a much more prominent role. Demands shifted away from defensive goals, such as job security, as strikers took the offensive for higher wages. Union membership rapidly increased among not only manual, but also white-collar workers.

The trigger for the wage-strike explosion is commonly found in certain economic changes. It has been argued that as resources were fed into the balance of payments, the virtual absence of an increase in living standards led to rising discontent which could only be exacerbated by the higher prices following devaluation in November 1967.[11] This explanation, however, raises the same question prompted by the excessive expectations of consumer groups. Did not trade unionists recognize the dangers of such heightened demands? A lowering of consumption was, of course, an intended and integral consequence of the policy to which the Government felt itself driven by the hard lesson of events. Are we to say in harmony with the Schumpeterian view, that the members of the Government were capable of learning this lesson but that trade unionists and their leaders could not?

9. *The Politics of Industrial Relations: The Origins, Life and Death of the 1971 Industrial Relations Act* (London, 1977) p. 31.
10. Cronin, *op. cit.*, p. 146.
11. See Cronin's discussion of this view *op. cit.*, 142, 145.

And again the reply is that these dangers were widely recognized by the public. Opinion surveys show that in the late 1960s and increasingly through the 1970s, trade unionists by and large did see the need for wage restraint; and, moreover, they approved the means to that end, whether it was put to them as an incomes policy or as a reform of trade union law. As we have seen, the public overwhelmingly came to recognize the relation between rising prices and rising wages. A 1974 survey showed that solid majorities of both Conservative and Labour voters preferred strict wage controls to spending cuts, more taxation, or more unemployment as a remedy for inflation. Surveys, concludes James Alt, have "long suggested that majorities of people are prepared to accept, and indeed welcome, incomes policies, at least until they demonstrably cease to work."[12] The same sort of public support was forthcoming if we turn to the other main device for moderating wages, viz., the restraint of trade union power. When Heath introduced his proposals for reform of industrial relations, an overwhelming majority of voters supported them, including a majority of trade unionists. Nor did general public support decline during the long campaign waged by the Labour party and the TUC against the bill, although the support of individual trade unionists weakened slightly.[13] Popular support for reform was in accord with the growing hostility to trade unions reported in opinion surveys. Already in the sixties, Butler and Stokes found such negative feelings on the increase—so much so that a four-to-one majority said that when they heard of a strike their sympathies were generally against the strikers, with union families themselves including more who said "against" than "for."[14]

One possible reason for greater militancy by trade unions is the rise to power of militants. Much has been made of the radicalism of Hugh Scanlon and Jack Jones who took over the leadership of the two largest unions, the engineers and the transport workers, in the late 1960s. The influence of single individuals is never to be disregarded in large or in small arenas. But as a major condition for the deep and persistent change in union behavior the "terrible twins"

12. Alt, *op. cit.,* p. 205, 270.
13. Moran, *op. cit.,* pp. 112–113.
14. David Butler and Donald Stokes, *Political Change in Britain: The Evolution of Electoral Choice.* 2nd ed. (London, 1979) p. 198.

explanation does not get one very far. It is not consistent with the fact that after these men were succeeded by moderates, thanks to the victories of Terence Duffy and Moss Evans, one of the most fateful defeats of incomes policy took place during the disastrous winter of 1978–79.

The Donovan Commission had reported the crucial change in the structure of influence: the shift of initiative to the shop floor.[15] During the interwar years a centralized national system of industrial relations had been established. Wages and working conditions were settled by industry-wide negotiations between the representatives of unions and employers. By the mid 1960s these national institutions—what Donovan called the "formal system"—remained, but in many industries they were in decline as pay and conditions came increasingly to be determined by the direct action of groups, often quite small,[16] under the leadership of a growing body of shop stewards and other local leaders—the "informal system." Various reasons account for this change. But full employment is often said to have played the major part by putting workers in a strong bargaining position and inciting managers of individual firms to compete with one another in offers to cope with the labor shortage. Mass unemployment had made possible the centralized national system; the full employment brought by the welfare state engendered the decentralized system that appeared in the 1960s. Neither stupidity nor radicalism but the pluralism of this fragmented structure propelled British trade unionists, against their express opinions, into the pay scramble that swept over the country in the late 1960s and continued with mounting disorder, only briefly remitted, through the following decade.

As the 1970s ended, this lesson of events was widely understood at all levels of the British polity, both by participants and observers. At Mrs. Thatcher's first press conference in the 1979 general election campaign, a West German correspondent asked her a question about government-labor relations that suggested an unfavorable contrast with the success of Bonn in that field. She immediately got to the heart of the matter by remarking that "in West Germany, you have only 14 trade unions, while we have over 400." About the same

15. *Report*, ch. III.
16. Moran, *op. cit.*, p. 25.

time, a leading authority on the law of British labor relations, having
traced how decentralized collective bargaining tends to pit groups of
workers against one another, concluded:

In this sense the strike as a social institution—once considered as the supreme
example of working-class solidarity—may have been dialectically trans-
muted into its opposite: action of groups of workers seeking advantage at the
expense of others.[17]

A perceptive and well-informed journalist has repeatedly driven
home the fact of labor fragmentation and its consequences. Far from
being "over-mighty, greedy giants holding the 'nation' to ransom,"
writes Robert Taylor, the labor correspondent for the London
Observer, the fault of British unions is "that they are not strong
enough." The TUC is and will remain "a weak, loose confederation" and "more and more decisions will be taken farther down the
union structure." Division at the national level is reflected in "a lack
of solidarity on the shop floor" where "workers in the same factory
often find it difficult to organize coherent action." In consequence,
having failed to achieve "the kind of collective solidarity that would
ensure the success of a permanent voluntary incomes policy," British labor is continually threatened by "the self-destructive bonanza"
of unfettered wage bargaining.[18] So also is the economic policy of
any Government.

The Self-destructive Bonanza

The wage-strike explosion of the winter of 1978–79 was such a
"self-destructive bonanza." The pay policy agreed between the
Government and the TUC in the crisis year of 1975 when the annual
inflation rate reached 26 percent had been renewed in each of the
following two years. An austere fiscal and monetary policy continued into 1978. By the fall of that year the inflation rate was down to
7½ percent, living standards were rising markedly, and the Government attempted to negotiate a new stage of the social contract that

17. Otto Kahn-Freund, *Labor Relations: Heritage and Adjustment* (London, 1979)
p. 78.
18. Robert Taylor, *The Fifth Estate: Britain's Unions in the Seventies* (London,
1978) pp. xiii, 337–338, 353.

would limit wage increases to 5 percent. As usual public opinion, including trade unionists, supported the pay policy.[19] When Ford workers struck for a bigger raise, a survey of trade unionists showed that 77 percent condemned the strike and a clear majority said the 5 percent offer should have been accepted. Most national trade union leaders probably supported a renewal of the pay policy. But the TUC, pressured by local leaders,[20] repudiated any renewal, as did the party conference. The general council and the Government could not achieve even a face-saving formula. In Parliament a left-wing revolt deprived the Government of its power to put pressure on employers to hold out for moderate settlements by the denial of various benefits such as contracts and financial assistance. Early in the year the country was swept by a big truck strike which was joined by widespread walkouts by public employees. As garbage men, ambulance drivers, hospital workers, and school teachers paralyzed crucial services, the public reaction was bitterly hostile. Wages rose, prices resumed their upward climb, and opinion shifted sharply to the Conservatives who were returned to power in the general election of May 3, 1979.

As this thumb nail sketch suggests, the reasons for the disaster were many. It also suggests that the enduring structural weaknesses of the trade union movement continued to prevent the participants in the managed economy from acting on their own better judgment. At the height of the disorder Robert Taylor explained what was happening and why: "Envy of the super-rich, or a revival of class warfare is not the inspiration behind the anger and frustration among tens of thousands of British workers which is boiling over in the form of big pay claims and industrial action." On the contrary, "workers strive, through fragmented and localised bargaining, to hold their position relative to workers in other work-places and other industries," seeking at most "to climb a rung or two above those whose pay they traditionally compare with their own."[21]

To illustrate his points, Taylor presented the table put out each year by the Government to show the relative gross weekly earnings of the main categories of workers, manual and white collar. (See

19. A Gallup Poll published in the week of Oct. 21 showed that two-thirds of the general public and fully 69 percent of trade unionists favored the 5 percent pay limit.
20. *Economist,* 30 September 1978, p. 101.
21. *Observer,* 28 January 1979.

TABLE 2.1
National Wages Table

April 1978		April 1975	
DIVISION ONE		DIVISION ONE	
Over £100 a week, gross		Over £70 a week, gross	
		Senior civil servant	£91.90
Electricity power engineer	£136.10	Teacher in higher education	£87.10
Marketing sales manager and executive	£131.40	Marketing sales manager and executive	£84.90
Teacher in higher education	£121.30	Electricity power engineer	£82.60
Office manager	£116.10	Office manager	£77.50
Senior civil servant	£113.70	Miner (face)	£75.80
Production and works manager	£110.50	Secondary school teacher	£73.50
Miner (face)	£109.20	Accountant and computer programmer	£72.90
Accountant	£107.40	Production and works manager	£72.80
Secondary school teacher	£102.70	Primary school teacher	£70.90
Primary school teacher	£99.90		
DIVISION TWO			
£84 to £100 a week, gross		DIVISION TWO	
		£60 to £70 a week, gross	
Electrician (industry)	£95.10		
Draughtsman	£92.00	Miner (surface)	£65.30
Steel worker	£91.70	Electrician (industry)	£64.90
Miner (surface)	£91.20	Railway engine driver	£64.30
Policeman	£91.00	Policeman	£64.10
Car worker	£90.70	Clerical/executive (post office)	£63.40
Toolmaker	£89.80	Steel worker	£63.30
Train driver	£86.00	Water worker	£61.80
Plumber	£85.30	Gas worker (manual)	£61.70
Clerical/executive (Post Office)	£84.80	Fireman	£61.40
Heavy goods lorry driver	£84.20	Toolmaker	£60.50
DIVISION THREE		DIVISION THREE	
£70 to £80 a week, gross		£50 to £60 a week, gross	
Gas worker (manual)	£81.50	Draughtsman	£59.90
Printer (outside London)	£81.10	Heavy goods lorry driver	£59.30

April 1978		April 1975	
DIVISION THREE		DIVISION THREE	
£70 to £80 a week, gross		£50 to £60 a week, gross	
Food process worker	£80.50	Car worker	£59.30
Fireman	£79.90	Plumber	£59.20
Bricklayer	£79.20	Bricklayer	£57.60
Railway worker	£78.80	Food process worker	£55.30
Electricity supply	£78.00	Electricity supply	£55.10
Water worker	£74.60	Railway worker	£54.60
Painter and decorator	£73.90	Print worker (outside	
Dustman	£70.40	London)	£52.80
		Painter and decorator	£52.60
		DIVISION FOUR	
DIVISION FOUR		Under £50 a week, gross	
Under £70 a week, gross		Dustman	£49.50
Nurse	£68.20	Nurse (female)	£45.70
General clerk	£68.40	General clerk	£45.70
Clerical officer (civil		Caretaker	£43.80
service)	£62.90	Clerical officer (civil	
Bank worker (woman)	£62.00	service)	£42.20
Caretaker	£61.50	Catering worker	£41.80
Farm worker	£57.70	Bank worker (woman)	£38.00
Catering worker	£57.00	Farm worker	£37.40
Bespoke tailor	£43.00	Bespoke tailor (woman)	£28.80
Retail food worker		Retail food worker	
(England and Wales,		(England and Wales,	
woman)	£42.20	woman)	£27.40

SOURCE: *Department of Employment Gazette: Earnings Survey*

table 2.1.) These figures, hierarchically arranged in four divisions, reveal what had happened to each category from 1975 to 1978. There is some evidence for the familiar explanation that the pay policy had been destroyed by workers, especially skilled workers, attempting to recapture their differentials. Power workers in the nationalized electricity industry had moved to the top of their division, enjoying an increase of 65 percent. Car workers had moved a whole division upward with an increase of 53 percent. The lowly dustman (garbage collector) had also moved up a division, improving his lot by a 42 percent rise. Post office employees had suffered a relative loss, as had workers in the gas supply industry. Others, like coal miners and school teachers, had just held their own, not far behind dons and senior civil servants. Overall, workers in the public sector, both manual and white collar, fell behind those in private employment.

Clearly, there are grounds for wage pressures here. But perhaps the most interesting and, in a sense, most ominous fact is the very substantial increases for all categories during the operation of a pay policy which was judged, in light of the circumstances, to be remarkably successful. Such continuous and substantial change in money wages, real income, and relativities must create a climate of uncertainty in which promises, however heartfelt, to abide by some fixed rule, could not last.

The National Union of Public Employees

The story of NUPE encapsulates the pay scramble. If it were not so sad, it would be a comedy of self-defeating industrial action. Composed of a miscellany of low-paid and semiskilled workers, most of them public employees, NUPE has little syndicalist power and its members rank in the lower levels of the lowest division of the pay league. The bulk of its members are part-time women workers, the largest single occupational group in the union being employees of local government who work in the school meals program. In the 1970s membership in NUPE grew enormously, rising in 1968–78 from 265,000 to 712,000 as employment in the public sector mounted. A principal object of the union, therefore, is to maintain and increase public expenditure and to resist any policy of cuts. At the 1979 annual conference, a banner at the platform accordingly read "Defend the Public Services."

At that conference, however, the main question was wages. Given its industrial weakness, the union would like to avoid strikes, preferring an incomes policy, but as its general secretary, Alan Fisher, remarked to me, "if the right kind." The "right kind" of incomes policy would be a legislated minimum wage setting the minimum at two-thirds of the national average wage.[22] In the wage round of 1978–79, this goal led NUPE to demand a minimum wage of £60 for a

22. Resolution 3, *Final Agenda*. 52nd National Conference of the National Union of Public Employees. Scarborough, 20–22 May 1979.

thirty-five hour week—a raise of some 40 percent, far in excess of the Government's figure of 5 percent.[23] But the basic problem was not Government policy, it was the fact that the two-thirds minimum would have compressed the differentials between NUPE workers and other workers, as a glance at the earnings table will show. The great diversity in the syndicalist power of the various unions has meant that any effort to raise the wages of low-paid workers immediately sets off a series of corresponding increases at higher levels, which in the end leave the low-paid in the same position of relative deprivation as before. These hard truths were brought home in an exchange between Alan Fisher and Sid Weighell, general secretary of the railwaymen, at the 1978 Labour party conference. Weighell was warning Fisher to support resolution 38 which expressed approval of the Government's pay policy. He said:

If Alan Fisher wants to get out from under the bottom of the pile—Alan, you have got to support 38, because if you do not I will tell you what is going to happen. You say 'Let's get 40 percent'. That is what you want. . . . Let me tell you this. If you get 40 percent, Alan, in your world, I am going to get 40. And the difference between you and me. I have got some power to do it with. (*Applause*)[24]

Fisher recognized the weakness of his union and in the course of the negotiations indicated he would settle for 9 percent. When this proposal went to the ballot, however, there was an outburst of opposition. The instructions sent out in response by the executive council reflected in their ambiguity the decentralized authority and great variety of attitudes and interests within the union. Local organizations were urged, but not instructed, to take "selective industrial action," where possible, and to do so in the ways they found suitable. Such permissiveness was inevitable since nurses, for instance, are far less willing to withdraw their services from patients than workers in a hospital laundry are to leave their machines. The national leaders had as little authority in conducting the resulting industrial action as in trying to head it off. In some respects it would have been advantageous to both sides to agree on a code of conduct—for instance, to permit school children to go through the picket lines set

23. Robert Taylor, *op. cit.*, 2nd ed. 1979, p. 352.
24. *Report of Annual Conference*, Labour party, 1978, p. 223.

up by striking caretakers. Other unions could make and keep such agreements. But NUPE was typically unable to speak for its locals.

What NUPE did, so to speak, had a minimum positive effect on wages and maximum negative effect on public opinion. The union settled for the 9 percent increase plus one pound a week and reference of its further claims to a government commission charged with bringing wages in the public and private sectors into line with one another.[25] But as stories spread of garbage piling up, ambulancemen refusing to take sick people to the hospital, grave diggers leaving the dead unburied, and so on—some true, some untrue—public hostility mounted toward NUPE, trade unions in general, and to the Labour party and its Government. After the general election when the House met to debate the Queen's speech, a newly elected MP, sponsored by NUPE, sat down on the Opposition benches beside a colleague, sponsored by the miners. Unaware of the new MP's connection, the miners' MP began his conversation: "It's bloody NUPE that got us into this mess!" A delegate from Nottingham to the 1979 conference, and himself a branch secretary, put the matter in a clearer perspective. Granting that the pay scramble is self-defeating, he recognized that its roots are in the fragmented structure of British labor. The National Health Service, he observed, must deal with some forty-seven separate unions. Most members of his union, he was sure, would favor an annual agreement among all British unions on how much wages could be raised, after which this amount would be divided among them. But, he claimed, the well-paid workers would not go along—the miners, for instance, and especially the power workers in the nationalized electricity industry. So "at present it is dog eat dog."

The union does have its radicals and, although they cannot win important votes, a good deal of time at conference and on the picket lines is taken up by members of the Workers Revolutionary party and the Socialist Workers party speaking what Alan Watkins, political correspondent for the *Observer,* has termed "the rancorous sub-Marxist terminology" of present day militants. The language of Marx, however, cannot mask the desperate Hobbesian struggle of union against union.

25. The Standing Pay Commission on Comparability in the public sector under Professor Hugh Clegg is discussed in Taylor, *op. cit.,* 2nd ed., 1979, p. 147.

THE SUBSIDY SCRAMBLE

The three purposes of Labour's National Plan of 1965 conveniently summarize the main economic and social commitments of the collectivist polity and focus attention on how pluralistic stagnation frustrated its promise.

The expectation of new and increased social programs was driven out of control by the benefits scramble. The hope for an incomes policy to restrain inflation was destroyed by the pay scramble. In the following pages we will consider how an industrial policy that was to boost investment and heighten productivity was defeated by the similar logic of the subsidy scramble.

If we may look at the benefits scramble as a disorder of parliamentary representation, the pay scramble and subsidy scramble appear as failures of functional representation. When the collectivist polity took on the responsibilities of economic management, it was obliged to seek the cooperation and consent of the producer groups that would carry on the relevant activities.

Functional representation began with this administrative thrust. It also developed a representative aspect as these groups, empowered by their control over resources and skills, bargained for consideration of their interests in exchange for the desired behavior. One might have hoped for a balance of power in which the particular interests of groups were reconciled with a view of the common interest. In some such way the parallel systems of representation, parliamentary and functional, could have been harmonized.

We have seen how this hope was frustrated in the relations of government and labor. The relations of business and government suffered a similar fate and for similar reasons. The world of business organizations in Britain is as fragmented as that of labor and its so-called peak organs have failed at least as badly as the TUC in mobilizing the consent of their members in the service of public purposes. A self-defeating pluralism undermined both the administrative and representative processes of functional representation. The subsidy scramble was another example of pluralistic stagnation.

Corporatism

Arrangements of this sort in which government is closely and continuously linked with bodies—*corpora*—performing important functions in the society are often referred to as "corporatism." It will help bring out the significance of the subsidy scramble, if we look at it in that context, viz., as a product, and a failure, of British corporatism.

As modern society became more interdependent, government was confronted with a new kind of power. Within this interdependent network, a group controlling a specialized function could paralyze the whole society by a withdrawal of its activity. The base of the power of such groups was twofold: the exclusive possession of a skill and the organization of those who possessed it. This kind of power may properly be called "syndicalist" and may be wielded by organizations of workers or of managers or—a possibility by no means to be overlooked—of workers and managers together. As we have seen, when government intervenes to regulate, or to manage, or to plan the economy, it needs the cooperation of these groups, whose syndicalist power is to that extent increased. In this sense the collectivist polity, with its commitment to planning, or at least to management, necessarily involves corporatism in some degree.

When I first took note of these linkages in Britain between government and producer groups in the 1950s, I called them "quasi-corporatism."[26] With the establishment of the National Economic Development Council (NEDC) in 1962, it seemed that this functional need of collectivism had advanced by a giant step. This council, backed by an expert staff, was organized on a tripartite basis to include representatives of government, trade unions, and industry, both private and public, and was linked with a score or so of little "Neddies," similarly organized tripartite bodies for particular industrial sectors. Its potential for becoming a full-fledged corporatist system seemed forbidding.

On looking again at the British system in the later 1960s, I concluded: "The further development of corporatism is surely to be expected. Planning is inevitable in an economy that seeks both sta-

26. "Pressure Groups and Parties in Britain," *American Political Science Review*, 50, no. 1 (March, 1956): 9 and *passim*.

bility and expansion . . . as planning develops, functional representation will likewise grow, becoming an even more important part of
the representative system of the polity."[27] In the 1970s various
events—the "social contract" would perhaps be the main one—made
it appear to some observers that important matters were increasingly
being determined through channels of functional representation rather
than those established by electoral politics and the parliamentary system. Frequently one heard that Britain was becoming a "corporate
state."[28]

The term has an ominous ring. One thinks of Mussolini and other
reactionary regimes. But there is of course a corporatism of the left
as of the right, of reformers as well as revolutionaries.[29] And beyond
these distinctions, corporatism may vary in other important ways. A
principal differentia is the balance of power between central government and constituent bodies within the corporatist structure. Insofar as government controls the flow of influence, thereby making the
administrative function predominate over the representative, the
relation is étatist. Insofar as the groups control, making the representative function more important than the administrative, it is syndicalist. Looking at the needs of the managed economy, one might
well expect this network of contacts to develop toward étatist corporatism. Looking at the syndicalist power of the producer groups,
one could equally well expect them to take over running the economy. These two contradictory possibilities should be distinguished
in any talk of "the coming of the corporate state." Do we mean by
that fearful prediction that a central planning apparatus, resting on some
independent political base, will dominate the constituent economic
bodies? Or do we mean that a cartel of these bodies will dictate to
the legitimate organs of the state?

There is, moreover, a third possibility that will be of special interest to the present inquiry. It is that a pervasive pluralism may destroy
the chances for a coherent solution of either sort, whether centralized
étatism or cartelized syndicalism.

27. *Modern British Politics,* 2nd ed., 1979, Epilogue, p. 429.
28. For summary and criticism of such comment, see Alan Cawson, "Pluralism,
Corporatism, and the Role of the State," *Government and Opposition,* 13, no. 2
(Spring, 1978).
29. *Modern British Politics,* "The New Pluralism," pp. 73–79.

For twenty years British attempts to plan the economy have been severely criticized for their lack of firm central direction by the planners and their excessive consideration for the wishes of the planned. In this attack the foreign model has been France with its supposedly étatist approach. In an article that has become something of a classic, Jack Hayward has summarized this perjorative comparison.[30] The problem is Britain's "institutional inertia"—meaning very much what I have called the "paralysis of public choice"—which he holds primarily responsible for Britain's inability, relative to France, to mobilize consent for change and to cope with economic failure. In this more traditionalist country, he believes, the structure of government has been weighed down with institutions and modes of behavior that have been valued for their own sake, rather than for their effectiveness as instruments of policy. But he is especially concerned with "the greater dispersal of power in Britain compared with France and the fact that the government is conceived as operating on the same plane as other political actors." In both countries, government has been confronted by an array of powerful producer groups. In France, however, a brilliant "techno-bureaucratic élite" has acted to impose policy on reluctant producers, while Britain has chosen the path of pluralism and incrementalism in which decisions are made—or avoided—in a "piece-meal bargaining process of mutual adjustment among the interested parties."

These weaknesses penetrate all levels. Governments have attempted to deal with inflation by recourse to "a toothless tripartism" with producer organizations such as the Confederation of British Industry (CBI) and the Trades Union Congress (TUC). But since their style of authority, like that of the Government, consists in a reliance on consultation and voluntary consent, they find it hard to make, and even harder to carry out, comprehensive agreements on behalf of their members. The self-defeating character of what happens is indicated in his summary that "the British political process may be said to have triumphed over its purpose."[31]

30. "Institutional Inertia and Political Impetus in France and Britain," *European Journal of Political Research,* vol. 4 (1976): 341–359.
31. *ibid.,* pp. 347, 346, 351.

The Modernization Drive

It will be easier to trace the logic of collective action that has blunted the étatist thrust of corporatism, if we look at one aspect of government-industry relations, the use of subsidies for modernization. The reason for the new step of government intervention was the growing recognition in the early 1960s of Britain's industrial backwardness in comparison with her continental rivals. In response, Macmillan in 1962 set up the National Economic Development Council for the express purpose of mobilizing consent for industrial modernization. In the same years, his Government also launched the new wave of industrial subsidies. Previously, subsidies for industrial purposes through such means as direct grants or tax reliefs had been slight. After 1959 each new Government accepted and extended this sort of intervention.[32]

These subsidies were an instrument of the managed economy and took government a long step beyond the other main approach to economic growth which looked to the social consumption of the welfare state for stimulation of greater production. Their purposes were manifold. They were often intended to sustain employment—for instance, in the depressed areas—and in this respect served a social purpose. They also sometimes had more political objectives, such as prestige (Concorde) or defense (Rolls Royce). But the subsidy strategy had the separate and distinguishable economic purpose of promoting growth, along with closely related objectives such as improving the foreign balance, by enabling firms to acquire the capital necessary for more productive enterprise. Since it was felt that investment had been inadequate in comparison with Britain's continental competitors, subsidies would tackle this failing directly, utilizing a kind of specific intervention which was very much in accord with the strong technocratic thrust of these years. In heralding its "plan for economic growth" in *Signposts for the Sixties* (1961), Labour put first "the investment drive" which would enable planners to harness "the scientific revolution" to reverse Britain's relative industrial decline. Some of the Wilson Government's measures along this line, such as

32. Geoffrey Denton, "Financial Assistance to British Industry," in W. M. Corden and Gerhard Fels (eds.), *Public Assistance to Industry: Protection and Subsidies in Britain and Germany* (London, 1976) p. 120.

the Selective Employment Tax and the Regional Employment Premium, were so complicated and technical as to be a kind of "fine tuning" of investment policy.

Spending on trade and industry surged in the late 1960s. By the end of the decade, subsidies to private industry amounted to nearly £1 billion per year, rather more than 6 percent of central government expenditures.[33] By 1970, however, it was apparent that these programs had not reversed the low levels of investment in British manufacturing and, while they may have directed some employment to the assisted areas, they were contributing little to the overall modernization of industry. Many firms received subsidies to do what they would have done anyway. And complaints from industry that subsidies gave unfair advantages to some firms over others led to increasingly standardized criteria for the distribution of aid, which undercut the subsidies' usefulness as a selective incentive. Moreover, if subsidies were to render industry more efficient, they had to be directed to sectors and firms capable of developing a competitive edge over their international rivals; yet many businessmen resisted the idea that their stiffest competitors should receive extra aid from the state. What was efficient did not seem fair. Similarly, while the intention may have been to provide seed money for industries short on capital but long on growth prospects, the more immediate demands from declining sectors invariably generated political pressures too strong to resist, and investment for the future generally gave way to alleviating distress in the political present.

For a brief moment in 1970–71, the new Conservative government appeared determined to resist the forces which had transformed the subsidy system from an investment program into a welfare program for business. The method was to be complete withdrawal—the elimination of state intervention in the industrial sphere. The Industrial Reorganization Corporation, which had been set up in 1966 by Labour, was abolished; the regional employment premium was given a death sentence; and subsidies were replaced with tax allowances designed to go only to firms that had already proved profitable on their own.

But exhortations to invest and grow seemed to have no effect on

33. Denton, *op. cit.*, p. 123.

British business. Few firms proved profitable enough to claim their new tax rewards, and Heath became increasingly frustrated with the slow pace of industrial growth. Within two years a new system of subsidies had been established under the Industry Act of 1972.[34] That act gave the government sweeping powers to assign grants to industry according to the public interest. Tony Benn later called it "the most comprehensive armoury of Government control that has ever been assembled for use over private industry."[35] The intention once again was to aid the strong and let the weak fall by the wayside. But once again, the lion's share of assistance went to "lame ducks" and declining sectors where jobs seemed immediately at risk. Rolls Royce and the remnants of the shipbuilding industry received most of the funds. Heath had executed a double U-turn—back to the techniques and good intentions of the preceding Government, and then back to the same results.

Labour's U-turn began from its initial effort in 1974 to revive a more centralized and socialist version of the National Plan. As set forth in party programs, this effort, if successful, would have been a triumph of étatist corporatism. The "new industrial strategy" would have been étatist in the sense that under "a powerful planning Ministry," compulsory planning agreements would have been negotiated with the largest manufacturing firms and all major public enterprises, old and new. Government would set the objectives and provide financial assistance at its discretion, leaving "the *tactics* which will be needed to achieve these objectives to the companies themselves."[36] The scheme would have been corporatist in that the negotiations would have been tripartite, involving the Government, the companies and the trade unions and in that the actual implementation would have been carried out by the firms, private or public. The tripartism of the Neddy structure would have also been used, but the Economic Development Councils with their sectoral concerns would have remained advisory, charged with "passing ideas to and from Government and industry."[37]

34. On Conservative industrial policy, see Stewart, *op. cit.*, pp. 134–138
35. Quoted in Trevor Smith, *The Politics of the Corporate Economy,* (London, 1979) p. 166.
36. *Labour's Programme 1973*, p. 18.
37. *Labour's Programme 1976*, p. 24.

In Labour's subsequent U-turn, étatism lost out to syndicalism. The idea of compulsion with regard to planning agreements and government acquisition of shares in private firms was the crux. Trevor Smith doubts that "such obedience could ever be achieved whatever the political regime."[38] In any case, industry, as one close observer has reported, was "hysterical," and in the hands of ministers and officials the new strategy was adapted to the old routines of consultation and consensus, the defeat for étatism being sealed by the removal of Benn as secretary of state for industry in the summer of 1975. Planning agreements and public acquisition of shares were to be voluntary and only those firms were to be assisted which were likely to achieve a commercial rate of return on the capital. For industrial policy under Labour's neosocialism, as under Heath's neoliberalism, the "resistances" were too strong to permit a "drastic move."

The Bottoms-up Exercise

This second phase of the new industrial strategy was shaped by an approach which came to be known among officials, who were its principal authors, as "a bottoms-up exercise."[39] While the overall Neddy structure was used, the approach was highly decentralized with regard to sectors of industry and areas of the country. Tripartite bodies would examine particular sectors of industry and recommend to government and to their constituent firms what needed to be done "to help bring about an improvement in competitiveness."[40] Called Economic Development Committees, or more commonly Sector Working Parties (SWPs), these tripartite bodies totaled fifty-nine by 1979.[41] Their work was guided by a steering brief composed by the NEDC, requiring them, for instance, to set "market share objectives," to help their respective sectors achieve these objectives and to assess "implications for resources."[42] They were not, no more

38. Trevor Smith, *op. cit.*, p. 167.
39. For help in understanding these matters I wish to thank Caroline Miles, a member of the National Enterprise Board, and Adrian Hamilton, industrial correspondent of the *Observer*, with whom I talked respectively on May 2 and June 6, 1979.
40. National Economic Development Council, *Annual Report, 1978–79*, p. 9.
41. *ibid*. Appendix A.
42. *ibid*. p. 9; *Industrial Strategy: Analysis of Sector Working Party Reports* (NEDO, February 1979) p. 1.

than NEDC itself, legislative or executive bodies. They could not order anybody to do anything, nor give anyone any money. According to their reports, they might establish "genuine dialogue" among firms in their sectors whose response to their recommendations was entirely voluntary. Although disposing of no money, they could "call firms' attention to the need to maintain investment and make use of Industry Act schemes" or "recommend more Government support for export-oriented activities" and "greater export-linked concessions in personal and corporate taxation."[43] The Neddy structure, in short, could take no action to carry out the new industrial strategy.

Since compulsion had been rejected as an instrument of economic control, action had to come from the use of public money. The money was to be provided by two sources, the National Enterprise Board and the Department of Industry. The board, a new body established under the Industry Act of 1975, which envisaged its having a capital of more than £1 billion, had as its mission to take permanent shareholdings in firms for the sake of investment, exports, or other national objectives.[44] The board sought to emphasize that it was not primarily meant to supply subsidized finance, but to extend assistance where there was "a real prospect of commercial return." This did not mean that it would allow "market forces alone to operate." It was rather, in its words, "reinforcing commercial drive with the impetus of public financial support."[45] In some sense, however, its technocratic judgment was considered superior to the unassisted mutual adjustments of the market. Following this strategy, the board acquired an interest in a number of small firms in such fields as computers and micro-electronics. But in an all-too-familiar pattern, the urgent needs of big lame-duck firms almost immediately preempted the larger share of its capital.

Acting mainly under the Industry Act of 1972, the Department of Industry administered some broad programs of aid for depressed areas.[46] We need not consider them, except to note that these programs, which involved large sums of money and thousands of firms, were primarily intended to sustain and increase employment. In con-

43. *Industrial Strategy,* pp. 2, 39, 40.
44. Michael Shanks, *Planning and Politics: The British Experience* 1960–1976 (London, 1977) p. 75.
45. National Enterprise Board, *Annual Report and Accounts 1978,* pp. 8, 9.
46. *Industry Act 1972, Annual Report.* H. C. Paper 206 (1979).

trast, the principal instrument of the bottoms-up approach was the program of national selective assistance schemes. They were available at the discretion of the department to firms in any part of the United Kingdom for the purposes of "modernisation, rationalisation, and restructuring."[47] Under this rationale, the schemes provided investment aid to major manufacturing projects "with significant benefits to the economy where these would not have gone ahead at all, or on the same timing, nature, or scale without the assistance." Over rather more than two years, out of 556 applications the scheme provided aid totaling £756 million to 115 projects promising a primary benefit to the balance of payments and significant benefit to employment.[48] On a sectoral basis fifteen schemes of selective assistance provided aid to particular industries, such as wool textiles, ferrous foundries, machine tools, cloth, paper and board, and so on. In some four years the applications totalled 4,018 leading to 2,839 grants, averaging a little under £30,000 per grant.

The thrust toward industrial growth was blunted by the usual pressures. The major portion of the funds went to provide employment in the development regions rather than to restructure or retool British industry. In many cases, the funds were dispersed in small amounts to large numbers of claimants: something for everyone. Under the wool textile scheme, often cited as a model project, 370 grants were made in response to 403 applications. Since there were only about 400 firms in the industry, it would seem that most must have been able to convince the department of their need and promise.[49]

When the Department of Industry made an award, it was by a straightforward administrative procedure involving "a thorough and professional review"[50] and free of the consultation with interests involved in corporate relations. At the same time however, the minister and the department's regional offices were advised by industrial development boards which included persons drawn from industry and which clearly had weight in the decisions, especially at the national level. If we are to look for producers' influence, a passage

47. *ibid.*, p. 3.
48. *ibid.*, p. 4 and Appendix 11.
49. National Economic Development Council, *Industrial Strategy Wool Textile EDC, Progress Report* 1979, pp. 1, 119.
50. Caroline Miles.

in the comment of the chairman of the board which advised on the selective investment scheme is suggestive. In accordance with their mandate, he notes that the "Board have paid particular attention to the effects of projects on the efficiency and quality of production." Sharpening the difficulties of that task, he goes on to say that, in every case "the Board has had to judge not only the economic benefits of the project, but also whether or not it would have been undertaken on the basis proposed in the absence of Government assistance." With masterly understatement, he concludes: "This is never an easy judgement to make, either in the case of domestic projects or of internationally mobile ones."[51] Even when backed by such expertise, in short, the department could not easily override the individual firm's own assessment of its needs and capacities.

While the individual SWPs could encourage firms in their respective sectors to take advantage of the industry act schemes, the Neddy structure was helpless to impose any overall order on the allocation of public money. But that structure did qualify the pluralism of the industrial arena. Each SWP brought together the unionists and employers in its sector to explore their mutual interests, and also gave them official channels for pressing their sectoral demands on government. In consequence, these institutions which had been designed to serve a central strategy for industrial development often became lobbies against the center for subsidies, tariffs, and regulations that would defend existing firms against encroaching competition from abroad. This thrust for protectionism was barely concealed in the sectoral reports. It expressed an interest which workers and managers might convince themselves they had in common. It exemplified a kind of worker-manager corporatism which, one might well conceive, would be even further encouraged by the introduction of full-fledged industrial democracy.

The Neddy structure has not been able to offset pluralistic stagnation. In a recent review of "the politics of the corporate economy" which starts from the interwar years and concludes with the 1970s, Trevor Smith summarizes his judgment of Neddy in these words:

An elaborate system of functional representation from the grass roots to the centre inhibits the articulation of the public interest. Functional claims are

51. *Industry Act 1972, Annual Report*, p. 12.

not easily aggregated; nor are sectoral policies easily summed. The electorate cannot be broadly appealed to by governments on the urgent issues of the day, above the clamant utterances of sectional interests, for it will have been all but dissolved into a series of introspective and covetous factions. All have a veto and none (including government) have the power of initiative.[52]

Process defeats Purpose

Looking back over some twenty years of public assistance to industry, one can hardly avoid being depressed by the record. "Industrial policy in the United Kingdom since 1960," concludes Geoffrey Denton, "can only be characterised as incoherent." On balance, he finds, the outcome has been to create a "dependency" syndrome in which the "incentive to efficiency and controlling costs in industry is lost" because "it is assumed that governments will always rescue firms that are in trouble."[53] The outcome, in short, of this long and varied effort is precisely the opposite of its goal. Aiming at greater efficiency, competitiveness, and economic growth, the subsidy strategy has encouraged inefficiency, complacency, and economic stagnation.

Such counterproductive results suggest that there is something in the process itself that defeats its purpose. That is precisely the point of Hayward's analysis. Denton, the economist, makes his findings of fact—the dependency syndrome—which he attributes to a bad policy choice, the "implicit political decision" that "no firm will be allowed to fail." Hayward, the student of politics, goes behind the bad policy choice, suggesting how it is produced and sustained by the pluralist and incrementalist process of government-producer group relations. In a succinct sketch of the motivation and behavior of managers who seek subsidies, Sir Keith Joseph outlines the logic of collective action that links Hayward's explanatory model with Denton's description. He writes:

One man's subsidy is another man's penalty, so he shouts for a subsidy, too. If you give vast grants and subsidies to some new factories, you are making life difficult for the rest, the more so if you tax them to pay for the lucky

52. Smith, *op. cit.*, p. 180.
53. Denton, *op. cit.*, p. 161.

ones. So in this way more and more firms can be forced to turn to government for help, which hardly helps self-reliance.[54]

The subsidy scramble is very much like the benefits scramble and the pay scramble. The problem is not motivation, but the situation. The manager will "shout" for a subsidy even if he recognizes the actual tendency of the subsidy policy to diminish the economic achievement of the whole and of its respective parts. For given the situation, that unhappy prospect is not diminished for him if he abstains; on the contrary, abstention will only increase his immediate disadvantage. Then, what about the government? The technocrats have their guidelines to favor only those firms that can use the money effectively. Such differentiation is essential to their industrial strategy. Why will they not, therefore, as good étatists, impose their judgment as to who is the more worthy candidate upon the clamant multitude? The rub is: how can they tell? As the chairman of the Industrial Development Advisory Board confirmed: "This is never an easy judgement to make . . ."

A principal source of syndicalist power is the "know-how" of the producer. A familiar problem of government regulation of industry is that this knowledge, without which the agency cannot achieve its purpose, is very largely a possession of the firm or industry being regulated. Such knowledge, moreover, may be not only technical, and thus accessible only to technocrats with the right training, but also quite particularistic and even personal, and thus radically decentralized to the firm or sector. The granting of subsidies for the purpose of growth and efficiency is a kind of regulation and in carrying it out the subsidy giver is very much dependent upon the industry and even the individual firm to know what is feasible. This decentralization of knowledge, technical and practical, thrusts back upon the regulated the power taken by the regulator. Thus étatism succumbs to syndicalism.

Finally as Sir Keith's paradigm suggests, in the British context syndicalism will be dominated by pluralism. The producers which exercise this syndicalist power are a vast array of firms united only in weak formal groupings. Even if their members were generally to

54. Keith Joseph, *Reversing the Trend: A Critical Reappraisal of Conservative Economic and Social Policies* (Chichester, Eng., 1975) p. 59.

recognize that differentiation is necessary if the industrial strategy is to succeed, the pluralistic structure within which they act would hinder their acting on that recognition. Thus the norms of ''subsidies for all'' and ''no firm shall fail'' unintentionally emerge, as the political process triumphs over its purpose. Like the benefits scramble and the pay scramble, pluralistic corporatism defeats social learning.

PART TWO

Class Decomposition

CHAPTER III

Class Decomposition

In the party politics of the 1970s, policy convergence gave way to policy polarization. At about the same time, paradoxically, the social polarization that had marked the two class-based parties gave way to social convergence. It is a curious sequence. In 1945 polarization marked both policy outlook and the social base. In the 1950s and well into the 1960s, when the two parties were drawing together in policy, they yet retained their strongly marked social differentiation. As their policy positions sharply diverged in the 1970s, however, their electoral supporters became more and more alike in social character. Clearly, the policy outlook of a party and the character of its electoral support did not keep neatly in step.

According to the collectivist model, such a change in the social base of partisanship could be expected to have some considerable effect upon party government. Class identification transferred to party identification had given a steady foundation to party government. One would expect the weakening of such identification to make it more difficult for party leaders to win the cooperation of their traditional constituencies. One might also suppose that such a loss of solidarity would disorient the leadership function itself. Weakening the ties between leaders and followers may not only make followers less faithful; it may also make leaders less responsible. In the 1970s, as we shall see, the declining power of party in and out of power to mobilize consent went along with a growing tendency of party to make excessive demands on traditional adherents and the general public. It seems that the less Governments could do, the more parties promised.

SOCIAL CONVERGENCE AND PARTY DEALIGNMENT

The social convergence of parties since the 1960s has received so much comment and confirmation that we need only review the main trends.

It is hard to think of a study of British politics at any time in history that does not give a major role to class. Some found class a divisive force in the nation; others found it a unifying one. British political culture was ambiguous on the function of class.[1] British political behavior, however, made it an indubitable reality. Using data gathered largely in 1963, Butler and Stokes reported that their "findings on the strength of links between class and partisanship in Britain echo broadly those of every other opinion poll or voting study."[2] Their findings showed that British voters tended strongly to think in terms of two classes, the working class and the middle class, and to use occupation rather than wealth, education, or other marks of status as their basis for assigning individuals to one or the other class. As indicated on table 3.1, the British voter did not draw the line precisely between manual and nonmanual occupations, but within the area of the nonmanual. The table shows the strong correlation between class and party preference, Conservative strength increasing and Labour strength decreasing as we move up the occupational scale.

But the deviations from this tendency were notable. At the upper end, among the managerial groups, Labour had a following. Here we would find those "middle class radicals" who have been influential in the party since the great days of the Fabian Society and who in recent years have played an increasingly important role in the party organization and in Parliament. Even more sharply deviating from the simple correlation of party and class was the substantial number of working class Tories. In the 1960s the Conservatives won the support of a third of the manual workers, which came to about one-half of the total Conservative vote.

Barely had one authority been able to state with confidence based on two decades of electoral studies, that "Class is the basis of British party politics; all else is embellishment and detail,"[3] when evidence

1. *Modern British Politics* pp. xi–xii.
2. Butler and Stokes, *op. cit.*, 1st ed. (1969) p. 76.
3. Peter Pulzer, *Political Representation and Elections* (New York, 1967) p. 98.

TABLE 3.1
Social Polarization 1963
(in percentages)

	Middle Class			Working Class		
	HIGHER MANA-GERIAL (A)	LOWER MANA-GERIAL (B)	SUPER-VISORY NON-MANUAL (C1)	LOWER NON-MANUAL (C1)	SKILLED MANUAL (C2)	UN-SKILLED MANUAL (D)
Conservative	86	81	77	61	29	25
Labour	14	19	23	39	71	75

SOURCE: Based on Tables 4.3 and 4.8 from *Political Change in Britain* by David Butler and Donald Stokes © 1976 by St. Martin's Press, Inc. and Macmillan (London and Basingstoke) and reprinted by permission.

of a decline in the class/party nexus began to come in. Using data for 1963–1970, Butler and Stokes found that "the declining strength of association between class and party is one of the most important aspects of political change in this decade."[4] But their evidence came from a time when a softening of class division might well seem a fitting complement to the still lingering convergence in policy outlooks. With the evidence of the early 1970s at hand, Ivor Crewe and his associates perceived and emphasized the striking contrast between the trends in social base and policy offerings. Given the "resurgence of ideological and class polarization" in party appeals, "the central paradox and puzzle of the February 1974 election," they observed, "is that the class alignment failed to revive."[5]

In their analysis of the previous ten years, however, they found something more than a growing homogeneity in class support for the parties. On both sides, the identification of voters with party had declined. In terms of attitudes this "party dealignment" consisted mainly in a decline in the number of strong identifiers, leading them to speak of the decade as marking "the decline of the party stalwart." In terms of electoral behavior, party dealignment took the

4. Butler and Stokes, *op. cit.*, 2nd ed., 1974, p. 203.
5. Ivor Crewe, Bo Särvlik, and James Alt, "Partisan Dealignment in Britain 1964–1974," *British Journal of Political Science*, 7, no. 2 (April, 1977): 135, 168. "The two main social classes," they write, "did not polarize in their partisanship."

form of a striking fall in the two party vote. While in 1951 Conservatives and Labour between them received 96 percent of the total vote, by February 1974 this figure had fallen to about 77 percent. Since turnout was down only slightly in comparison with 1951, this meant spectacular gains for the "third" parties, Liberals, Scottish and Welsh nationalists, and anti-Conservative Ulster Unionists. Along with greater instrumentalism in attitudes toward party performance and increasing volatility in voting from one election to another, the evidence clearly showed that the old unthinking loyalty of British partisans to the two big parties and through them to the party system, which had flourished during the hotly contested elections of the era of policy convergence, had been deeply eroded.

On balance, Crewe found that the partisan decline on both sides reflected "a continuing erosion of the class-party tie." Among Conservatives the causes were fairly immediate, many switching, for instance, because they thought Labour could handle the unions better than Heath had done. But the case of the Labour party was more serious. For the old fundamentalist view that a solidary working class strains toward socialism in harmony with the unions, Crewe's findings are devastating. The decay of partisanship among Labour's supporters, he found, went back to the 1960s; and far from expressing an aspiration for a more radical policy stance, "had its origins in a growing rejection of the Labour party's basic tenets on the part of its own rank and file during the late 1960s, in particular in a rising hostility to the disruptive powers of trade unions and to their close involvement with the party."[6] As voters, in short, the working class (if one can still use the singular in referring to so fragmented a social category) had no more proclivity to support a coherent break from the consensus than did the trade unions.

In the behavior and attitudes of voters, the general election of 1979 further confirmed these conclusions. As table 3.2 shows, the trend to social convergence continued. Labour lost the election because of an immense shift of working class support to the Conservatives. Among both skilled and unskilled workers, Conservatives made large gains. Even among occupational classes D and E, which include unskilled and semiskilled workers as well as persons dependent on welfare or pensions, the Labour party did not quite get a

6. Crewe *et al.*, *loc. cit.*, p. 183.

TABLE 3.2

Social Convergence 1974–1979

Middle Class				Working Class	
PROFESSIONAL/MANAGERIAL (A,B) OFFICE/CLERICAL (C1)		SKILLED MANUAL (C2)		SEMI/ UNSKILLED MANUAL (D,E)	
	1979	Oct 74 to 1979	1979	Oct 74 to 1979	1979	Oct 74 to 1979

	1979	Oct 74 to 1979	1979	Oct 74 to 1979	1979	Oct 74 to 1979
Conservative	59	+3	41	+15	34	+12
Labour	24	+5	41	− 8	49	− 8
Liberal	15	−6	15	− 5	13	− 3
Other	2	−2	3	− 2	4	− 1
	100%		100%		100%	

NOTE: The table shows how the voters in each of the main occupational groups distributed their support among the parties. It also shows the net change in percentage points between the general election of October 1974 and the general election of 1979.

SOURCE: Market & Opinion Research International, *British Public Opinion. General Election 1979*, Final Report (London, 1979), pp. 6–7.

majority. But the most striking result is the even distribution of skilled workers' support between the two main parties. As usual, the middle class gave its support overwhelmingly to the Conservatives. The trend to social convergence, however, was furthered by Labour's gain among the higher occupational groups. "Both parties," Dennis Kavanagh has recently concluded, "have been making their electoral gains among their 'deviant' classes."[7]

REPOLARIZATION AND U-TURNS

Let us look first at the political behavior that accompanied class and party dealignment and then turn to the question of explanation.

In Britain during the postwar period, the tendency of the policy outlooks of the main parties to converge did not erase the underlying values that differentiated them. It did, however, so broaden and intensify the parties' competition during those critical years from

7. "Still the Workers' Party? Changing Social Trends in Elite Recruitment and Electoral Support" in Dennis Kavanagh, ed., *The Politics of the Labour Party* (London, 1982).

Macmillan to Heath that they could appear to some acute observers as nothing more than teams competing for the support of groups, which thereby became the most important channels for "the transmission of political ideas from the mass of the citizenry to their rulers."[8]

If such convergence precipitated pluralistic stagnation, the remedy, it would seem, was some degree of repolarization. What was needed was a set of coherent initiatives by each party which would help it discipline what it promised when in opposition and order what it did when in power. The parties still retained the moral resources for such an effort in the opposing values which had long motivated their competition, but which had been subdued by the emergence of the consensus of the 1950s. Repolarization in this sense did not necessarily mean a turn toward violent ideological conflict. Properly it meant rather that the parties would recognize and try to cope with the new realities of the collectivist polity and especially its tendency to strengthen and multiply group pressures. Each had a broad, humane, and not overly restrictive tradition by which it could orient its attempts to frame the particulars of a new strategy in policy-making. Such repolarization would mean in short that the parties would confront the political ambiguities of the consensus and act, each in its own way, to resolve them.

The U-turn from Neoliberalism

Edward Heath made a deeply serious, thoroughly prepared, and coherently formulated effort to break with the consensus. When he promised "a new style of government" in his foreword to the 1970 manifesto, he was in part expressing his personal antipathy for what he took to be Harold Wilson's opportunism and shallowness. But above all he was projecting the results of five years of program-making while in opposition on which he had imposed his "determination to change Britain"—indeed, "his passionate determination" to do "for Britain what Adenauer and Ehrhard had done for Germany and de Gaulle for France."[9]

In his first policy statement as party leader, he had signalled his break with the paternalistic interventionism of Butler and Macmillan

8. R. T. McKenzie, *Political Quarterly*, 29, no. 1 (January–March, 1958): 10.
9. Douglas Hurd, *op. cit.*, pp. 13, 139.

by dropping two crucial items of the 1964 manifesto, the commitments to national planning and to an incomes policy. Between 1965 and 1970 he developed his new departures through an elaborate network of consultation with experts from government, business, and the universities which reflected the technocratic tendencies that were running strongly in both parties at the time and which will claim more of our attention at a later point. On taking office, he carried out his plans and promises with clarity and firmness of will. "I take election promises seriously," he remarked after a year in office, "and we have been at great pains to fulfill them. I find that many of my colleagues bring a copy of the election manifesto to Cabinet meetings. At the last count we found that we have already redeemed 79 election pledges."

"Set the people free!" had been the catchword of the Conservatives since 1945, but Heath took it in dead earnest, making a more competitive economy the key to his economic and social policies. Like Labour he aimed at growth, but would achieve it, not through planning, but through encouragement of the market. His centerpiece was the reduction of direct taxes on companies and individuals in order to encourage saving and provide incentives for enterprise and effort. The other measures were logically related to this goal. The lost revenue would be made good partly by shifting the burden to indirect taxation, but mainly by cutting public expenditure. Those cuts would fall on nationalized industries which would lose their subsidies, on business which would be offered investment allowances (tax credits) in lieu of investment grants, and upon social services which would be made more selective by being concentrated especially on those in need. As for inflation, faster growth, it was expected, would dampen price rises, but the upward pressure on wages received most attention. Reduction of income tax would help. Fiscal policy would allow a slightly higher level of unemployment in order to moderate wage pressures. In the public sector the Government would "stand firm" on pay claims,[10] while private companies would be obliged to do the same because of the no lame-duck policy. Not least important, industrial relations reform would reduce the power and propensity of unions to push up wages.

As the application of forethought based on the best available

10. Michael Stewart, *op. cit.*, p. 157. I have found Stewart very helpful in putting together this summary of Heath's economic policy and its outcome.

knowledge to the whole range of economic policy, Heath's preparation was a remarkable achievement. Douglas Hurd is probably right in saying that it was "greater in quantity and higher in quality than any which a political party had previously attempted in opposition."[11] A Labour critic concedes coherence: "Selsdon man," writes Stewart ". . . at least knew where he stood."[12]

With the benefit of hindsight, one can find almost too many reasons for failure. Heath's personal style, as one close associate recalls, reflected his experience as an officer during the war: meticulous preparation combined with loyal reliance on an efficient machine for execution. But this was not the time to trust current orthodoxies or obedient hierarchies. The economic science that had served the country so well during the postwar years and into the era of hubristic Keynesianism and fine tuning was breaking down, but policy makers did not yet fully perceive its failings. According to the Phillips curve Heath's fiscal policy should have held unemployment and the increase in wage rates to 3 percent in 1971; instead unemployment rose *and* wages soared. Stagflation had made its appearance. But the subsequent attempt to cope with it by a "dash for growth" through an expansionist fiscal and monetary policy, although supported by almost all expert opinion at the time, only made matters worse. Well before OPEC struck in November 1973, prices were rising steeply and the foreign deficit was piling up.[13]

The record of Heath's steps in making his U-turn away from neoliberalism and back to the consensus again reveals the character and the power of the pressures generated by the collectivist polity and discussed earlier. There were four main steps. First, the expansionist policy begun in mid-1971 and leading to the dash for growth in 1972; second, the reversal of the subsidies policy by support for Rolls Royce and nationalized shipbuilding and by passage of the sweeping Industry Act of 1972; third, the failure to hold the line on public sector wages when confronted by the miners strike in early 1972; and finally the breach with a fundamental election pledge by the turn toward

11. Hurd, *op. cit.*, pp. 12–13.
12. Stewart, *op. cit.*, p. 112. Heath had launched his new policies early in 1970 at a conference at the Selsdon Park Hotel, enabling Wilson to conjure up the sinister specter of "Selsdon Man."
13. *ibid.*, p. 142.

incomes policy, at first voluntary, and then when that effort failed, statutory, from late 1972 to 1973. The return to the old practices of spending to combat unemployment, subsidies to save jobs and businesses, and a readiness to bargain with organized labor over a wide range of policy did not, however, moderate the most disruptive pressures. The miners refused to accept the third stage of the incomes policy in a strike that led to the three-day week and the election of February 1974.

Some Conservative critics have found the source of Heath's misfortunes in his failure to follow the right policy, viz. strict monetarism. In their view "the correct line" would have averted the bad effects of the oil price rise, the need for an incomes policy, the temptation to bargain with the trade unions, and indeed the whole sad retreat of the U-turn. In rebutting that criticism, Douglas Hurd observes that "Britain cannot be governed dogmatically or by the exercise of willpower," but "only . . . with the consent of people of widely different opinions."[14] What from one viewpoint looks like yielding to pressure, from a wider perspective appears as recognizing the need to mobilize consent. A spectacular illustration of that necessity and of the increasing difficulty of meeting it was Heath's failed attempt to reform industrial relations.

Noncooperation and Confrontation

As Michael Moran observes, Heath's industrial relations act "was not 'class' legislation."[15] Perhaps it would have had more of a chance if it had been. Opinion among the general public and trade unionists strongly favored it. But support was diffuse and opposition concentrated. Since the legislation was not what employers wanted, it drew on itself the opposition of organized business as well as organized labor. Both sides, although not to an equal extent, so far refused cooperation as to make the legislation hopelessly ineffective.

In a sense Heath and his advisers invited this refusal and provided the model for it. Unlike the Tory paternalists who had very much fancied tripartism, as in Macmillan's NEDO, the lawyers and others

14. Hurd, *op. cit.*, p. 140.
15. Michael Moran, *The Politics of Industrial Relations* (London, 1977) p. 152. I have based my account largely on this excellent study.

who designed the act took only party and expert advice and refrained from consulting seriously with the Confederation of British Industry or the Trades Union Congress while the measure was being deliberated within the party, discussed during the election and introduced and debated in Parliament. Yet at point after point its complex provisions required action on the part of employers and employees which sheer coercion could not motivate. The fate of two provisions will illustrate the point: the attempt to make collective bargaining agreements legally binding and the attempt to control internal union rules by means of registration.

The purpose of the act was complex and its gestation had been long, but the wage strike explosion of the late 1960s focused attention on the effect of strikes, especially unofficial strikes, in heightening cost-push inflation and disrupting production. One main purpose of the reform, accordingly, as stressed in the manifesto of 1970, was to create "a framework of law" that would "provide for agreements to be binding on both unions and employers." In Britain, under long standing practice, since collective bargaining agreements were not legally enforceable, unions could take industrial action whenever they liked, an option that favored unofficial strikes, i.e., local walkouts without official union sanction. The new mechanism, like the American Taft-Hartley law, would enable employers to sue unions for breach of contract. It did this by establishing the presumption that collective agreements were intended to be legally enforceable, unless express provisions, to which, of course, both sides acceded, said they were not. The loophole is evident: employers could go along with unions in adding such provisions to their agreements. After the passage of the act, the CBI, reflecting the coolness of big business toward it and acting in parallel with a similar recommendation by the TUC to its members, encouraged employers to insert such exclusion clauses in their collective agreements. Large industrial undertakings virtually boycotted the National Industrial Relations Court (NIRC) which had been set up as the legal forum for enforcement of the new law. And generally managers went to great lengths to ensure that the legislation did not disturb existing arrangements.[16]

A few years later I talked with Mr. Heath about the relations of

16. *ibid.*, pp. 128, 153, 154.

modern governments with trade unions. Agreeing that no government could avoid close consultation, he observed that in the United States the authorities enjoyed the advantages of a stronger legal background. I asked how he explained the failure of his effort to supply that deficiency in Britain by making collective agreements legally binding on the model of our Taft-Hartley act. "The employers would not make use of the law—which they had clamored for—because of fear of the unions," he replied with unconcealed bitterness.

The focus of the union resistance was nonregistration. Failure to register with the newly created Registrar's office would deprive a union of all the significant rights guaranteed by the act. These included crucial immunities gained in earlier struggles, especially the Trades Disputes Act of 1906 which exempted unions from action for tort, thereby making it legal for pickets to encourage workers to break their individual contracts of employment. In the future the unregistered union which sanctioned such everyday acts of industrial relations would be open to a suit for damages. On the other hand, registration would have subjected unions to additional restrictions, and moreover, as they exercised the rights deriving from it, in time would have made repeal very difficult.

The TUC tactic of nonregistration was perfectly legal and constitutional. It was also risky, since it confronted the unregistered union with the option of giving up industrial action or of practicing it under the threat of heavy penalties. This danger did materialize. In the confusing and sometimes farcical narrative of the ensuing struggle between government and unions, one must not lose sight of the coercive power applied to unions in the form of sequestration of assets and big awards of damages. The unions did not win this struggle easily.

Two deployments of syndicalist power turned the tide. The balance of power was first tipped toward the unions as the Government, in the course of executing its U-turn, early in 1972 switched its strategy for fighting inflation to an attempt to win union cooperation with an incomes policy. Success was obviously incompatible with continued coercive action. The unions also pushed the use of their syndicalist power beyond the limits set by the original constitutionalist stance of the TUC. The use or threat of strikes to reverse legislative or judicial action presumably transcends that limit. In July 1972 the National Industrial Relations Court sent five shop stewards to prison for refusal to comply with an order of the court. In response the general council of the TUC voted a one-day national strike, but deferred the determination of a date until the courts had an opportunity to act.

Many unions, however, did not preserve this veil of constitutionalism, and strike action spread throughout the country, preventing publication of newspapers for five days.[17] The law lords, working with unusual speed, as Moran reports, "did as was hoped," securing in effect the release of the prisoners, and the TUC withdrew its threat. Again in the next year, and after the Labour Government had taken office, the engineers refused to pay heavy damages awarded by the NIRC and instead called a national strike of indefinite length which was averted only when an employers association anonymously made the payment. In these cases, trade union power shifted from the negations of noncooperation to confronting legal coercion by the state with syndicalist coercion by the unions. In Michael Moran's terms, functional representation defeated parliamentary representation.[18]

The U-turn from Neosocialism

Heath's attempt to break from the consensus foundered on his inability to mobilize consent. The Labour party's subsequent thrust to make a "drastic move" failed for the same reason. But in the mid-1970s some observers on the Left read into the widespread and successful resistance of the unions to the Conservatives an expression of working class solidarity that would carry Britain forward toward socialism.

Writing with a wide and scholarly knowledge of the Labour party, Lewis Minkin offered a persuasive analysis of these expectations.[19] In the 1950s, he argued, successive defeats had led the party leadership to desert its traditional goal of a socialist society achieved incrementally by successive acts of nationalization and its traditional

17. *ibid.*, p. 142.
18. *ibid.*, p. 157.
19. "The British Labour Party and the Trade Unions: Crisis and Compact," *Industrial and Labour Relations Review,* 28, no. 1 (Oct. 1974).

concern for the interests of the unions in favor of the revisionist strategy of a "people's party" operating a mixed economy in an affluent society. As a result the first Wilson Government came increasingly into conflict with the party and especially with its major working class base, the trade unions.[20]

At the party conference, this growing conflict took the form of unprecedented defeats for the leadership, mainly on incomes policy, trade union legislation, and deflation. In the electoral arena likewise, according to Minkin, revisionism alienated the working class, whose low turnout led to the defeat of 1970.[21] That lesson, however, he thought, had been learned. While some on the Right of the party still regarded the unions as an electoral handicap, the "dominant tendency," with which the Left strongly concurred, was to restore them to their old position of influence, as in the "compact" of 1974. Taking stock in 1974, Minkin concluded that there was danger of disruption if the leadership again resorted to deflation or wage control. On the other hand, the historic "symbiosis of British unions and the Labour party" might well prove to be "a mainspring of the party's ability to carry through a successful radical administration and of the unions' ability to secure the equitable social and economic development that they seek."[22]

Minkin's informed and balanced account, I should say, echoes the ancient orthodoxy of the Labour movement: that there is such an entity as the British working class which is solidary in political and industrial behavior; that the working class seeks incrementally and democratically not just social reform, but a truly socialist regime; and that the trade unions as well as the party in their fundamental aspirations are moving toward this goal.[23] In the light of this political sociology, revisionism was, so to speak, not only a crime, but also a blunder. This blunder was corrected by the forces of class struggle which produced the "social contract" with its promise of a "radical administration." In such an effort of reconstruction, the role of the

20. *ibid.*, pp. 16–18, 30.
21. *ibid.*, p. 36.
22. *ibid.*, p. 37.
23. This belief had a good deal of historical truth in it during what I have called "the socialist generation" in *Modern British Politics,* Chapters V and VI. See also below on the composition and decomposition over time of the British working class, pp. 138–140.

unions would be crucial. It was from their "bowels" that the party
had been born which broke from liberalism, declared for the "socialist commonwealth," and developed during the interwar years the
programs of nationalization which it put into effect under Attlee.
After the diversions of affluence and technocracy, it was logical to
expect these historic forces to reassert themselves. Accordingly, the
role of the unions would be to use their power, recently revealed as
of a new order of magnitude, not merely to defend their respective
interests, but rather to construct a new social and economic order.

There are two things wrong with this vision: its view of trade
union behavior and its view of working class behavior. The unions
did not use their power in this way, nor did they show any intention
of so doing. Indeed, they were quite devoid of positive ideas for
governing Britain, socialist or otherwise. In this lack of interest in
neosocialism, moreover, the unions were entirely in step with the
working class. Its electoral behavior showed further decline of solidarity and ever greater indifference to socialist appeals. It will be
convenient to take the two points in this order.

The Unions and the Social Contract

In the early 1970s the Labour party swung sharply to the left. I
recall the contrast between the 1973 conference and my first conference twenty years earlier. Then also electoral defeat had led to fierce
doctrinal strife, the focal issue also being public ownership. Repeated
defeats of the nationalization proposals in 1953 were a harbinger of
the ultimate victory of revisionism, but out of the later conflict came
massive new commitments to the ancient orthodoxies. In contrast
with their evaporation from the manifestoes of the 1950s and 1960s,
these orthodoxies were reaffirmed ardently in the manifestoes of
February and October 1974. Proclaiming its "socialist aims," and
proposing "a fundamental and irreversible shift in the balance of
power and wealth in favor of working people and their families,"
the February statement in seventeen carefully numbered pledges
promised higher social spending, price and rent controls, central
planning, massive extensions of public ownership, and a series of
specific acts of legislation on industrial relations. While the manifesto was based on the program approved by the conference in 1973,
it is more important to know that the main items had also been agreed

upon over the past couple of years in discussions within the newly established Liaison Committee representing the parliamentary party, the National Executive Committee (NEC) and the TUC. Out of these discussions came the "new social contract" proclaimed in January 1974 between the party and the unions and reaffirmed in the manifesto.

At the heart of the social contract was an agreement to cope with the contribution—nominally denied—of rising wages to inflation. For its part, the party pledged a return to free collective bargaining along with a range of social and economic measures substantially the same as those in the manifesto except for much less stress on public ownership. For their part, the unions promised nothing specific, insisting that "wages and salaries are very far from being the only factors affecting prices"; but they did indicate that the "alternative strategy" would favorably "influence the whole climate of collective bargaining."[24]

How did the two sides carry out their parts of the bargain? The Labour Government quickly set to work to carry out its pledges, in the next few months restoring free collective bargaining, increasing pensions, freezing rents, imposing price controls, subsidizing foods, making redistributive income tax changes, and repealing the Industrial Relations Act. At the Trades Union Congress in September, 1974, "a check list was drawn up of what the Government had achieved during its short spell in office and it amounted to a virtual item by item implementation of the February 1973 Liaison Committee statement on economic policy."[25] After a narrow victory in the October election, the Government set forth a parliamentary program for further steps, as promised, with regard to taxation, education, nationalization of the shipbuilding and aircraft industries, the National Enterprise Board, and a system of planning agreements. "Despite its minuscule majority," writes Stewart, "the new Labour Government came back in October 1974 determined to press on towards socialism. . . . Although one or two items in this programme had not made much headway a year and a half later, a great deal had."[26]

How about "responsible collective bargaining"? The February

24. TUC-Labour Party Liaison Committee, *Economic Policy and the Cost of Living,* (February 23, 1973) p. 4.
25. Robert Taylor, *op. cit.,* 2nd ed. 1979, p. 132.
26. Stewart, *op. cit.,* pp. 200–201.

manifesto had stated the necessity for "money incomes to grow in line with production."[27] In March the general council, however, went no further than recommending to union negotiators that they limit their claims to "compensation for the rise in the cost of living since the last settlement" and that "the twelve month interval between major increases should in general continue to apply."[28] No rule to bridge the gap between these recommendations and the criterion of the manifesto was agreed. No numerical targets for wage increases were suggested, except for a minimum for the low paid.

In the following months although the OPEC oil crisis necessarily imposed a fall in the British standard of living, wage settlements met and more than met the sharply rising rate of inflation. The general council cautioned against "self-defeating" wage increases. "Very few negotiators," reports Taylor, "appeared to take much notice during the winter of 1974–5 when pay rises began to rise over 25 percent."[29] Having risen by about 13 percent in 1972 and 1973, average earnings shot up by 17.5 percent in 1974 and 26.7 percent in 1975. Inflation broke the single digit barrier, the percent change in prices over the previous year rising from 9.2 percent in 1973 to 16.1 percent in 1974 and 24.2 percent in 1975.[30]

That latter year of desperate crisis forced Labour to make its U-turn back to the consensus. Within those boundaries, as we have seen, the Government and the unions then worked out the moderately successful arrangements that lasted until the new wage explosion of 1978–9.

In the frantic failure of the social contract in its early neosocialist phase, the events are interesting for what they tell us about what the unions really wanted. To keep "money incomes . . . in line with production" is as much a necessity of a socialist as a capitalist economy. If in any serious sense the unions had sought to advance toward the socialist commonwealth, they would have acted to meet that necessity. The obvious fact is that the leadership at national and local levels could not or would not deliver those "responsible" wage claims

27. *The Labour Party Manifesto 1974*, p. 9.
28. Trades Union Congress, "Collective Bargaining and the Social Contract." Adopted by the General Council, June 26, 1974 and by the Trades Union Congress, Sept. 4, 1974.
29. Taylor, *op. cit.*, 2nd ed. 1979, p. 134.
30. Stewart, *op. cit.*, pp. 169, 262.

that had been promised. As a result, the Labour party was even less able to mobilize consent for neosocialism than Heath had been to rally the support of business for his neoliberalism.

What then did those promises mean? One must take care in pronouncing on the sincerity or substance of the socialist beliefs of British trade union leaders. To hear someone with the incontestable integrity of Len Murray, general secretary of the TUC, affirm his commitment to equality with a fervor reminiscent of William Morris or Tawney, while at the same time fully recognizing the fierce combat over differentials within the movement to which he has dedicated his life is to confront a moral and psychological snarl that is not easily untangled. It is a pity we do not have a study of the beliefs of union leaders comparable to what we have learned about British politicians.[31] But in reply to our question, the first step is to see that in these critical years when the TUC seemed to be joining strongly in the reassertion of the socialist commitment, there was within that body virtually no serious discussion or study of what that commitment entailed. The unions were clear about those laws that would promote "the interests of labor," specifically the repeal of hostile Conservative legislation and further measures "to strengthen the legal protection of the right to strike."[32] They also were strongly committed to spending on social programs from which their members benefitted and for the sake of full employment. But for action as "a mainspring" of a "radical administration" by a neosocialist Labour party, they were intellectually unprepared.

Stephen Bornstein and Peter Gourevitch have traced in detail the "economic thought" of British unions in preparation for, and response to, the crisis of the mid–1970s. It is a story of insignificant effort and meager achievement. A few leaders did take an interest in the "alternative strategy" being worked out by leftwing intellectuals led by Stuart Holland of Sussex University. But the bulk of the TUC's general council members did not regard these schemes as central to their own concerns and to the interests of their members. In one of their milder comments, Bornstein and Gourevitch conclude that "in the

31. Robert D. Putnam, *The Beliefs of Politicians: Ideology, Conflict and Democracy in Britain and Italy* (New Haven, 1973) p. 4.
32. *NUPE Guide to the Employment Protection Act and the Trade Union and Labour Relations Act.* (Labour Research Department, London, 1977) p. 3.

early days of the Labour Government, when the industrial side of the
Social Contract was still a serious possibility if the unions had pushed
it, the TUC and most of its affiliates lacked a sound intellectual basis
for believing in the necessity of such a program."[33]

THE POLITICS OF CLASS DECOMPOSITION

In the palmy days of the collectivist polity, party government had
been undergirded by the still flourishing solidarities, horizontal and
vertical, of the British class system. Policy convergence intensified
the pressures of the new group politics which threatened to reduce the
party battle to a mere competition for power and to paralyze public
policy. The attempt to escape from incoherence first through neoliberalism, then through neosocialism was frustrated by the inability
of the parties to mobilize the organizational cooperation of even those
occupational groups which had traditionally identified with them.
Heath had hardly more success in winning the support of organized
business than in stirring a response among the unions to the old hierarchical appeal of Toryism. Labour found that its old class catch-
words had no more success at the polls than in rallying organized
labor to the discipline of social reconstruction. The fragmentation of
producer and consumer groups frustrated repolarization, while continuing to make the consensus inviable. In retrospect, the old class
system, as a behavioral reality in politics and government and not
simply the rhetoric of manifestoes and agitation, might well appear
to have some advantages.

The causes of the decay of these social foundations of party government are complex. In some respects class decomposition follows
naturally from modern economic evolution. In Britain, occupation
has been a good indicator of the class to which a person is assigned
by himself and by others. When we ask what it is about an occupation that has led people to assign it to one class or another, no simple
answer appears. One aspect is standard of living. In this respect an
age of unprecedented productive power greatly weakened the objective basis of class identification during the rise of affluence in the

---

33. Stephen Bornstein and Peter Gourevitch, "Unions in a Declining Economy: the
Case of the British T.U.C." in Andrew Martin and George Ross, eds., *European
Trade Union Responses to Economic Crisis*, Vol. 2 (London, 1982).

postwar years. Another basis of class has been found not on the consumption, but on the production side of economic relations, the owners of the means of production being set off from the nonowners. In recent phases of modernization, this distinction also has been lessened by bureaucratization. In many instances the control of economic enterprises has shifted from owners to managers, while on the lower levels trade unions provide workers with channels for dealing collectively with management.

The fact that public ownership has not abolished class conflict suggests a further and more enduring basis of class differentiation. This is power: the ability of one person to impose his will upon others, whether by economic, or political, or other means. In this sense, following Dahrendorf, a class may be defined as a collectivity sharing interests that arise from the authority structure of the imperatively coordinated association.[34] This definition is in conformity with the fact that class conflict occurs in socialist as well as capitalist economies. It is also in accord with popular conceptions of class in which degree of power is a major determinant of social evaluation. For instance, in distinguishing between the two main classes, British respondents, as we have seen, draw the line not precisely between manual and nonmanual occupations, but between the nonmanual occupations with supervisory duties and those without supervisory duties. (See table 3.1.)

Private ownership and differences of wealth and income are two of the forms taken by the differentiation of power. Managerialism, not capitalism, however, is the root of the relative deprivation of power that identifies the manual and nonsupervisory occupations as working class. In this respect the relative deprivation of power has been diminished by the rise of trade unions and various forms of influence exercised by employees over the operation of their firms, ranging from collective bargaining to functional representation. In modern bureaucratic society, however, an objective basis of class consisting of a differentiation of power is still a major feature of both public and private enterprise.

34. Ralf Dahrendorf, *Class and Class Conflict in Industrial Society* (Stanford, 1959) p. 238.

Social Mobility and Class

If the members of an inferior class reject their inferiority, there are, broadly, two ways they can change matters. One is to act together to use their collective power to change the system that has put and kept them in this position. The other is to act individually to rise out of a position of inferiority and join the superior class. Like many sociologists, John Goldthorpe believes that if social development hinders the second option, the chances of the first being taken will be increased. Since he is one of those socialists who look to the working class as an important social vehicle for achieving a socialist society, he is concerned to see whether recent changes in social mobility have increased or decreased the potential of the working class for solidary action. As set forth in his authoritative study, *Social Mobility and Class Structure in Britain* (1980), his reply, in brief, is that, while for the middle class these changes have diminished the chances of solidarism, for the working class they have greatly enhanced them.

Goldthorpe starts from a classification grouping together occupations which are similar with regard both to material circumstances and position of authority. Seven main occupational classes are divided into a "service class" of managers, independent businessmen, professionals, and high-grade technicians and supervisors, constituting about a quarter of the total labor force; an "intermediate class" of clerical employees, petty bourgeois owners and artisans, and lower-grade technicians and supervisors, constituting about 30 percent of the total; and a "working class" of skilled and unskilled manual workers, constituting rather more than 40 percent of the total.[35]

Much of his discussion goes to show how very greatly upward mobility has increased from the beginning of World War II to the seventies. In Britain, as in all advanced industrial countries, the proportion of nonmanual to manual workers has risen markedly, widening the class structure at the top and narrowing it at the bottom. Expanding "room at the top" has been filled by men from all classes. The top rank of the service class, for instance, while drawing about a quarter of its members from families similarly placed, also drew

35. Goldthorpe, *op. cit.*, Table 2.1, p. 44.

rather more, nearly 30 percent, from working class families. "The dominant feature of the pattern of absolute mobility," Goldthorpe finds, has been "the relatively high and increasing rate of upward movement from working- and intermediate-class origins into the ranks of the service class."[36]

Prospects for solidary action on the part of the service class, he believes, are reduced by the heterogeneity of its social derivations, although the lack of much downward movement and the similarity of economic function may promote solidarity in the future. At present, as he notes, the findings of sociologists are that the service class has a relatively low sense of identity and class consciousness. The potential for solidary behavior by the working class, he finds, has, on the contrary, increased. Although the working class is a somewhat smaller portion of the labor force than in the interwar years, the lessening of recruitment from other classes makes it more homogeneous. Moreover, the chance of any of its sons getting a top job is still far, far less than that of someone born at the top. In Goldthorpe's calculations, the chance of a son of the service class remaining in it is four times the chance of a son of the working class rising into it.[37] More families are moving up, but once they get there they seem to have the same superior ability to stay there that top people have had in the past. Absolute mobility has increased; relative mobility has not. In the confrontation of this continuing and "enormous discrepancy" by a "mature" working class that is increasingly homogeneous and "second generation blue collar," Goldthorpe sees "a distinctive potential" for the pursuit of "strategies of solidarism."[38]

From Class to Groups

What light does this study of the changing class structure throw upon the decay of the social foundations of party government? In electoral behavior, as we have seen, class solidarity has declined. In economic management likewise the parties when in power have faltered in attempts to mobilize cooperation from traditional clienteles. Nor did those groups show a positive class-based drive to master the

36. *ibid.*, p. 147.
37. *ibid.*, p. 75.
38. *ibid.*, pp. 256, 252, 271.

state and reconstruct society. They would defend themselves and the norms of the consensus conforming to their particular interests. But otherwise, the economic actors that appeared in politics were not classes, but groups deeply engaged in rivalry within, as well as between, classes.

In trying to understand this development, we must grant that economic modernization by way of affluence and bureaucratization has greatly reduced some of the older bases of class solidarity. In accord with Goldthorpe's analysis, an increase in absolute mobility has no doubt also directed into individual advancement energies which in another era would have gone into collective effort. His depiction of the service class with its bureaucratic functions and heterogeneous social background accords with the increasing ambiguities of the middle class vote. The service class is primarily "the class of those exercising power and expertise on behalf of corporate bodies" along with its appropriate "subaltern or *cadet* levels." Diverse in social origins and oriented by occupation toward collectivist solutions, with many of its members employed in the management tasks of the public sector itself, such an occupational grouping, one can readily grant, would have a low sense of class identity. One can understand also how, accordingly, this class could contribute to the social convergence of the parties over the past two decades in the form of that growing middle class vote for Labour.

In his portrait of the "mature" working class, however, Goldthorpe has argued that modernization has left intact strong economic bases for solidary behavior. If we are to understand why such behavior has failed to materialize, we must turn not to economic, but to political developments. In the changes engendered by and within the collectivist polity, we can find abundant reason for class decomposition.

In saying this I am in a sense simply repeating the old liberal formula, familiar since the days of Emile Durkheim and L. T. Hobhouse, that social reform and democratic participation can reintegrate the working class into society. In Britain for reformist liberals and social democrats this has been a promise of the welfare state. In major respects that promise has been fulfilled as social mobility has increased and class conflict has declined. Yet the collectivist polity has diverted energies from class conflict not only by improving the chances for individual self-advancement, but also and especially by strengthening the power of groups. The decomposition of classes, therefore, has led not to old-fashioned atomistic competition, but to the pluralistic competition of the new group politics.

If we keep in mind that class is based on relative power and consider the reallocation of power accomplished by the collectivist polity, we can readily understand this transformation. The process underlying class decomposition was that reallocation of power by which the welfare state and managed economy strengthened the position of groups commanding electoral or syndicalist power. The grounds of pluralistic stagnation and class decomposition are the same.

Reintegration

Our discussion of social mobility was premised on the common notion that individual self-advancement and class conflict are alternative responses to social inferiority. By promoting social mobility, the collectivist polity has undoubtedly helped diminish class conflict and class solidarity. But the course of political development in Britain in the past two decades shows that there is a third option, viz., group competition. We have looked at this option in its various forms as the benefits scramble, the pay scramble, and the subsidies scramble.

Social mobility reintegrated the working class into society by directing the energies of individual members into the competition for self-advancement. The new group politics reintegrates the working class into society by directing the energies of component groups into the competition for group advantage. As Goldthorpe has pointed out, the collectivist polity meant that a further step had been taken toward fulfilling Durkheim's hope for greater "equality of conditions of conflict" and this "new power of labor" has been used to engage "forcefully, but severally in distributional conflict along with other interest-groups."[39] In so doing, organized labor, he believes, is simply learning the lesson of the capitalist market. The market which has, so to speak, taught organized labor this lesson, however, is not an atomized, free market, but the managed market of the collectivist

39. *ibid.*, pp. 202, 208.

polity, peopled largely by actors with some intermediate degree of market power. A socialist may wish that the unions would use their power in a concerted way for broad social reconstruction. In fact, they reflect the conditions of this managed market in their fierce determination to defend their rights under it and in their unwillingness to go beyond. "There is," as Colin Crouch observes, "a powerful working class collectivism, but paradoxically this remains, in its fragmentation, defensiveness, and essential lack of politicization, more consistent with the classical liberal economy than with current state co-ordinated forms."[40]

"Sectionalism," i.e., interunion and interoccupational rivalry, has always plagued the labor movement in Britain, as elsewhere. But from one generation to another, the broad direction toward or away from solidarity has shifted profoundly. Over the past hundred years, one can trace a cycle with a rising and declining phase. The "new unionism" of the 1880s, marked by the rise of the general unions, is generally considered to express a growing self-consciousness in the working class and a consequent tendency toward unity in political and industrial action. This tendency was displayed in the founding of the Labour party and its break from liberalism and in the trend toward density and amalgamation in trade union organization. This was a period of class composition when working class solidarity emerged from dispersed centers of activity.

The "new unionism" of the 1960s, on the other hand, marked the declining phase of the cycle in which fragmentation and decentralization engendered increasing interunion rivalry. Class composition was succeeded by class decomposition into local and occupational fragments. In this phase of union development, the defensive interest of the unions in maintaining and strengthening their legal and organizational power was as great as ever, as was their concern for maintaining the general and specific conditions of the collectivist polity which had called forth the new phase of sectionalism.

In this sense the working class was reintegrated into competitive society, although the basis of reintegration was neither a solidary class nor a set of individuals but a plurality of groups. In so promoting the decomposition of class, however, the collectivist polity

---

40. "Inflation and the Political Organization of Economic Interests," in Hirsch and Goldthorpe, *op. cit.,* p. 232.

undermined the social foundations of party government and of the mobilization of consent in the welfare state and managed economy. Individual membership in the Labour party fell to less than half a million out of an electorate of forty-one million at the end of the 1970s, while outside the party the revolutionary left splintered into many small, raucous factions.

PART THREE

The Collapse
of Deference

CHAPTER IV

The Romantic Revolt

The discovery of structural explanations is probably the most prized achievement of the social scientist. This is his *métier:* to show how a certain pattern of action regularly leads to consequences unintended by its institutional norms or by its human participants. Such a sequence may support the pattern. Or it may be counterproductive, as when the collectivist polity leads to developments that produce pluralistic stagnation and class decomposition. Whether counterproductive or not, the sequence of manifest structure and latent function resembles those uniformities of unthinking nature that justify calling the study of it "scientific."

Yet in social studies there is always a certain looseness in such a structural explanation arising from the fact that its subjects are thinking, feeling beings. For that reason you can never quite tell what they will do next. Therefore, powerful as the situational compulsion on them may appear, you can usually imagine them responding differently to the situation if they took it into their heads to have different thoughts and feelings about it. Nor does the problem vanish when the social scientist pursues the pressures into the psyche. There he meets with the same indeterminacy. You can never be quite sure what a person will do with his compulsions.

The previous discussion of the contradictions of collectivism shares the strengths and weaknesses of structural explanations. The weakness is that one can imagine these processes being impeded or reversed by a different state of mind. This reflection prompts the hypothesis that they may have arisen not only because of the developments we have examined, but also because of a change in the ideal foundations of the collectivist polity. Doubts of this sort arise with regard to all the forms of self-defeating pluralism that we have examined, but for

107

illustration we may look again at the failure of incomes policy. Given the fact that most of the time, most trade unionists and many of their national leaders have favored an incomes policy, it is hard to understand why a government guarantee that all groups will play according to the rules did not sufficiently assuage their competitive fears as to bring about the "concerted action" that was generally desired. Allegations of stupidity, lack of information, extreme self-interest, or widespread radicalism among trade unionists and their leaders do not correspond with the facts. One must suppose some lack of trust in government and in one another, if one is to understand why the situation had such power over so many for so much of the time.

"Concerted action" would involve agreement, tacit or explicit, among unions and between unions and government in the manner of classic social contract theory. To say that such a political contract requires trust is common sense. The everyday contracts of the market place, which are usually seen as no more than instruments of enlightened self-interest, likewise require trust by the parties in one another and in the agencies responsible for enforcing them.[1] An effective free market, in short, depends on a generally accepted system of norms and beliefs to promote enlightened calculation among its participants and their conformity with the rules of the game.

In the political forum as in the economic market place, likewise, trust rests on a cultural foundation in which norms and expectations are mutually reinforcing. When these beliefs are widely and firmly shared, the choice mechanism of the polity is equipped to cope with the inevitable tensions of individual and group conflict. As doubt of the legitimacy and effectiveness of established authority rises, the polity loses its capacity to mobilize consent and to act in concert. The sharp onset of pluralistic stagnation in the 1960s is incomprehensible until we recognize the sudden and radical change in British political culture that released these self-destructive tendencies.

Class decomposition is also a puzzle that points to the same line of inquiry. Perhaps one can put the question by asking how some-

---

1. In the economy, Kenneth Arrow observes, "trust in each other's word among traders makes possible a whole range of mutually beneficial exchange that without it would not be feasible." "The Organization of Economic Activity: Issues Pertinent to the Choice of Market versus Non-market Allocation," in R. H. Haveman and J. Margolis, eds., *Public Expenditure and Policy Analysis* (Chicago, 1970) p. 70.

thing so useful as class struggle in organizing and rationalizing the
political process could be so gravely weakened in so short a time.
Objective bases for class differentiation in politics and industry could
still be found. Inequalities of power persisted, although some forms
were new. British political culture, moreover, embodied ideas and
sentiments that could crystallize on these objective formations in such
a way as to retain, suitably adapted, the familiar vertical and horizontal solidarities of the class system. Attitudes supporting both broad
organic connections and hierarchic relations within and between such
connections have survived over the centuries. In the course of modernization these attitudes have been projected upon and helped sustain many different economic, social, and political structures. Why
could they not have survived and assimilated the new pluralistic
structures of the collectivist polity? It must have taken something
more than the new group politics to reduce to so enfeebled a condition those ancient organic and hierarchic powers.

The structural explanation has real value. It is useful to see how
the collectivist polity inherently but unintentionally tends to create a
new group politics which fragments power among producer and consumer groups. Yet in Britain as in any polity, power in a sense has
always been fragmented; at some level of analysis there is always a
group politics. The task is to explain the weakening, not to say disappearance, of the conditions which over a long past have normally
aggregated these fragments. Analytically speaking, if we are to
understand pluralistic stagnation and class decomposition, we must
first look at the collapse of deference.

POLITICAL IMAGINATION AND POLITICAL VALUES

The weakness of structural explanations is that they make insuffi-
cient allowance for the operations of the human imagination. There
is no good reason for social science to blind itself to this reality. On
the contrary, as Clifford Geertz brought home to social science in his
interpretation of ''ideology as a cultural system,'' the necessity is
rather to recognize and study systematically ''the autonomous process of symbol formulation.'' The sociological and psychological
background of new ideas is, of course, relevant. It cannot, however,
explain away the contribution of man, the ''agent of his own reali-

zation,'' who through the construction of "schematic images of social order . . . makes himself for better or worse a political animal.''[2] Some of the main currents of political thought have always sustained and given direction to this fundamental insight. Still today one can hardly ask for a more instructive guide than Shelley's *Defense of Poetry* (1821) to the ways in which imagination gives rise to values that transform the political world.

In *Modern British Politics,* I took political culture to be "one of the main variables'' of the British political system and "a major factor in explaining the political behavior of individuals, groups, and parties.''[3] In saying that political culture is a variable, I mean not only that over a period of time a certain complex of values and beliefs—such as those I term "collectivist''—oriented feeling and behavior. That view of political culture is compatible with its being regarded as merely a reflection of, or an adaptation to, nonpolitical changes, which, once formulated, condition behavior until again remolded by outside forces. I mean to take this variability seriously by recognizing that political culture may also be shaped by "the autonomous process of symbol formulation'' or in Shelley's words, "the imaginative and creative faculty'' which makes "poets . . . the unacknowledged legislators of the world.''[4]

The theme of the following pages is accordingly how the British political imagination has operated within a given tradition and structure to formulate new symbols and elicit new attitudes that are transforming that tradition and structure.

THE DECLINE OF THE CIVIC CULTURE

Although I have entitled this section "The Collapse of Deference,'' it is concerned with what is more broadly called "the decline of the civic culture.'' This profound and well-documented change has affected both the hierarchic and the organic values embodied in the traditionalism of Britain's unique political culture, but "defer-

2. "Ideology as a Cultural System,'' in Clifford Geertz, *The Interpretation of Cultures: Selected Essays* (New York, 1973).
3. *Modern British Politics,* pp. xii and 389.
4. "A Defense of Poetry'' in Roland A. Duerksen, ed., *Percy Bysshe Shelley: Political Writings* (New York, 1970) pp. 196–197.

ence'' as the most celebrated, although not necessarily the most important, of these traditionalist elements, serves to focus attention on the seriousness and depth of the change.

While we will be concerned with the unique ways in which in Britain new attitudes have been articulated and have influenced events, it will throw light on their character to see them as part of a general transformation of political culture in Western countries. The thrust has been twofold. On the one hand, a powerful, indeed an exaggerated and unbalanced assertion of the values of scientific rationalism engendered a trend toward technocracy. At the same time, a romantic revolt in politics gave rise to a new populism that embodied a hardly less exaggerated expression of democratic values.[5] Both the technocratic and populistic impulses arise from the culture of modernity that is shared by all these countries. Each is an exaggerated expression of the elements of that culture. The transformation has been characterized in different countries by sharply different emphases and by impacts that are sometimes more, sometimes less serious. In Britain both the populistic and the technocratic tendencies have undermined the civic culture, but the populistic has had much the greater effect on attitudes and behavior and it is this effect, its source, and its significance for British politics, that will occupy virtually all our attention in the following pages.[6]

To give such emphasis to the new populism in Britain is not to say that Britain has become more radically participatory than other countries. In the United States, for instance, the surge of populism in the past two decades has affected behavior and institutions at many levels—as in the explosive growth of presidential primaries. But in American history, populism is so familiar and recurrent that these

5. I have examined the impact of these two forces on American politics in ''In Search of a New Public Philosophy'' in Anthony King, ed., *The New American Political System* (Washington, D.C., 1978).

6. For the sake of a definition, let me say that by populism I mean an exaggerated assertion of the values of radical democracy. These values are individualist, participatory, majoritarian, and egalitarian with regard to power rather than rewards. See the discussion in *Modern British Politics*, pp. 39–43. The exaggeration came when, in their excesses, the romantic rebels of the 1960s asserted these values in word and deed with a disregard for other values and often indeed for objective reality itself. As the romantic passion subsided, however, the thrust of radical democracy continued increasingly to affect political attitudes and behavior, so providing the culminating theme of this book in Chapter V.

changes, while important, are, so to speak, more of the same thing. In the case of Britain—a country that has never experienced anything like Jacksonian democracy—the new stress on participant attitudes and behavior collides with values anciently embedded in the political system. The threat to British institutions, therefore, is much greater, not because populistic forces are stronger there than in America— they surely are not—but because their criticism attacks values that are central to those institutions and would, if carried into effect, fundamentally transform them.

The term, civic culture, comes from the well-known study by Almond and Verba. I am shading its meaning, however, to allow for other recent work as well as for older and more literary descriptions of the ideal foundations of the British polity. In Almond and Verba's account, the civic culture in Britain was "characterized by a mixture or balance between participant and deferential or acquiescent attitudes; between a consensus on the rules of the game and disagreement on specific issues; between commitment and pragmatism."[7] In a recent summary of the concept Almond gives the first and the last of these characteristics—deference and pragmatism—special emphasis. "From enlightenment and liberal political theory," he writes, "it drew the 'rationality-activist' model of democratic citizenship, the model of a successful democracy that required that all citizens be active in politics and that their participation be informed, analytic, and rational." At the same time, the concept reflected the fact that "this participant-rationalist model of citizenship could not logically sustain a *stable* democratic government." "Only when combined in some sense with its opposites of passivity, trust, and deference to authority and competence," he concludes, "was a viable, stable democracy possible."[8]

In essentials this sketch restated, in the language of, and with the support of contemporary political science, a view that other perceptive observers had reported in the past. Among foreign observers, a quite similar understanding of the stability and effectiveness of the

7. Dennis Kavanagh, "Political Culture in Great Britain: The Decline of the Civic Culture," in Gabriel A. Almond and Sidney Verba, eds., *The Civic Culture Revisited* (Boston, 1980) p. 125.
8. "The Intellectual History of the Civic Culture Concept" in Almond and Verba, *op. cit.*, (1980), p. 16.

British polity was shared by Alexis de Tocqueville, Hippolyte Taine, Gaetano Mosca, Joseph Schumpeter and A. Lawrence Lowell. As an historical explanation, their approach emphasized the exceptional degree to which Britain retained elements of its traditional, premodern political culture during the centuries of modernization. Their admiration was attracted especially by the survival of a responsible and able governing class into the era of popular government and by the adherence of participants to a nonideological and pragmatic mode of intercourse in the context of wide-ranging debate and adaptive government. These same points of excllence were celebrated by Walter Bagehot whose authoritative account put into circulation the term "deference" as a description of a central feature of the system.[9]

These observers saw the political culture of Britain as a balance or integration of two orientations, the modern and the traditional. On the one hand, the civic culture embraced the premises of modernity, voluntarism, and rationalism. In its voluntarist outlook, modernity turned away from the old teleological restraints on individual and collective action. Legitimacy for the regime or for individual purpose came to be founded on subjective human needs and wishes, rather than on the objective standards of a divine or natural order. Even for the conservative Burke "the satisfaction of human wants" was the purpose of the state. In the pursuit of these satisfactions, moreover, whether through public or private means, the attitudes of scientific rationalism gained influence. Under this influence, action was not only instrumental, but also sought a basis in knowledge that was universally valid, systematically ordered, and empirically founded.

The conflict of such values with traditionalism is implied in this description. In any country, the story of modernization is in great part simply the displacement of the old by the new in outlook and institutions. On the other hand, in Britain, as we have seen in tracing the stages of modernization, much of the traditional world survived, sometimes alongside, sometimes fused with the modern. Values of hierarchy and organic connection that were medieval in origin adapted to and strengthened successive systems of stratification, even as power

9. Bagehot, *The English Constitution* (first published in 1867) Fontana Edition. With an Introduction by R. H. S. Crossman (London, 1963), *passim* and the famous passage in the 1872 Introduction on England as "a deferential country," p. 270.

and participation were extended. As deference, these hierarchical attitudes supported much independent authority for government, respect for leadership in political and organizational life, and in the bureaucracy "a due sense of subordination and superordination."[10] Inseparable from such hierarchical values, a propensity to identify with large social bodies—the organic sense—sustained the horizontal groupings of modern social and political structures, so that, as we have seen, the objective bases of the modern class system were colored and strengthened by premodern survivals. Moreover, as these attitudes descending from the traditional order qualified the liberating spirit of modern democracy, so also an attachment to custom, precedent, and history moderated the scientific thrust of modern rationalism. It was the British style of government to avoid any excess of systematic thought or empirical research in policy making.

Against these restraining influences of traditionalism the cultural revolution in politics directed its force in the 1960s, and in their weakening the decline of the civic culture was measured in the 1970s.

The Survey Evidence

Having reviewed the survey evidence in light of recent political developments, Dennis Kavanagh concluded at the end of the 1970s: "What does seem clear is that the traditional bonds of social class, party, and common nationality are waning, and with them the old restraints of hierarchy and deference."[11] We have already examined the decline of the class/party nexus and at least glanced at its association with a rising instrumentalism—an increase, in Almond's terms, of the attitude of the "informed, analytic, and rational" citizen. "The decline in strong partisanship and the erosion of both the working-class deferential Tory and the 'traditionalist' Labour voter," writes Kavanagh in his summary of these changes, "has made support for party and government more instrumental, tying it to actual performance."[12]

The decline of attitudes supporting hierarchy deserves more specific attention. One aspect of deference is diffuse support for the

10. H. E. Dale, *The Higher Civil Service in Great Britain* (London, 1941).
11. Kavanagh, *loc. cit.,* p. 170.
12. *ibid.,* p. 146.

political system independent of policies and performance. Reporting such support as very high, Almond and Verba found in Britain "a deferential political culture."[13] They saw "deferential and subject orientations" as linked attributes, "the sense of trust in the political elite" making "citizens willing to turn over power to them."[14] One measure of deference, therefore, was the level of trust in government, which the 1959 data showed to be very high, 83 percent of respondents saying that they expected to get equal treatment in dealings with government officials.[15] A 1972 survey—admittedly of young people only—showed a strikingly lower figure in response to a very similar question, only 18 percent of those questioned saying they expected to be treated evenly by government.[16] In 1980 Kavanagh, although not satisfied with the trend data, felt secure in saying that the survey evidence showed "a low level of confidence" in government and "a general lack of trust in the country's leadership."[17]

A sense of the magnitude of distrust of government and politics that had arisen in Britain in the 1970s is conveyed by a table in which Alan Marsh reported some of his findings. Marsh used four questions to probe attitudes relevant to political trust and mistrust. Table 4.1 summarizes the results. The totally cynical are a small number— only 10 or 15 percent. But for none of the four measures did a majority of respondents offer a "trusting" response. Only 40 percent trusted the Government to do what is right most or all of the time. Seventy percent had grave doubts about the truthfulness of politicians. Sixty percent had grave doubts that a Government would put the interests of the country above those of party. Significantly more believed that the country was run by a few big interests than believed it was run for the interests of all the people.

The question of timing is crucial if one is interested in the source

---

13. Almond and Verba, *op. cit.,* (1963) p. 455.
14. Vivien Hart, *Distrust and Democracy: Political Distrust in Britain and America* (Cambridge, Eng., 1978) p. 44; Almond and Verba, *The Civic Culture,* p. 490. In that context Almond and Verba also write: "The role of social trust and cooperativeness as a component of the civic culture cannot be overemphasized. It is, in a sense, a generalized resource that keeps a democratic polity operating."
15. Almond and Verba, *op. cit.* (1963) Table 2, p. 109.
16. Hart, *op. cit.,* p. 44.
17. Kavanagh, *loc. cit.,* p. 147.

TABLE 4.1

Political Trust in Britain (in percentages)

	JUST ABOUT ALWAYS	MOST OF THE TIME	ONLY SOME OF THE TIME	ALMOST NEVER	DON'T KNOW
(1) How much do you trust the government in Westminster to do what is right?	7	32	47	10	3
(2) When people in politics speak on television, to the newspapers, or in Parliament, how much in your opinion do they tell the truth?	3	22	60	10	4
(3) How much do you trust a British Government of either party to place the needs of this country and the people above the interests of their own political party?	7	28	45	15	5

	ALL THE PEOPLE		FEW INTERESTS		DON'T KNOW
(4) Generally speaking, would you say that this country is run by a few big interests concerned only for themselves or that it is run for the benefit of all the people?	37		48		15

SOURCE: Alan Marsh, *Protest and Political Consciousness* (Sage: Beverly Hills & London, 1977), Table 5.5, p. 118.

of these changes. They were far advanced, I emphasize, well before the economic deprivation of the 1970s had set in. Indeed, an article in the very first issue of *The British Journal of Political Science* in January 1971 set off rather an explosion in political studies by revealing what had already happened to the civic culture.[18] This study, Vivien Hart says in summary, showed that "British teenagers, soon to become British voters, massively rejected existing government, and even more fundamentally, questioned the usefulness and benevolence of any government."[19] Compared with three other national samples, the British sample was lower in positive affect for government on almost every one of the items in the questionnaire. When the authors of the study called this a "surprising conclusion given what was in the not very distant past an accepted judgment that the government in Britain enjoys exceptional legitimacy among its people," Dr. Hart commented: "In the space of a decade, the civic culture is declared to have collapsed."

Based on field work done about the same time, a study for the Kilbrandon Commission revealed a similar mood among adults.[20] Two points should be noted. Taking care to distinguish dissatisfaction with performance of the system from dissatisfaction with its accessibility and responsiveness, which was their main interest, the Kilbrandon survey found widespread evidence of the latter, as revealed in feelings of powerlessness and in concern for more participation.[21] Moreover, dissatisfaction was found in all sections of the population. In this sense the new climate of opinion did not derive from or characterize only one party or class, but was a society-wide change in orientation as one would expect of a genuine change in political culture. In sum, the decline of the civic culture that Kavanagh's review confirmed at the end of the 1970s had already gone very far by the end of the 1960s.

Yet to speak of the change only as "decline" is to miss its essential content and, moreover, major aspects of its potential influence.

18. Jack Dennis, Leon Lindberg, and Donald McCrone, "Support for Nation and Government among English Children," *British Journal of Political Science*, I (1971).
19. Hart, *op. cit.*, p. 32.
20. Commission on the Constitution (Kilbrandon Commission) *Research Papers*, no. 7, *Devolution and other Aspects of Government: An Attitudes Survey* (London, 1973).
21. Discussed by Hart, *op. cit.*, pp. 60–68.

As Vivien Hart has shown, the values that have informed this decline embody a positive commitment.[22] In her view the demands for more responsive and more open government and for a more participatory politics that have been reflected in surveys and put forth in public debate marked a new phase in the old thrust toward radical democracy. If those values inspire distrust, that is in her judgment only the natural, indeed the logical, consequence of a perceived discrepancy between the way the system works and the norms by which it is judged, following on "the collapse of the myth of deference."

In his study of the attitudinal background of protest politics, Alan Marsh came to not dissimilar conclusions. While his study, based on 1974 data, focused specifically on political protest, he also argued that Britain no longer had a deferential political culture. Without claiming that the evidence demonstrated a decline in deference, he felt justified in concluding that the new behavior reflected a change in values.[23] Refining Inglehart's thesis[24] that generally in Western countries "postmaterialist" values had begun to supplant "materialist" values, especially among the young, he showed that in Britain material and security needs remained important even while a concern for participation increased. "The British," he wrote in summary, "want to be secure, certainly, but they want to be *consulted* even more than they want to be rich or powerful. This finding seems to accord well with the general theme of this study: that deference is no longer a force in British political culture but has given way to a concern for influence in the decisions of the political community."[25] His emphasis, we should note, like Hart's, is not on the negative aspects of distrust, but rather on the positive demands underlying it. "The growth of protest potential among the young, while often concerned with the demands for better material conditions," he concludes, "is strongly influenced by the need to maximize other goals which include the creation of a more humane, sensitive, and concerned community. This conclusion does not rest on rhetoric, it rests on empirical observation."[26]

22. Hart, *op. cit.*, pp. xi–xii and *passim*.
23. Marsh, *op. cit.*, p. 174.
24. See below p. 146.
25. Marsh, *op. cit.*, pp. 176–177.
26. *ibid.*, p. 96.

The rhetoric is also worth examining. Hart connects the shift in opinion shown in the surveys with a decade of debate from the late 1960s in which "there has been a gradual accretion and clarification of the parts of a full democratic critique of the British polity."[27] Discussion of this critique properly belongs with the history of the cultural revolution of the 1960s to which we will shortly turn. That discussion will support and clarify the evidence of the opinion surveys. Before turning to it, however, it will be helpful to take stock of where our inquiry now stands and where it will go in the following pages.

In the light of the survey evidence it is no exaggeration to speak of the decline of the civic culture as a "collapse." The change in attitudes toward politics and government since the 1950s has been deep and wide. What is the significance of this change for the British polity? If one accepts the crucial role attributed to political culture in the collectivist model, one would expect major impacts on behavior and institutions. Broadly speaking, one would expect that insofar as the old institutions failed to adapt to the new expectations, the legitimacy of government would falter, and trust in its equity and effectiveness would decline. More specifically, one would hypothesize consequences very much like the main behavioral components of pluralistic stagnation and class decomposition: a loosening of the class/party nexus, a greater self-assertion by participants, a decline of leadership, and a weakening of party government.

The selections from cultural history in this and the following chapter will make more precise the substance of the new outlook and compare it with corresponding changes in behavior. The matching of those behavioral changes with the changes in political culture helps us understand the background of expectation and motivation that sustains the processes of pluralistic stagnation and class decomposition. To clarify in this way the new political orientation is a step toward answering the questions with which this chapter began and toward filling out the analysis put forward in the first two parts of this book. To see this new cultural context also throws some light on future possibilities. In particular it compels one to ask whether the new values have the potential for restoring authority to the polity and trust

27. Hart, *op. cit.*, p. 201.

to its relations with its members and their relations with one another.

In an effort to identify the main elements in the new orientation, our first task is to characterize the new populism and to show that it is widely and seriously accepted. Another task, as difficult as it is important, is not only to describe but also to explain the change in political culture. How shall we account for the collapse of deference and the rise of populism? Students of politics might well agree that deference has declined and populism acquired new strength, yet differ sharply over the source of the change. Some surely will feel that the causal background is to be found in socio-economic developments. Needless to say, that is not my approach. I have broadly hypothesized that the collapse of deference is a contradiction of collectivism and so in some essential sense is a political development. After completing the descriptive tasks of this chapter I will turn to this question of causation.

THE TECHNOCRATIC ATTACK

The assertion of technocratic values will be considered here primarily in order to help isolate and characterize the more powerful influence of populistic values.

The faith that science can transform society for the benefit of man goes back to the beginning of modernity. In *The New Atlantis* (1627) Francis Bacon with dazzling foresight sketched the outlines of a technocratic utopia. The promise of science also informed Enlightenment thought. And in fact during the centuries of modernization in all Western and westernized countries, the slowly developing knowledge of the various sciences was increasingly used by government in fields such as engineering, sanitation, and the conduct of war on land and sea. The great promise of power, however, came into its own only during and after World War II when the scientific and technological revolution entered a new phase. A principal reason was the action of government itself in financing and promoting research in science and development of technology. In those years physicists invented nuclear weapons, transforming foreign and defense policy. Advances in medicine made possible a great expansion of programs in public health. Economics was given a form enabling it to be used in fiscal policy and planning.

In Britain as in the United States, as we have observed,[28] these developments led toward greater professionalism in the public service. Such advances in knowledge and the consequent increase in the role of people with specialized training, however, were only the background for the spasm of fear and hope that gripped élite opinion in the early 1960s. Out of these rapid, but fragmented and incremental developments emerged an exaggerated assertion of the scientific ethos, a veritable ideology of technocracy.

In the forties and fifties, although more and more money was being spent on research and development, public interest, as reflected, for instance, in the little time devoted to the subject by Parliament, was low. Then suddenly from the very late fifties the level of concern rose sharply. An intense science policy debate took place during the next few years.[29] The positive thrust of this debate was technocratic in the double sense of urging a greater role for science and technology both in making policy and in the personnel of policy makers. The immediate constructive purpose was to raise the British growth rate in comparison with its Continental competitors, as well as, along with other Western countries, to keep up with what was then thought to be the rapid economic advance of the Soviet Union.

Both the major parties adopted the new rhetoric. Perhaps the best remembered utterance was the speech of the newly chosen leader of the Labour party, Harold Wilson, at the 1963 conference when, declaring that "we must harness Socialism to science and science to Socialism," he promised a Britain "forged in the white heat" of "the scientific revolution."[30] This theme had entered party statements only after the defeat of 1959 when its development was offered as giving to revisionism a "framework of principle" which the new political strategy might theretofore have seemed to lack.[31]

But Labour did not originate or monopolize the new ideas. Technocracy and planning go hand in hand and during these same years the Conservatives under Macmillan—"I have always been a planner"—vigorously pressed the technocratic case. Indeed, during the

---

28. Above p. 34.
29. Norman J. Vig, *Science and Technology in British Politics* (Oxford, 1968), pp. ix, x; Chapters III and IX.
30. *Report of Annual Conference,* Labour Party, 1963, pp. 134, 140.
31. Morgan Phillips, *Labour in the Sixties* (Labour Party, London, 1960) p. 5.

general election of 1959, it was Macmillan who first promised a "Minister for Science." The word that focused the new issue was "modernisation." Soon after that election, the Conservative back-room boys started to develop program proposals whose main theme was "modernisation" along with Europe. In the following years it was stressed in Parliament and in the country.[32]

The Two Cultures

Thinking back to those years, however, I recall the negative undertones of the technocratic attack as dominant. In what one might regard as the opening salvo, C. P. Snow's *Two Cultures and the Scientific Revolution* (1959) had proclaimed the scientific culture as the hope of a Britain held back by its traditional literary culture. Another scientist turned novelist was less restrained. In *The Black Cloud,* also published in 1959, the Cambridge astronomer Fred Hoyle summed up the British political system in these words: "'Politicians at the top, then the military, and the real brains at the bottom. . . . . We're living in a society that contains a monstrous contradiction, modern in its technology but archaic in its social organization. . . . We scientists do the thinking for an archaic crowd of nitwits and allow ourselves to be pushed around by 'em in the bargain.'"[33]

A climax was reached in a special symposium issue of *Encounter* published in July 1963 under the editorship of Arthur Koestler and entitled "Suicide of a Nation?" The titles of some of the articles will convey the drift: "Amateurs and Gentlemen, or the Cult of Incompetence," "The Comfort of Stagnation," "Taboo on Exper-tise," "The Price of Obstinacy, or Crises in the Trade Unions." The contributors were remarkably in agreement. The causes of decline were not material, but ideal ("we are dying by the mind. . . .") taking the form of the class system—the "psychological apartheid between the bourgeoisie and the proletariat"—and, closely related to class, the traditionalist style—the "cult of amateurishness and the contempt in which proficiency and expertise are held."

Pressing the technocratic case, Koestler summed up: ". . . Ama-teurs and Gentlemen . . . fight valiant rearguard actions in the merry

32. Butler and King, *op. cit.,* pp. 87–92.
33. Quoted in Don K. Price, *The Scientific Estate* (Cambridge, Mass., 1965) p. 9.

civil war between Eggheads and Engineers; and they see to it that
their sons are educated in the same spirit by becoming thoroughly
immersed in Homer's universe, but not in the world of Newton."
While in this sense the main weight of the attack was directed against
Toryism, the division of social forces was not conceived in class
terms, but as modernity versus tradition—"the new elite" of managers and technocrats against the powerful rearguard of "Blimps and
Trade Union bosses."

These phrases are worth quoting because they convey the message
of an outpouring of self-criticism in speech and print in the early and
middle 1960s. As for the contribution of this flood of words to the
decline of the civic culture, I doubt that it stirred for long a public
much beyond Bagehot's "educated ten thousand." Surveys showed
that voters did strongly prefer things that were "modern and up to
date" rather than "traditional and well-tried"; and in the mid-sixties
Labour briefly enjoyed a small though real advantage over the Conservatives by being seen as more "modern."[34] But as an election
appeal the "modernisation" theme, although exploited by both parties, did not catch on with the voters,[35] nor, judging by the high
level of contentment and optimism among the general public, which
we have recorded above, did the negations of the technocratic critique. So while Wilson as prime minister continued to air his hopes
for "technological socialism"—as at the 1969 party conference—
the technocratic attack faltered and faded from public debate in the
1970s. Conceivably, of course, the growing instrumentalism of voters' attitudes that surveys revealed may have been reinforced by the
rationalist emphasis of the critique. That growing presence of the
"informed, analytic, rational" citizen, however, would seem to owe
more to the uncorseting effect of weaker party and class identifica-
tions than to the reassertion of scientific rationalism.

The technocratic attack, however, did shape behavior in critical
ways among those upper ranks of the "service" class who "exercise
power and expertise on behalf of corporate bodies." In the 1960s
and 1970s the elites of this class carried through a remarkable series
of reforms in British government which were very much in the spirit
of the technocratic critique, often had been advocated by its propo-

34. Butler and Stokes, *op. cit.* (1974) p. 349.
35. Butler and King, *op. cit.*, pp. 92, 128–129.

nents, and reasonably can be thought of as being influenced by that agitation. The great expansion of higher education following the Robbins report of 1963, for example, was intended to add to the scientific and technical capacities of the country.[36] Since 1961 changes broadly of the sort proposed in the report had been urged by Labour under the rubric of meeting the challenge of "the scientific revolution." When the report came out, the new Conservative prime minister, Sir Alec Douglas-Home, "demonstrated his intention of taking seriously the 'modernisation of Britain' " by immediately accepting the expansionary goals set by it.[37]

Not every effort to introduce order into some social or political arrangement is to be taken as resulting from the technocratic urge. The change must have something to do with the method or substance of science or technology. The creation of the Department of Education and Science and of agencies such as the Council for Scientific Policy and the Science Research Council are obvious examples. But it is reasonable also to include reforms in process and organization, such as the many changes in the central machinery of government in the 1960s and 1970s that L. J. Sharpe characterizes as "the new managerialism."[38] In the realm of administration, the hubris to which the technocratic spirit may succumb is illustrated by the huge ministry of technology which did not begin to achieve and probably could not have achieved the grandiose purpose assigned to it by the 1964 manifesto, "to guide and stimulate a major national effort to bring advanced technology and new processes into industry."[39]

But probably the most serious and long-lasting outcome of the technocratic attack was the reform of the civil service resulting from the Fulton Report of 1968.[40] Appointed by Wilson in 1966, the committee attacked head on the twin pillars of traditionalism in the British bureaucracy, its implicit class bias and its explicit preference for generalists in the higher posts. The intake of candidates from Oxford and Cambridge headed for the top posts remained high. But profes-

---

36. *Higher Education* (Robbins Report). London, 1963. Discussed in Vig, *op. cit.*, pp. 47–50 and *passim*.

37. Butler and King, *op. cit.*, p. 21.

38. "Whitehall: Structures and People" in *New Trends in British Politics: Issues for Research* (London, 1977), p. 55.

39. Vig, *op. cit.*, p. 149.

40. The Civil Service. vol. I. *Report of the Committee 1966–68*. Cmnd. 3638. (London, 1968).

sionalism, which, as we have seen, was already on the rise, was further advanced. The number of trained economists in government and the mass of statistical and other data available became almost American in their amplitude, and quite transformed Whitehall from what it was a generation ago. "Think tanks" made their appearance in modest numbers.

Technocracy and Toryism

As one would expect, the impact of technocratic values on administrative behavior and structure was marked. What was the impact on élites in the more political realm? The immediate effect on the Labour party was considerable. Along with the political realities of three successive defeats, the new technocratic rationale gave the party leadership cause to separate itself from the party orthodoxies of nationalization, class struggle, and intraparty democracy. Public ownership was largely irrelevant to the need to raise productivity by the application of advanced technology. Solidarity with the trade unions would be a dead weight on the more mobile and flexible economy envisaged by central planners. Conference resolutions could not be permitted to override the judgment of experts. Given the ethos and structure of the Labour party, however, it was a forlorn hope to attempt such a transformation. Economic failure and electoral defeat sealed the fate of this effort and for a time even put revisionism in the shade. Revisionism revived in the mid-1970s, but its new rationale was not government by experts, but what came to be called "social democracy."

The Conservative party was a more promising subject. Technocracy is élitist and can utilize hierarchy so long as it is functionally based. In the modern literature of utopian tracts and futuristic fiction, visions are common of societies ruled by men who owe their authority to their command of science and technology. Coinciding precisely with the technocratic attack in Britain and in part responsible for it, the novels of C. P. Snow portrayed the "new men" of World War II and after as such a class. When the Conservatives chose a new Leader in 1965, one might reasonably have predicted that in shifting from Home, the fourteenth earl, to Heath, the self-made scholarship boy, Toryism was simply preparing to take another new lease on its long life. And indeed, in a fascinating exercise in political hybridization, Heath, on the one hand, did fully exploit the old powers of his position as party leader to prepare a program, while, on the other hand, showing little respect for ancient ways as he ranged widely through the world of expert advice for new ideas. Having learned about the latest methods of policy analysis and budget control in the United States, his emissaries brought back the ideas for a similar effort, Programme Analysis and Review. From his original idea of a central cost effectiveness department responsible to the prime minister, the Central Policy Review Staff finally emerged, heavily staffed with varied experts, half drawn from outside the civil service and advising the cabinet as a whole.[41] Although a neoliberal and not a planner, Heath legitimately could be and often was referred to as a "technocrat."

But the predictable did not happen. Toryism sharply declined. Dennis Kavanagh puts the point almost too strongly. Having observed that in the past the Conservative party has been "suffused with the values of upper-crust England," he declares that "in little more than a decade that apparently secure ruling class has almost disappeared." The "watershed" was the election of Heath as leader, who as prime minister put "few old Etonians and aristocrats" in his cabinet, preferring "self-made, professional politicians" to "the traditional 'magic circle.' "[42] Even more important for Tory values, Heath was not a "strong" leader. He could not mobilize consent among organized business or organized labor. In Parliament, as we shall see, he was confronted with unprecedented resistance. In sum, while among political élites the technocratic attack may well have weakened traditional sentiments of deference and solidarity, it failed to provide a new and positive basis for legitimate authority. The example confirms Sanford Lakoff's generalization:

In no actual society is scientific or technological knowledge considered to be a sufficient source of moral or legal authority, and since the exercise of power entails considerations of group and national interest, as well as representation and legitimacy, there is little reason to expect the rise of outright technocracy.[43]

41. Heclo and Wildavsky, *op. cit.,* pp. 267–268.
42. Kavanagh, "Political Culture in Great Britain," *op. cit.,* p. 158.
43. "Scientists, Technologists, and Political Power," in I. Spiegel-Roesing and D. de Solla Price, eds., *Science, Technology and Society: A Cross-Disciplinary Perspective* (London, 1977) p. 371.

THE ROMANTIC EXEMPLAR

A contemporary, but diametrically opposite and far more formidable assault on the civic culture was the outburst of populism which swept through the 1960s and which, shedding its violence but gaining in acceptance, provided the doctrine and motivation for the "full radical democratic critique" of the 1970s.

If we are to understand the message and the power of this populistic upsurge, we must see its roots in modernity and its parallel with similar outbursts in the past. Populism is the political manifestation of the romantic ethos. An exaggeration of the liberating spirit of modern culture, romanticism bursts forth periodically in literature, the arts, and social life, often with a political message of utopian expectations. It is as deeply rooted in modernity as the technocratic thrust. Indeed, for Irving Babbitt "romanticism was the causal nexus explaining the modern epoch . . . because it had captured men's minds and altered their values on so unprecedented a scale."[44] In Babbitt's interpretation, the humanism of the Renaissance undermined the old restraints of an external moral standard and internal self-discipline. Carried too far, it produced in time the literary, philosophical, and political movement of the late eighteenth and early nineteenth centuries whose famous spokesmen gave romanticism its most notable expression: in France, Rousseau, Chateaubriand, Victor Hugo; in Germany, Herder, Schiller, von Schlegel and Goethe; in England, Blake, Wordsworth, Coleridge, Byron, and Shelley.

One could not ask for a more faithful or more compact statement of the romantic message at any time and place than these lines from Wordsworth:

> One impulse from a vernal wood
> May teach you more of man
> Of moral evil and of good
> Than all the sages can.
> Sweet is the lore that Nature brings;
> Our meddling intellect
> Mis-shapes the beauteous forms of things:
> We murder to dissect.

44. Harry Levin, *Irving Babbitt and the Teaching of Literature* (Cambridge, Mass., 1960) p. 28.

> Enough of science and of art;
> Close up these barren leaves;
> Come forth, and bring with you a heart
> That watches and receives.
> *(Lyrical Ballads,* 1798)

That is the message: for guidance in conduct, trust the heart not the head; emotion not reason; spontaneity not calculation; nature not civilization. Subjectivity, moreover, not only controls the mode of conduct, but also dictates its ends. The important thing is not the fruit of experience, but experience itself; not utility, but sentiment; not wealth, power, or any external possession, but feeling. "Feeling is all" in Goethe's words, and from so indefinite a purpose romanticism draws a sense of longing and boundlessness that gives great power of arousal to its poetry, music, and political rhetoric.

The flight from external and internal restraints upon subjectivity leads toward models of conduct drawn not from organized society, but from physical nature—the "vernal wood"—and toward teachers found not among persons of authority or knowledge, but among those closest to nature—children and the young, the "noble savage" of Rousseau, the simple peasant of Wordsworth's Lake District.

The hostility to hierarchy is obvious. But any organic connection that is fixed or imposed is equally abhorrent to the romantic impulse. Any vertical or horizontal solidarity therefore must be freely, immediately, and only contingently willed. Romantic sentiment dissolves not only the authority that comes from above, but also the class identification imposed from outside by inheritance or objective function. In this sense, the romantic tendency is radically individualist. On the other hand, a group formed by the free and immediate assent of sovereign individuals—or whose members believe it is so formed— can become a mighty power. This radical individualism contains the possibility of a radical populism through which the solvent negations of the romantic attack on traditionalism can be converted into a new basis for legitimacy. In the nineteenth century, the rise of the democratic nation-state displayed this dialectic, and today in Britain it is just conceivable that the populism that has ravaged the civic culture in Britain might in similar fashion repair the damage it has done.

The romantic message indicated not only how the group was to be constituted, but also why. Here again its approach was dominated by subjectivity. The basis of group life was found not in universal values, but in a common culture, a distinctive way of feeling and acting. In Herder's powerful formulation of this approach, the concept of the *Volksgeist* swept over Europe as a doctrine of cultural nationalism. This doctrine soon took on a political form as the early advocates of the nation-state claimed that such a "people's spirit" provided the only legitimate foundation for authority. The romantics did not create the nationalities of Europe, which had deep historical roots. But in formulating and spreading the ideology of nationalism they had an impact that was hardly less revolutionary than that of the new ideas of individual equality. Nationalism brought warmth and emotion to the modern state. It glorified diversity within the framework of universal liberal values that was gradually spreading over Europe. In consequence it had powerfully disruptive effects. The new view of the rights of the national group supplied the rhetoric of rebellion against the old multiethnic regimes, arousing the Irish against the British, the Poles against the Russians, and a host of nationalities against the Austrian and Turkish empires. In that context romantic populism was as radically decentralizing as it had been radically centralizing in the days of the Jacobin revolution in France or national unification in Italy.

A few general points in summary. Romanticism is celebrated for its works of high culture. It can also, however, generate styles of life that spread throughout society and have a wide popular acceptance. While romantic movements, therefore, may be confined to an élite—for example, that brief flowering of Georgian poets in Britain before World War I—they may also embrace a large following from many classes as in the first great outburst of romanticism after Rousseau. These larger movements may or may not have an explicit connection with a political theory. The first romantics did vitally contribute to the democratic and liberating impulse of their day. Shelley's *Queen Mab* (1813) became the Bible of the Chartists and Blake's *Jerusalem* is still sung at Labour party conferences. Whether or not there is such an explicit connection with political theory, the intrinsic message expresses an attitude toward authority and society. In one perspective that attitude is radically antiauthoritarian and individualist to the point of solipsism. Yet the same disruptive impulse can engender lasting structures of social and political action.

The New Populism

The first romantic revolution is significant to our inquiry not because it was equalled politically or culturally by the upheavals of the 1960s, but rather because as an exemplar, so to speak, it enables us to perceive more clearly its real, though diminished, reflection in those upheavals—and obliges us to take them seriously, whether we like them or not.

As the comparison suggests, the romantic message in politics is populist, yet also ambiguous toward the conventional classification of regimes. Romantic values cut across the usual range of "isms." There surely are ideologies with which it is incompatible. Only heroic efforts of textual distortion could reconcile it with the Marxism of *Das Kapital* or the liberalism of *The Wealth of Nations*, not to mention the Toryism of premodern regimes. When the romantic impulse again burst forth in the populism of the 1960s, it was as hostile to the current orthodoxies of the Labour party as to those of the Conservative party. Whatever the specific locus of its reincarnation, the new populism spread across the political and social spectrum into all parties and among all classes. The doctrine which it conveyed echoed basic themes from that earlier time. It emphasized cultural values and a concern for what we today would call "the quality of life." It demanded a wider and more intensive participation. As against the centralized bureaucratic state, it was radically decentralizing.

This populist trinity emerged suddenly in the early 1960s, informed a harsh attack across the board on the values of the existing polity, gradually won a wider acceptance, and by the 1980s, while by no means dominant, had become an orthodoxy of dissent in all sectors.

To my knowledge the first clear statement of the new populist doctrine appeared in the initial issue of the *New Left Review* in January 1960. In a lead editorial the editors summarized the new outlook. As socialists they took a stand for a common ownership and economic equality. But their claim to be "new" appeared in how they proposed to realize and utilize these familiar goals. And in these respects the novelty of their proposals was not specifically or exclusively socialist. On the contrary, it arose from their adoption of the populist trinity of the romantic model: they stressed culture, not economics, participation against bureaucracy, and local control against centralization.

Repudiating economic determinism, they spoke of the New Left as "a movement of ideas" and declared that there was no law of history that said that Labour like "a great inhuman machine" was going to "throb its way to socialism."[45] They did not call for greater economic growth, nor even for more radical redistribution. Rather they celebrated "the humanist strength of socialism," which they asserted ". . . must be developed in cultural and social terms, as well as economic and political." Nationalization was denounced as "not a socialist form," because it failed to give ordinary men and women direct control over their own lives. Workers' control, a neglected tradition in socialism, needed to be "rediscovered." Deploying the same decentralizing line of argument against the authority structure of unions and party, they called for "rallying points of disturbance and discontent within the local community" against "the frozen monoliths of the Labour movement." They shared William Morris' contempt for "the thousand follies of party politics," scorned the rituals of Parliament from Black Rod to committees and commissions and delegations and admired the methods of "direct action" being used by the Campaign for Nuclear Disarmament.

This declaration of aspirations was radically opposed to the technocratic case then being elaborated by the revisionist leadership. Yet in a real sense, the program of the New Left was also revisionist when compared with the orthodoxies of the socialist generation or the position defended by the fundamentalists of the recent past. The Bevanites had fought Morrison and Gaitskell in favor of a centralized bureaucratic socialism based on nationalization as the predominant form of common ownership. In those days, attacks on "bureaucracy" were the exclusive ammunition of the Right. Nationalization was so authentically socialist as to have been advocated by Keir Hardie from the earliest days of his agitation[46] and, while contested at times by the idea of workers' control, had so dominated party opinion

45. I cannot exaggerate how far this approach departs from that of the Old Left in the 1930s. For a powerful and accurate summary of the Old Left's view of "culture," I refer readers of later generations to Louis MacNeice's poem of 1939, "Goodby to Plato and Hegel" which ends with that definitive sentiment: "There ain't no more universals in this man's town." The Old Left did believe that the international working class movement like "a great inhuman machine" was going to "throb its way to socialism." Some called it the "locomotive of history."

46. In the July, 1887, issue of *The Miner,* Hardie outlined the program he favored which included immediate nationalization of land, railways, minerals and mines. *Modern British Politics,* p. 166.

that in 1946 Attlee could identify "our socialist policy" with "our policy of nationalisation."[47]

If widely adopted, the new antibureaucratic, participatory, decentralizing doctrine would transform the Labour movement in both its industrial and political aspects and in its policy outlook as well as in its own internal methods of decisionmaking. But the vision of the small permissive commune where culture and consciousness were valued above any material qualities, which lit up the polemic of the New Left with the romantic anarchism of William Morris, was no less alien to the ideology developed in the previous generation of mass politics and central planning than the brassy élitist collectivism of the growth-minded technocrats.

This power of negation, directed against enemies on the Left as well as the Right, was displayed in a culminating exhibit of New Left rhetoric, the *May Day Manifesto 1968*. Put forward as "a counter-statement to the Labour government's policies and explanations" and edited by Raymond Williams with help from other New Left writers, its descent from the editorial of 1960 is plain.[48] The organizing theme is "democratic participation," branching into corollary demands for decentralization in many forms. On this ground the case for the extension of workers' control is elaborated and urged. Scots and Welsh nationalism is looked on with favor. So also are "single issue" campaigns, especially those with strong "local democratic organization." "Student power" is singled out for special praise.

As an affirmation of these ideas, the manifesto has a positive message. In style and substance, however, it is overwhelmingly negative, a corrosive indictment of the institutions blessed by the civic culture and embodied in the collectivist polity. The enemy is, of course, capitalism. But the centralized bureaucratic state, instead of being seen as the instrument by which the working class would revolutionize the economic system, appears as the agent of continued domination. In contrast with the old doctrine of socialist democracy through party government, the notion of "more powerful Labour majorities in parliament" becomes "reactionary," since such party

47. *ibid.*, p. 134.
48. See especially the concluding sections, which are mainly concerned with politics, pp. 133–190.

majorities only maintain "an insulation from *popular* pressures." Hence, rightly, toward the "theatrical show" of Parliament, "the young, especially . . . are less deferential" and display "little surviving respect."

The attack upon the parliamentary system extends to and depends upon a thoroughgoing rejection of the legitimacy of the Labour movement itself. The "organized working class" is still termed the "central strength of the Left." But the ways in which that social entity actually appeared and operated in political and industrial life are almost totally condemned. The Labour party has been so far co-opted as to become "an alien form." Its real function is fixed by the "managed politics" of the new corporatistic capitalism. In that politics, "the political parties and parliament itself, are necessary to legitimate this essentially centralized and bureaucratized form of government." As for its socialist commitment, the Labour party is no longer even a coalition: for "what starts as a coalition ends as a confidence trick."

The trade unions come off only slightly better in this harsh assessment. Along with "the banks, the corporations, [and] the federations of industrialists," the TUC has accepted a place in the new corporatist system. The principal example is their involvement in an incomes policy. Bracketing incomes policy with the Vietnam War as a strategy of "the forces we oppose," the manifesto finds in "the local militants" the one healthy element in the trade union movement and urges "socialists" to lend them their support, for "unofficial strikes . . . are at the heart of the democratic struggle."

Morrisians and Freudo-Marxists

The survey evidence gave a quantitative dimension to our assessment of the decline of the civic culture. Citing the New Left rhetoric above serves a qualitative purpose: with the help of the romantic model to give greater definition to the populistic attitudes revealed by the surveys. That model also suggests that populism is by no means confined to socialists but may arise from nonsocialist sources and spread to nonsocialist sectors. In the next chapters we shall have occasion to show not only how populism has been reflected in behavior, but also how it has affected the Center and Right, as well as the

Left, winning a powerful, though not dominant role in the political culture of the 1970s.

Having defined and measured the force that attacked the civic culture, we may appropriately turn now to another implication of the romantic model, viz., that populism tends to arise as an integral element in a larger cultural transformation. This hypothesis bears on the basic problem of causation by directing attention to the source of the new values. By the same token it also may throw light on how the new values were spread through the society on so wide a scale.

Like the first great romantic movement, the romantic revolt of the 1960s affected not only politics, but also social life generally. It is hard to think of any aspect of personal or social behavior that was not affected: sex, music, clothing, marriage, the family, work, crime, sport, education, religion, race relations. The attack upon the civic culture was one aspect of a far-reaching assault upon established values throughout society by the counterculture. In the service of the permissive society, as of the populist polity, the counterculture summoned up the romantic values of liberation from conventional morality, authority, and society in the name of freely rendered mutuality and love. The ethos was the same in all spheres. No explanation of political developments can satisfy that does not recognize this connection.

The immediate antecedents of the New Left on an intellectual plane can be readily identified. The *New Left Review* itself incorporated two short-lived anti-Communist journals. But the revulsion against Stalinism does not define a new position. As Raymond Aron remarked, there is something of a puzzle in the way so many disillusioned leftists in the 1960s turned not to "realism" but to a "radical utopianism" emphasizing national traditions and pre-Marxist solutions.[49] In the British case the forefather of the romantic populism set forth in that first editorial was explicitly William Morris. For two of the editors the connection with Morris went back to the early 1950s. E. P. Thompson has recalled how he and Raymond Williams, unknown to each other, had been working on "different aspects of the Romantic criticism of utilitarianism," a concern issuing respectively in Thompson's biography of Morris in 1955 and Williams'

---

49. "The Exaltation of Folly and Reason," *Encounter*, August, 1969.

Culture and Society three years later.[50] The imprint of Morris is clear not only in the general romantic ethos of New Left utterance but also in its specific advocacy of cultural, participatory, and communal values. This national, not to say parochial, posture is confirmed by the sharp criticism directed against Morris in the *Review* in its later phase after it had been taken over by editors who were bent on making it an organ of Marxist scholarship and who accordingly felt the customary Marxist disdain for the romantic and utopian critique of capitalism. In this later time when Williams' outlook was termed "Romantic populism" it was as an accusation.[51]

As an explanation of the origins of the new populism, this Morrisian perspective is too narrow not only because it is national and so leaves out of account events which, as Aron's comment suggests, were producing similar outbursts of political utopianism in other countries, but also because it does not connect the new populism with the wider changes of the counterculture. That connection is suggested by works of literary culture, other than socialist scholarship, which appeared in the 1950s. In this time of economic affluence and political consensus, the "Angry Young Men"—as they came to be called after the opening of John Osborne's *Look Back in Anger* in May 1956—put forward in plays and novels a biting criticism of the social and political order that accompanied the welfare state. Some see these writers as heralds of the New Left.[52] Their mood and message, however, make a much better fit with Aron's category of realism. My own recollection accords with Kenneth Allsop's judgment that the right word to describe their outlook is not "anger," which suggests some positive standard of reference, but rather "dissentience," which implies simply disillusionment and rejection.[53] Their politics was accordingly "a lukewarm and perfunctory socialism,"[54] quite lacking in utopian or romantic overtones. If their work presages

50. "Romanticism, Moralism and Utopianism: the Case of William Morris," *New Left Review*, no. 99 (September/October 1976).

51. *ibid.*, "Afternote."

52. For example, George Watson in his *Politics and Literature in Modern Britain* (Totowa, N.J., 1977).

53. Quoted in Gilbert Phelps, "The Novel Today," pp. 487–88, in the *Pelican Guide to English Literature*, Vol. 7 *The Modern Age* (London, 1961) edited by Boris Ford.

54. *ibid.*, p. 488.

anything, I should say, it is not the spirit of revolt that one finds in the popular upheavals of the 1960s, but rather the mood of irony that pervades drama and fiction in the following two decades.

A source of the new political attitudes which was comprehensive in its concern with culture and international in its impact is found in that amazing hybrid which the Manuels have termed "Freudo-Marxism."[55] The examples were many and influential. Norman O. Brown (*Life Against Death,* 1959) and Erich Fromm (*Beyond the Chains of Illusion,* 1962) were widely read. Surely the leading figure, however, was Herbert Marcuse (*Eros and Cvilization,* 1955; *One Dimensional Man,* 1964) who reached a pinnacle of prominence when he became the sage of the student uprisings on two continents in 1967 and 1968. While rarely specific, his criticism of existing society was comprehensive, finding all sectors and institutions dominated by "surplus repression."[56] Once the fetters of capitalism and the instinctual repressions of civilization had been broken, however, the liberated individual would achieve self-actualization through the release of the Eros of sexual-aesthetic values. As for the agent of this revolution, Marcuse changed his mind from time to time. Having lost faith in the revolutionary proletariat, he looked to other groups, such as rebellious students and oppressed minorities, finally placing his trust for deliverance in a "vanguard" which would, it seems, spontaneously arise in the course of the great transformation.[57]

In the Marcusian scheme the Freudo-Marxist synthesis is achieved by a selection from the masters controlled by an impulse foreign to both. To criticize its logic would take us far from our present inquiry. Even this brief summary, however, plainly shows the power of the romantic ethos—to force into its service two of its most irreconcilable enemies.

One should not underestimate the influence of Marcuse and the New Left writers generally upon the rapidly growing numbers of young people in higher education—older universities, new red bricks, polytechnics—after the Robbins report. No one who was a university

55. Frank E. Manuel and Fritzie P. Manuel, *Utopian Thought in the Western World* (Cambridge, Mass., 1979), p. 788.
56. *Eros and Civilization: A Philosophical Inquiry into Freud.* With a new introduction by the author (New York, 1962) p. 40.
57. Manuel and Manuel, *op. cit.,* p. 798.

teacher in those days can doubt the power of a book, such as Brown's *Life Against Death* or Marcuse's *Eros and Civilization,* to work a "conversion." These young people were of an age that hungers for ideology, as Erik Erikson and our own experience tells us. The themes of the student rebellion of the late 1960s echoed the rhetoric of the Freudo-Marxists as well as the Morrisian fathers of the New Left. Yet the new populism reached far wider sectors of the society than the several hundred thousand undergraduates of the late 1960s. Not even the paperback revolution in publishing can explain how it managed to affect so wide a public. The transmission belt that was carrying the new values was reaching not hundreds of thousands, but millions of people—especially young people, as suddenly revealed by those shocking views of British teenagers in 1970.

The Unacknowledged Legislators

This transformation of mass culture was accomplished by the instruments of mass culture. If one has eyes and ears for the time—especially ears—one will immediately recall how from the 1950s on Britain was swept by a quite new kind of popular music, rock and roll, which in lyrics and tunes carried a message that broke with established values as radically as did the thought of the revolutionary sages. This wave of pop music was a means of transmission with the capacity to reach the millions.

Once while discussing mass culture, André Malraux remarked that "never before has civilisation had at its disposal such powerful means for the dissemination of dreams, above all the film."[58] Rock and roll hit Britain in 1955 when *The Blackboard Jungle* brought Bill Haley's "Rock Around the Clock" from the United States and the cinema seats began to be ripped up, with such inevitability indeed that many towns banned the film for fear of violence.[59] Later, film also brought Elvis Presley and the Beatles to a large public. Radio and television were other means of transmission. For the Beatles, according to their biographer, Hunter Davies, it was when they were televised for an audience of fifteen million on the night of October 13, 1963, as top

58. "André Malraux," *Encounter,* January, 1969, p. 52.
59. Anthony Bicât, "Fifties Children: Sixties People," in Vernon Bogdanor and Robert Skidelsky, eds., *The Age of Affluence 1950–1964* (London, 1970) p. 324.

billing on "Sunday Night at the London Palladium" that "they stopped being simply an interesting pop-music story and became front-page news in every national newspaper."[60] The boom in record sales in the 1950s was floated on the new affluence which provided the material basis for the vast teenage market with its own tastes and style that arose in those years. Some £15 million, nearly half the total amount spent each year on records and record players in Britain at that time, came from "the pockets of the economically emancipated teenager."[61]

Yet this picture of mass culture in which some distant source provided by impersonal means a product consumed by the millions quite misses a crucial aspect of the pop music revolution. This was its intrinsic stimulation of the small group. Alongside the mass market for records and the huge screaming concerts, countless small groups for making the new sort of music flourished. That happened because their members chose to use instruments far simpler than those earlier staples of home music, the piano and violin. The skiffle group, such as the one formed by John Lennon when he was sixteen, might consist of a washboard, a tea chest, banjo, drums, and, of course, guitar. "It was the first time for generations," writes Davies, "that music wasn't the property of musicians."[62] "All the Beatles, like millions of lads of the same age," he reports, ". . . have the same sort of memories, of groups springing up in every class at school and in every street at home. There were overnight about a hundred dances in Liverpool with skiffle groups queuing up to perform." By the late 1950s, Davies asserts, "almost half the teenage population of Liverpool was in groups."[63]

The career ladder for these rising musicians was as different as their instruments from previous models. Formerly a singer might rise to prominence after "an apprenticeship with a professionally competent commercial dance band."[64] That sequence bears no resemblance to the Beatles' story. Even after they had acquired a manager (Brian Epstein) and a publicity man (Tony Barrow) the latter could

60. Hunter Davies, *The Beatles* rev. ed. (New York, 1978) p. 180.
61. Brian Groombridge and Paddy Whannel in *New Left Review*, no. 1 (January/February 1960) p. 54.
62. Davies, *op. cit.*, p. 20.
63. *ibid.*, p. 57.
64. Groombridge and Whannel, *loc. cit.*, p. 52.

confess: "I would love to say that it was my brilliant handouts which built the Beatles, but they didn't. The press was very very late catching on. Kids everywhere were starting to go wild about them, not just in Liverpool. . . . But nobody seemed to notice." "The simple explanation," in Hunter Davies' words, "is that as it had never happened before in Britain, the British press had no way of recognizing it."[65] But "it" did happen—for the first time—and by these various means, Beatlemania swept the British Isles and indeed most of the Western world. And the tunes and lyrics were as unprecedented as the means of their production and transmission.

How closely can one relate the new pop music to the counterculture? May one dare to suggest that the Beatles were the "unacknowledged legislators" of Britain's populist revolt?

Most spokesmen of the New Left, whether Freudo-Marxist or Morrisian, would probably frown on that hypothesis. In the early 1960s T. W. Adorno of the Frankfurt School of Marxism reiterated his earlier disdainful criticism of popular music as mere social cement.[66] A few years later, however, a younger member of the School, Jürgen Habermas, found that "Pop Art" "by creating images of a dehumanised world" could produce "a salutary shock-effect" which served "the radical purpose of debureaucratising the power-structure" and "opening up new, concrete potentialities for human freedom."[67]

The British New Left displayed the same ambivalence. In that innovative first issue, the *New Left Review* could see no health in this new departure in the arts, finding it "bad music" and "mass produced."[68] But a later critic for that journal rejected the Adorno analysis and called the "introduction of rock 'n' roll in the middle 50s a real revolution," perceiving and praising it as "small group music," which enabled the musicians to achieve greater autonomy and better resist standardization in composing and performing. He pronounced Mick Jagger "the greatest artist ever to come out of British popular

65. Davies, *op. cit.,* pp. 169–170.
66. Adorno, *Introduction to the Sociology of Music* (German 1963; English trans. 1968, New York), chapter on "Popular Music."
67. *Encounter,* September, 1968, p. 58.
68. pp. 48, 52.

music'' and found the lyrics of the Rolling Stones in their "narcissism'' and "arrogance'' to be "very much related to social life in the 1960s, even specifically to London life.''[69]

In time, professional critics did take the new pop music seriously. By 1972 Wilfrid Mellers, composer and professor of music at the University of York, while commenting in *The New Statesman* on a new album by John Lennon could write of the Beatles in "their glorious hey-day'' as "a foursome that created a communal mythology of the young, pertinent and potent because their songs also sprang from individualised experience.''[70] So far had this organ of the Left progressed from "The Menace of Beatlism,'' a classic bit of vituperation by Paul Johnson, which it had published eight years before.

The counterculture of the 1960s reincarnated the romantic impulse. For all its variety this transformation of values in many spheres of social life was impelled and informed by an exaggerated reassertion of the liberating spirit of modernity. In tunes and lyrics the new pop music expressed that spirit and carried it to the far reaches of society—and one might say without perjorative intent, its depths—as no other artistic medium did or could have done. One must still wish to press the question of the primacy of its influence: was pop music simply one among many cultural responses to a common originating condition, or was it itself that source of change?

Needless to say assessments differ. "Though changes in the other arts *reveal* the sixties and expose its sensibility,'' writes Morris Dickstein with reference to the United States, "rock *was* the culture of the sixties in a unique and special way . . . the nexus not only of music and language but also of dance, sex, and dope, which all came together into a single ritual of self-expression and spiritual tripping.'' But Dickstein shies away from making rock "the center and navel of the universe,'' and treats it as "part of the broader culture of the '60s''—thereby offending some eminent rock critics.

Views attributing primacy to the influence of pop music were much fancied during the 1960s. A forceful and documented analysis of the British case was put forward at the end of the decade by Anthony

69. Alan Beckett in *New Left Review,* no. 39 (September/October 1966) pp. 87–90.
70. Mellers, *Twilight of the Gods: the Music of the Beatles* (New York, 1973) p. 196.

Bicât, a director of experimental theatre. What he says is of special interest to our inquiry as his discussion appears in a study devoted primarily to the politics of "the age of affluence." A child of the same generation as Dickstein, Bicât, who "grew up to the songs of the Beatles, the Stones, and Bob Dylan," testifies even more emphatically to the impact of the new music, entitling his analysis "Fifties Children: Sixties People." His premise is bold:

The popular song is the lyric evocation of the collective dream. In its nostalgia and its myth-making it provides people with something much nearer their real spiritual needs than does conventional poetry. Its very need to be popular, the way it is tied to commercialism, ensures its relevance. It is a debased currency, but a genuine one.[71]

In the fifties the older style of popular music, such as jazz or swing, he writes, was "specifically designed for adults," and projected "a dream of affluence." "Men in white dinner-jackets sung to ladies in evening gowns on romantically lit terraces or the first-class decks of ocean liners." A music of social cement, one might well say, thinking perhaps of Noel Coward, Cole Porter, or Jerome Kern. In contrast, according to Bicât, the "great virtue" of rock and roll, the music of the teenagers of the late 1950s, was that "it generated a spontaneous liberation in its young listeners."

As one reads Bicât's account, one senses that this liberation, like the counterculture generally, had two aspects. One was Edenic and utopian, captured in what Bicât calls the "unaffected simplicity" of the Beatles' tunes and lyrics. This forceful and often satiric rejection of the materialism and power-seeking of contemporary society was converted by the Rolling Stones into its other aspect, a fierce and devastating assault.

The Rolling Stones [writes Bicât] are, indeed, the most obvious example of the young turning against the values of a whole society in their music. . . . Their revolt was much more obvious than that of the Beatles, and though in the long run their songs were not so revolutionary, Mick Jagger's words were the most striking expressions of hatred for the Affluent Society that have ever appeared in any medium whatsoever.[72]

71. Bicât, *loc. cit.*, p. 321.
72. *ibid.*, p. 327.

If Biĉat writing in 1970 found the music of the Beatles more "revolutionary" than that of the Stones, he could not, of course, have been thinking of the explicitly political songs of John Lennon after he plunged into the avant-garde at about that time. Nor if we are looking for the political message of the Beatles should we, in my opinion, try to find it mainly in the intentionally satiric or critical pieces of earlier years, such as *Taxman, Nowhere Man, I Am The Walrus,* or *Revolution.* "The basic Beatle song," writes Wilfrid Mellers, "is Edenic."[73] He is thinking of the early compositions, expressing "the euphoric happiness of togetherness," such as *She Loves You, I Saw Her Standing There, Love Me Do.* A Wordsworthian innocence also informs the great songs of their more mature years: *A Hard Day's Night, Help!, Norwegian Wood, Eleanor Rigby, Yellow Submarine, Sergeant Pepper's Lonely Hearts Club Band, Strawberry Fields Forever, A Day in the Life.* One does not have to hunt very hard to find in them the political theory of the *Lyrical Ballads.*

In these songs, the Beatles did not in so many words come out for the populist program. They did not tell people to cultivate their inner cultural life. But *Strawberry Fields Forever,* in Professor Meller's words, discovers "a *new* Eden . . . within the mind."[74] I doubt that they ever used the word "democratic" or "participation" in a song, but it would be hard to find a stronger case against exclusion than *Eleanor Rigby* or in favor of inclusion than *Sergeant Pepper.* And if you are looking for a secular hymn to *agape, All You Need is Love* should do. The localism of their songs is fundamental. Open as is their appeal to universal human feelings, they also have a pervasive "sense of place." Liverpool—"we were hicksville," Lennon recalls—is always there. Penny Lane and Strawberry Fields are real places in that area. The imagery of *A Day in the Life* started from two news stories, one about a London car crash and the other about 4000 holes in the streets of Blackburn, Lancashire. With William Blake, to again quote Professor Mellers, the early Beatles knew that "generalities signify only in relation to particularities." It takes no

73. Mellers, *op. cit.,* p. 33.
74. Jann Wenner, *Lennon Remembers: The Rolling Stone Interviews* (San Francisco 1971) p. 184.

ingenuity to see in that proposition a normative ground for decentralization.

A scholar, composer, critic, and man of an older generation, Professor Mellers restates in a sophisticated anthropology the essentials of Bičât's premise. He finds "obvious parallels" between the "rituals" of pop music and those of genuinely primitive cultures. Both are what he calls "music of necessity"; that is, music which "cannot be described as entertainment, let alone evasion" but "is also a way of life." "To a large number of young people, pop music seems passionately to matter" he writes, "it is not an embellishment of living which one can take or leave; it *does* something, being 'music of necessity' in somewhat the same sense as this phrase is applied to the musics of primitive peoples."[75] As a part of social history, the Beatles have had many functions, he concludes. "As pop musicians they are simultaneously magicians (dream weavers), priests (ritual celebrants), entertainers (whiling away empty time), and artists (incarnating and reflecting the feelings—rather than the thoughts—and perhaps the conscience of a generation)".[76]

EXPLANATIONS

This chapter has argued that the 1960s witnessed a profound change in British political culture, one that disrupted the balance of traditionalist and modern elements in the civic culture which for generations had sustained the British polity. The distrust of government and politics arising from this value shift makes more intelligible the onset of class decomposition and pluralistic stagnation. To take note only of the negative aspects of the cultural transformation, however, is misleading as to its origins and its effects. For the old hierarchic and organic values were being challenged by the rise of a new and radically democratic outlook. That new and positive force is hard to see and impossible to explain unless we understand it as an integral part of the broad cultural revolution of the time. As often in times past, a romantic revolt brought with it a new populism. Unlike those other outbursts of romanticism, however, this one sprang not from the

75. Mellers, *op. cit.*, pp. 23–24.
76. *ibid.*, p. 183.

élites but from the masses and was generated and transmitted by means unique to the day and age.

In this chapter we have observed the first manifestations of the new populism in the 1960s and in the next chapter we will take some soundings that show its spread into all sectors of British opinion in the 1970s. My description of the new outlook concludes by raising the question of explanation.

One can see how the collectivist polity itself engendered the new group politics. One can see how the social basis of party government was undermined as the collectivist polity promoted class decomposition. But how does one explain the decline of the civic culture and rise of the new populism which constituted the crucially necessary condition for the emergence of these other contradictions of collectivism?

In what people have said about this question in recent years, one can detect three approaches to an answer. Two find the source in economic change and contradict one another. The other is political.

When one asks observers today why so many of the British public have become dissatisfied with government and politics, the usual reply takes an economic turn. There will be some reference to the relative deprivation of the times and to the perceived responsibility of governments for it, especially in face of the repeated promises of parties and politicians to set things right. While voters are sensibly skeptical of such promises, they do tend to hold government responsible for the health of the economy and so with the onset of hard times turn away from those in power. Some such assumption informs and is confirmed by studies of the "political business cycle." When, moreover, the Opposition takes office and does no better than the former Government, and indeed may be unable to prevent times from getting even worse, one would not be surprised if, as these failures are repeated, the public becomes disenchanted with the charade of party politics and, in time, with the whole system of government. The examples of democratic regimes destroyed by the Great Depression seem to support this common-sense hypothesis.

In Britain, survey evidence indicates that "after the elections of 1974, the failure of *both* parties to deal with inflation was a source of weakened attachment to the two major parties." "One would expect," also observes James Alt, "years of economic failure to loosen people's ties to the political parties and the political system."[77] James Douglas, a Conservative, has developed the possibility that under these conditions "at each swing of the pendulum the whole two-party system loses some of its legitimacy." In time, he concludes, "the absence of popular support must undermine the authority of government and ultimately the authority of Parliament and the whole parliamentary system."[78] From an opposite ideological perspective James O'Connor argues rather similarly, that a capitalist state cannot retain its legitimacy if it does not keep benefits flowing to its citizens even though this diverts resources from investments.[79]

One must agree that in the 1970s such failures must have weakened trust in the political system. As an explanation of the change in political culture, however, this approach has several major flaws.

One is the matter of timing. The hypothesis of economic deprivation is not compatible with the fact that, as I have emphasized, the shift in values began while times were good in the late 1950s and early 1960s and had already brought the civic culture to a low estate by the end of the 1960s. When, for example, people were asked in the mid-1960s whether they thought they would be better or worse off in the next few years, only a very small minority took the pessimistic position.[80] Satisfaction relative to the past and optimism about the future were the general rule. Yet it was in these years that the attack on the civic culture was gathering force as revealed in the end of decade studies.

The second approach allows for this fact of timing. In sharp opposition to the previous hypothesis it finds the source of the values shift not in deprivation, but in affluence. This is a much harder explanation to fit into common-sense assumptions about motivation. Ordinarily, one would suppose that if conditions were getting better and especially if governments could plausibly claim some credit for the change, the public would respond with greater support for the political system. Reasons why the opposite should take place have been

    77. Alt, *op. cit.*, p. 200.
    78. "The Overloaded Crown," *British Journal of Political Science,* 6 (1976), p. 488.
    79. James R. O'Connor, *The Fiscal Crisis of the State* (New York, 1973).
    80. Butler and Stokes, *op. cit.*, (1969), p. 403.

developed in the most sophisticated way by Inglehart.[81] In his comparative study of cultural change in Western countries during the 1960s and 1970s, he finds "a shift from overwhelming emphasis on material consumption and security toward greater concern with the quality of life." His explanation of this change is based on Abraham Maslow's psychological theory that human needs are pursued in hierarchical order, so that once material needs, such as sustenance and safety, are taken care of, the individual will turn his energies toward "self-actualization needs" such as love, belonging, esteem, and intellectual and aesthetic satisfactions. It follows that as the prolonged boom of the 40s and 50s brought affluence to the West, prevailing values tended to shift from "materialist" to "postmaterialist."

In his emphasis on cultural and affectual values, the postmaterialist, I should say, is in the romantic mainstream; and in his high valuation of participation in economic and political life at all levels, he is something of a populist. The affinity between these attitudes and the positions taken by the New Left is acknowledged by Inglehart when he finds that the New Left showed "above all a tendency to be inspired by Post-Materialist goals and to recruit among a Post-Materialist constituency."[82] In contrast to the hypothesis of economic deprivation, this approach has the twin strengths of bringing out the positive side of the new values and of suggesting that what was happening affected not only political attitudes but a much broader range of values. The main difficulty with following this line of explanation is its attempt to ground the value change in the economic fact of affluence. If that were the case, one would have to suppose that the new values would wane with the arrival of hard times in the 1970s. On the contrary, of course, the attack on the civic culture and the spread of the populistic outlook gained force in those later and less comfortable years.

The third approach is political, finding in the centralized bureaucratic state, which had emerged by the later 1950s, an oppressive presence and future threat against which the new populism arose as a reaction and an alternative. This is surely the New Left's conception of its origins: a response to the élitist and corporatistic preten-

81. Ronald Inglehart, *The Silent Revolution: Changing Values and Political Styles Among Western Publics* (Princeton, 1977).
82. *ibid.*, p. 241.

sions of the system shaped and approved by Macmillan and Gaitskell. Looked at as an explanation, this approach makes the attack on the civic culture an unintended and dysfunctional effect—a contradiction—of the collectivist polity itself.

Such a focus on political action and reaction as the source of changing values makes a great deal of sense. A major difficulty, however, is that it explains very little about the specific character of the new values which emerged from the process. People could have reacted against the centralized bureaucratic state in a number of other ways. They might, conceivably, have sought a return to Victorian individualism and the free market, as in time the small band of neo-liberals did. The imaginative reader can think of other possibilities. Populistic democracy with its emphasis upon quality of life, participation, and decentralization is only one. Indeed, in order to see the attack as a reaction to the collectivist polity one must first adopt the values which it asserts. One cannot think of the object reacted against as itself determining the character of the reaction. For the items that are chosen for attack are those which are selectively perceived to be in conflict with the new populism. The process points to the primacy of a value change which, breaking sharply with prevailing outlooks, gives form and shape to the reaction. In the assertion of this new viewpoint there was an essential autonomy which escapes structural explanation.

The incursion into politics that produced the new populism was part of the romantic revolt which transformed values in many spheres of British life. The breadth of this change took it well beyond the bounds of organized political activity. In many respects the new outlook, like the ethos of "swinging London" in the 1960s, included a rejection of politics. On the other hand, however, even when expressed in nonpolitical spheres, the romantic revolt was so much an attack on authority and order that an implicit political message was unmistakable. As a broad social transformation the romantic revolt was not confined to the Left, but affected all sectors and classes. So also its explicitly political manifestation, while in the beginning most vividly articulated by the New Left, was taken up among élites and masses of all partisan tendencies. One can trace the broad affinity with the older romanticism. One can see how this reformulation of radicalism would produce a reaction against the collectivist polity.

But why this sudden, strong, and widespread resurgence of romanticism should take place and why the radical tradition should be reformulated in this way, I do not know. This epoch in British political culture was unprecedented and, I should say, unpredictable. ''By its very nature,'' conclude the Manuels, ''the utopian breakthrough is unannounced.''[83]

83. Manuel and Manuel, *op. cit.*, p. 802.

CHAPTER V

The New Populism

As a movement the New Left faded from the political scene in the early 1970s. The new populism which it had articulated for leftwing politics, however, continued to spread, although usually in less extreme forms, through industrial and political life. That is the usual pattern for radical movements in politics and culture. As they make their way in the world, they lose their character as the vanguard of something new and shocking and their function as agents for spreading the word. Thus, it can often be said that a conservative is simply a person who was a radical when young and has not changed his mind.

Writing about the United States toward the end of the 1970s, Theodore Roszak observed that "the counterculture has become less visible over the past decade only because it has dissolved into its surrounding social medium."[1] Today in Britain, as in the United States, the fighting causes of the counterculture have in great degree been absorbed into the fabric of everyday life for a large part of the society. Consider, for instance, how readily people put up with, accept, and where appropriate, practice: cohabitation, abortion, homosexuality, pornography, protesters blocking traffic, squatters occupying buildings, tenants going on strikes, school-teachers going on strike, undergraduates sitting on university committees, women doing jobs traditionally considered men's work, blacks in jobs formerly performed by whites, and most impressive to the returning foreigner, very little "Sir" and "Ma'm." Shorn of some of its wilder fantasies, the new populism has been institutionalized in political

1. Theodore Roszak, *Person/Planet: The Creative Disintegration of Industrial Society* (New York, 1978) p. xxi.

debate, constituting a new orthodoxy of dissent, and in political behavior, informing new patterns of dissentience. We shall have occasion to consider various examples. Here one illustration may be cited because of its great symbolic potency: the Official Secrets Act has fallen into desuetude not only as law, but also as a norm of ministerial and official behavior, so that unauthorized leaks torment the chief executive with almost American license.[2]

The task of this chapter is to illustrate the spread and impact of the new political attitudes. Our "tracer," so to speak, is in general the romantic outlook and in particular the populist trinity of quality of life, participation, and decentralization. We shall be looking for rhetoric that echoes these themes and for any associated behavior that conforms to them.

Before looking at the 1970s, however, we must quickly take note of two examples of behavior which exemplify the new populism in the late sixties, both climaxing in 1968—which, if any one year is to be so singled out, was the turning point.

STUDENT PROTEST

The student revolt is so familiar that it hardly needs comment. Its material background was the great increase in the number of students in higher education. In the four years from 1962 to 1966, membership in the official and long established National Students Union, embracing virtually the whole student population, rose from 150,000 to 366,000. In this context of rapid growth, advocates of "student power" produced the Radical Students' Alliance in 1967. In comparison with what happened in American, German, and French universities, the British protests were moderate. They did, however, involve an unprecedented outburst of direct action: demonstrations, sit-ins, occupations, and assaults as well as a great deal of rhetoric. As we have seen, that rhetoric echoed the ideas of both the Freudo-Marxist and Morrisian fathers of the New Left. The "vocationalist" spirit underlying the expansion and organization of higher education

2. A spoof in the *Economist* of Mrs. Thatcher's efforts to prevent leaks reflected what was actually going on, as when the imaginary minute read: "It seems to me that some ministers may be using the press to fight their private battles against the collective view of the Cabinet." *Economist,* 6 September 1980, p. 51.

was denounced. Participatory rather than representative democracy was acclaimed. Hierarchy in any sphere or in any form was rejected.[3]

Critics quickly sensed the dominance of the romantic ethos. Examining the student revolt generally, comments in *Encounter* took note of this inspiration with perceptive scholarship and a good deal of alarm. (And why not? Many of the authors were objects of the attack.) The uniformity of sentiments from country to country was remarked and, in contrast with the 1930s, so was the curious lack of organization or class affiliation. Characterizing the student revolt as "an explosion of radical Utopianism," Raymond Aron observed how it continued "the essentially romantic criticism of modern society": opposing the worship of money, the inhumanity of interpersonal relationships, the dessicating effects of specialization, and the alienation of the producer from the things he produces.[4]

The wave of protest subsided fairly quickly. But it left its mark. In the universities there were all those committees, which still today continue to meet and from time to time to provide a center for protest. Also, if we can believe Richard Lowenthal, writing in 1973 on the "prospects for socialism," the cultural revolt of the younger generation was the "most powerful" of the new factors of popular dissent.[5]

STRIKES AND THE NEW CONSCIOUSNESS

The wage-price explosion of 1968–72 coincided almost exactly with the student revolt. Although I would not suggest any serious direct connection—there was nothing like the old-time Communist party to bring students and workers into a single organization—and although the rhetoric of the striking workers was sparser by far than that of the students, there were harmonies between the respective motivations that impelled these two unprecedented outbursts.

The wage-price explosion, as we have observed, constituted an abrupt and puzzling discontinuity in the history of industrial relations in Britain, as strike activity and wage demands rose to quite new

3. See Alexander Cockburn and Robin Blackburn, eds., *Student Power: Problems, Diagnosis, Action* (London, 1969).
4. "The Exaltation of Folly and Reason," *Encounter*, August, 1969.
5. "What Prospects for Socialism," *Encounter*, February, 1973.

levels. The main structural condition leading to this new behavior was the fragmented and decentralized "new unionism" which had been fostered by the reallocation of power by the collectivist polity. Yet this structural explanation, helpful as far as it goes, leaves important questions unanswered. As Thomas Balogh in his poignant retrospect observed, the unions could have gained so much by using their massed syndicalist power to strike a bargain with the Wilson government in which they would have accepted an incomes policy "as a definite price of social progress." Union members generally, moreover, as well as their national leaders, were aware of the need for such a policy in order to avoid the counterproductive consequences of the pay scramble. The ideal barrier to acting on the implications of collective rationality was, therefore, not informational. What then was the attitude that prevented organized labor from resisting or correcting the structural compulsions on its behavior?

Was it a surge of radicalism in the working class? Were they rejecting the kind of "social contract" for which Balogh had hoped because they sought a more decisive advance toward the socialist commonwealth? At a superficial level there was a shift to the Left in the Labour party, but among the main body of the movement these were the years that saw "the decline of the party stalwart" and growing hostility among working class respondents toward trade unions and their connection with the party. Goldthorpe and Lockwood in their famous Luton study had already spotted some of these trends in the mid-sixties. They found that affluent workers were withdrawing their allegiance from national unions and focusing instead on cooperation with their mates on the shop floor. Union activity was looked on not as an end in itself, but as a means to personal ends, as, in Goldthorpe's words, workers practiced "instrumental collectivism—the achievement of individual private goals outside the workplace."[6] Such an attitude, if not radical in the old Bevanite sense, was radical in the new populist sense: hostile to hierarchy and large-scale organization, essentially individualist, but capable of making the local group a powerful instrument of industrial action.

In the later sixties, Fox and Flanders perceived the increasing tendency of such local work groups in industry to regulate indepen-

6. J. H. Goldthorpe and D. Lockwood, "Affluence and the British Class Structure," *Sociological Review,* 1963, pp. 133–163.

dently and informally their own work behavior—a tendency which they held responsible for "chaotic pay differentials" and extensive wages drift.[7] The Donovan Commission also reported this shift of authority within unions toward work groups and shop stewards which they likewise deplored because of "the tendency of extreme decentralisation and self-government to degenerate into indecision and anarchy." The commission regarded such localism as normal in the British labor movement, thanks largely to the "strange structure" of multiunionism.[8] It is historically correct, as the commission observes, and as we have previously remarked, that in an earlier period before World War I labor organization was fragmented. But one must doubt that the "new unionism" of the sixties was only the reappearance of an historical pattern. The commission held that the cohesion of the labor movement of the interwar years had arisen from the exceptionally high and prolonged unemployment of the time and therefore it dissolved when that condition was brought to an end under conditions of full employment. But that cohesion survived during two decades or more of full employment during and after the war.[9] Nor is the explanation sufficient if we take into consideration multiunionism as well as full employment. In the 1960s, the outburst of localism in the world of organized labor was not confined to Britain, but appeared generally in western Europe—Germany being the main exception—even in countries without the burden of multiunionism.

The main difficulty with the commission's attempt to find nothing unprecedented in the localism of the 1960s, however, is the way this condition developed into and impelled the unprecedented and unexpected outburst of the later years of the decade. Impelled by highly local pressures and certainly not set off by national leadership, the wage-strike explosion reflected a radically new offensive stance on the part of trade unionists. It is indeed as if they had taken to heart the harsh populistic rejection of party, government, and trade union movement put forth in the May Day Manifesto of 1968.

James E. Cronin, who identified the magnitude of the discontinu-

---

7. Allan Fox and Alan Flanders, "The Reform of Collective Bargaining: from Donovan to Durkheim," *British Journal of Industrial Relations,"* 7, no. 2 (1969).
8. *op. cit.,* pp. 33, 29–30.
9. The postwar union leaders, writes Lewis Minkin, were "a 'Praetorian Guard' against both the political Left and shop-floor militancy." Minkin, *loc. cit.,* p. 13.

ity in industrial behavior, has also directed attention to the "novel ideological impetus" which provided the dynamic.[10] Disagreeing with a common approach to the history of organized labor which regards workers as people "to whom things happen," he takes into account "the creative element in labour's adaptation to external realities" consisting in "the process of ideological change and organisational innovation." "The impact of structure on behavior," he contends, "must be mediated by workers' attitudes and consciousness . . . [C]onsciousness intervenes between structure on the one hand and organisation and behavior on the other." He is aware of the attempts to explain the strike wave as proceeding from an essentially defensive reaction against a stagnation of real income and "badgering" by the Government. These explanations, he finds, "fail to consider the workers themselves as actors in the drama" and cannot account for their new offensive stance in adopting a higher standard of wage demands and backing it up with a strike action on a wider scale throughout the labor force. "A new set of attitudes towards society and towards social inequality lay behind the new militancy of 1969–72."

In the evidence he cites as defining the "new consciousness" it is not hard to see reflections of the positive values of the new populism. Some quotations will convey the tone and temper:[11]

One worker has argued . . . that when asking for more cash, workers are actually "seeking those things that make them human—a certain dignity, a measure of equality, and above all their self-respect. In our culture . . . a man's pay is a status symbol as well as a means of existence, so 'not getting the rate for the job' is a blow to a man's pride as well as pocket. . . ."

Frequently, workers on strike have expressed a lack of concern with the actual monetary gains and losses. "Money don't count when you're fighting for principle," proclaimed a striking seamstress from Dagenham in 1968. "In the ultimate no strike is worthwhile [economically]," argued another striker, "but there are principles." These sentiments were echoed by many other workers, especially by opponents of the Government's White Paper, *In Place of Strife,* who felt, "This is our last right—to strike."

In summarizing this "major transformation in worker attitudes" Cronin terms it "an erosion of deference and a rising demand for a

10. Cronin, *op. cit.,* pp. 6, 37, 142.
11. *ibid.,* p. 143.

greater share of society's goods and services.'' The rhetoric is mainly concerned with outcomes, specifically, greater equality of rewards and opportunities, but the insistence on ''workers' rights'' also shows a concern with the exercise of power. Behaviorally, the decline of deference appears both in the higher standard of wage demands and in the wider assertion of the right to strike.

In precipitating and perpetuating the pay scramble, fragmentation and decentralization did indeed set in motion compulsions that thwarted the dictates of collective rationality. But the populistic attitudes that supported and helped bring about this ''new unionism'' were *a fortiori* barriers to correcting it. The old trust in leadership and organization, industrial and political, had declined as had the strong class identification that had once supported union solidarity. The pay scramble of the 1970s, inaugurated by the wage-price explosion of 1968–72, was a reflex of pluralistic stagnation and class decomposition. But supporting and fomenting these structural conditions was the cultural revolution of the preceding decade.

Populism in the Labor Party

In the rest of this chapter we will be concerned with the influence of the new populism upon the political parties during the 1970s and after. Three areas of inquiry are in order: electoral behavior; attitudes toward public policy; and power relations within the parties and Parliament. Probes along these lines will help us see what has been happening in the main sectors of British political life, Labour, Conservative, and Liberal. How about the new political formation, the Social Democratic party? How does it fit with my view of the influence of the new populism? I will not be tipping my hand if I say that the fit seems to me quite impressive.

We will first turn to the Labour party.

The relation of the new attitudes to electoral behavior, while of great importance, has already been discussed and requires only a brief reference at this point. Under the guidance of Kavanagh and others, we have seen how the decline of the civic culture has been manifested in the weakening of the traditional bonds of class and party generally and especially in the decline of ''the 'traditionalist' Labour voter.'' Along with this uncorseting of his attitudes and in some considerable degree as a result of it, the voter has become more pragmatic and more individualist in his political preferences. These changes in outlook, in turn, have promoted greater volatility in electoral support, the social convergence of parties and, integrally with these effects, the inability of parties and governments to mobilize consent. As expressed in the decline of the civic culture, the negative impact of the new populism has had and continues to have great consequences for the Labour party and indeed for the party system as a whole.

The tendency of the new populism to raise new issues of public policy and to thrust forward new attitudes toward them is a second effect on Labour that needs more attention. One can catch sight of this process by sampling the rhetoric of program making. In the 1970s, as we have seen, the Left within the party gained as the author of party statements, and these more and more reflected the ideas of the New Left in contrast with the party's Old Left. The New Left, although moribund as a movement, took on life as what I have called the rising orthodoxy of dissent within the party. The language of Aneurin Bevan was mixed with and in vitally significant ways was supplanted by the language of Tony Benn.

Even at the very beginning of the 1960s, when *Signposts for the Sixties* (1961) was being drafted, attempts were made to introduce populistic themes. As one might expect, they dealt with culture and the media, participation and democratic control in a mass society, and specific proposals for more participation in local government and industry. Such thoughts, however, were quickly weeded out of an early draft, so that in the final version the then new emphasis on modernization and technological advance was unqualified. In later party conferences the claims of "participation" were advanced and the case for workers' control was urged, but without great force or impact. In 1968, for instance, in a listless debate a skimpy statement favoring industrial democracy was discussed and carried.

When the party swung sharply to the Left in the early 1970s, it still made its case for a more thoroughgoing socialism largely in terms of the centralized bureaucratic model championed by the previous generations of fundamentalists. In the big program of 1973, from which, as we have seen, the radical manifesto of the next year was taken, industrial democracy received only brief attention and workers' participation, but not workers' control, was mentioned with approval. The Foreword, perhaps echoing resentment against Wilson's disregard for conference, emphasized that in the Labour party "policy is made by the members," citing the words of Clause V of the party constitution vesting in conference the power to make the "party programme." Attlee and Gaitskell would not have demurred. In contrast, however, with the documents published in their day, the 1973 statement was called "the" Party Programme. This status and function was made more emphatic three years later when in *Labour's Programme 1976* it was claimed that in publishing the previous statement the NEC had "for the first time, published a comprehensive and detailed Programme as provided for by this Clause." This new and ambitious self-definition may have been intended to justify, and may also help account for, the inordinate and unprecedented length of the 1973 and 1976 documents, which respectively ran to 122 and 147 pages.

The 1976 document was drawn up by the NEC after it came under the control of the Left in 1974. A massive and radical statement, approved by conference in 1976, it echoed in its political passages the populistic themes of the New Left. In setting forth the "new industrial strategy," as we have seen, the program again followed the old model of centralized planning, now with corporatist additions. The novelty came in a set of detailed and forceful proposals for industrial democracy, specific ideas for devolution for Scotland and Wales, and two long sections elaborating on "Human Rights" and "A Wider Democracy." Some of the detail of the program provides a sense of the new values in the background.

The paragraphs on industrial democracy went beyond demanding mere participation. Workers must not only be consulted; "they must at all levels have a decisive voice in the decision-making itself," including representation "in the Boardroom itself." And beyond "joint control," progress must be made "in the direction of employee's control and self-management." This new emphasis on industrial democracy, we should note parenthetically, was raised at a time when the Bullock committee, appointed at the urging of the TUC, was debating and formulating what became its quite radical proposals for worker directors.[12] In dealing with "human rights," the new party program recognized the dangers of the "age of

12. *Report of the Committee of Inquiry on Industrial Democracy* (Bullock Report). London, 1977.

bureaucracy" and suggested measures to tip the scale "back in favor of the individual" in both "private and public concentrations of power." Devolution for Scotland and Wales was advocated because "the time is now right for reforms making our system of government more democratic, more accountable and more open to the people." For England "directly elected regional authorities" would have charge of "planning and infrastructure development" and perhaps also independent taxing power. Since "the higher civil service" is "an important political force in its own right," its decision-making must be opened up to "much greater scrutiny and political control." For the sake of "an open democracy" the Official Secrets Act must be liberalized. To offset the influence of "closed and almost autocratic institutions," the structure of broadcasting must be reformed to make it "truly diversified, open, and accountable."

Tony Benn and Populism

The populist overtones were emphasized when, in presenting the document to the 1976 party conference on behalf of the NEC, Tony Benn drew "special attention" to its section on "A Wider Democracy."[13] Explicitly recognizing the contrast with the views of the Old Left, he remarked on the new value given to "the meaning of industrial democracy which now illuminates, as all democratic themes do, the programme of our party." As chairman of the NEC's home policy subcommittee which drafted the programme, Benn bore considerable responsibility for the new emphasis. His views and position in the party measured the advance of the new populism in the political side of the Labour movement. By the later 1970s Benn had become the principal leader of the Left. Regularly he topped the poll for the constituency section of the NEC, as Aneurin Bevan had done in the 1950s.

The profound changes taking place in the party will be illuminated by a comparison of the two men: Bevan, the Welsh miner, who, coming up from the pits with the help of scholarships paid for by his union, led the failing fight of the fundamentalists against the revisionists in the 1950s; and Benn, that familiar figure in British his-

13. *Report of Annual Conference,* Labour Party, 1976, p. 157.

tory, the rich and radical aristocrat who, having been educated at Westminster School and Oxford, rose to prominence on the populist wave of the 1970s and mounted a powerful challenge for the leadership in the early 1980s. First we may look at their views and then at their positions in the party.

Benn like Bevan was a committed democrat but by the mid-seventies he had become a democrat cast in the new populist mold. Like Bevan he was for public ownership, economic planning and control, and egalitarian social services. But his views on the distribution of power put him in a world apart from the old fundamentalists. Bevan's views of how power was won and exercised were uncritically collectivist. When he was a young coal miner in South Wales, wrote Bevan, he was concerned with one practical question: "Where does power lie in this particular state of Great Britain and how can it be attained by the workers?" This question, he said, did not shape itself in some such fashion as "How can I get on?"

The texture of our lives shaped the question into a class and not into an individual form. . . . For us power meant the use of collective action designed to transform society and so lift all of us together. . . . We were the products of an industrial civilization and our psychology corresponded to that fact. Individual initiative was overlaid by the social imperative. The streams of individual initiative therefore flowed along collective channels already formed for us by our environment. Society presented itself to us as an area of conflicting social forces and not as a plexus of individual striving.[14]

By contrast Benn feared bureaucracy as much as capitalism.[15] In his eyes the old fundamentalist collectivism threatened to lead to "the corporatist nightmare" which would permit "the worst forms of managerial authoritarianism to creep back through the back door of the public service, public agencies, and publicly owned industries." For him "the *first* and central problem of nationalisation" was, therefore, industrial democracy, by which he meant not co-ownership, profit-sharing, or workers councils, but full "workers' self-management." This would be based on the trade unions, but

14. Quoted in *Modern British Politics,* pp. 84–85.
15. The following discussion of Benn's views is based on Tony Benn, *Arguments for Socialism,* edited by Chris Mullin (London, 1979). References are to pages 172, 42, 170, 173, 110, 111 and 131.

under a structure and with responsibilities profoundly different from
what they had been in the past. From the time of the Attlee Government ''the trade union leadership'' had belonged to ''the Establishment''—that is, ''the body of key people whose assent is required to
govern.'' To avoid corporatism, the unions too must be democratized and the people at their top made more closely accountable to
their rank and file in the shop stewards movement.

In the same spirit he denied that government any longer ''rotates
entirely around Parliament and the old cycle of inner-party policy
formulation—intense electoral propaganda, voters' mandate, and
legislative implementation—important as they are.'' Power based only
on consent given at an election in his eyes was hardly less authoritarian than power based on feudal inheritance or military dictatorship. If government was again to enjoy ''general assent'' the ''social
contract . . . upon which parliamentary democracy was based . . .
needs to be renegotiated on a basis that shares power much more
widely.'' In the light of these sentiments, he supported a series of
far-reaching reforms to secure ''open government.'' With regard to
Parliament, they included abolition of the House of Lords, power for
parliamentary committees to interrogate ministers and officials, a
Freedom of Information Act, and greater accountability for the security services. With regard to the Labour party, reform would include
annual election of the cabinet and relaxation of the fictions of collective responsibility, when the party was in power, and the three reforms
of party organization taken up by the Left in the later seventies: compulsory reselection of MPs, full power over the manifesto for the
NEC, and the election of the party leader by an electoral college
representing the various elements in the party. His proposals, industrial and political, could be matched point for point with the main
items in the May Day Manifesto of 1968.

Power on the Left

To say that Benn was any more than the ''principal'' leader of the
Labour Left would be an exaggeration and herein lies another crucial
difference between him and Aneurin Bevan. Whether or not he had
any personal inadequacies, the political situation would not have permitted Benn to achieve a position of leadership comparable to that

enjoyed by Bevan. The radical fragmentation that had disrupted British politics generally affected no less its left-wingers both inside and outside the party. One reason for this loss of solidarity was the changed position of the Soviet Union in the politics of the Left throughout the world. In the first postwar years, Russia continued to exercise that polarizing power on the politics of all countries which it had gained in the interwar years. Its satellite parties of the Comintern uniquely defined the far left in their respective countries without serious competition from Trotskyite groups that might oppose them. In consequence, socialist belief extended in a continuum from the democratic forces toward those who would compromise democracy for the socialism they saw in the Communist cause. In Britain Bevan dominated that democratic left wing of this socialist continuum.

By the 1970s, however, the Communist party had not only long since been discredited by the unveiling of Stalinism, but also in recent years had gained a host of new rivals as champion of the far left.[16] In 1947, for instance, when the Revolutionary Communist party had a split, there were only two Trotskyite organizations. By 1980 internal fission had given rise to some fourteen descendants.[17] Meanwhile, the Labour party in 1973 had dropped its old list of "proscribed organisations" which had been adopted during the interwar period in order to protect against Communist infiltration and to which individual members could not belong. Although technically still ineligible for party membership, adherents of the splinter groups gained a fair amount of influence in some constituency parties, especially as the membership of the latter plummeted. Of the various Trotskyite groups, the most successful by far was the Militant Tendency fathered in 1950 by Ted Grant when the Revolutionary Communist party split. Publishers of *Militant* and with several thousand supporters, drawn especially from students and faculty in higher education—polytechnics rather than universities—they had by 1980 won "total control" over the Labour party's youth organization, could name the party

16. At the NUPE Conference of 1979 while talking with an ardent young member of the Workers Revolutionary party, I made some reference to the Communist party as "leftwing" only to be interrupted by a shout: "The Communists are the most reactionary party in the world!"

17. Tom Forester, "The Labour Party's Militant Moles," *New Society*, January 10, 1980, pp. 54–55.

conference delegate in 50 to 100 of the 635 parliamentary constituencies, but had not yet managed the election of any "100 percent Militant MPs."[18] Tony Benn, needless to say, could not be identified with them. Yet neither did he disavow their support.

While in some localities a clique had become dominant, leftwing politics in the party was deeply disoriented. Typically, to be sure, leftwing politics does splinter. But by the 1970s the structural and cultural conditions that in the past had enabled the Labour Left to offset these tendencies were no longer present. Confronted with such confusion in his natural constituency, Benn could not hope to acquire the breadth and solidity of support that Bevan had enjoyed. Moreover, as the confused and bitter wrangles within the party from the later 1970s demonstrated, the capacity of the party to produce effective leadership of any sort—of a faction or of the party as a whole—had been gravely weakened.

The organizational reforms advocated by the Left which have aroused such bitter controversy in recent years would dissolve even further the old power structure of the party. Again the contrast with the Left/Right struggles of the 1950s illuminates what has been happening. When the fundamentalists supported Nye Bevan in that ferocious struggle for the succession and for "full-blooded socialism," they sought to put their champion in the same position of authority that had been occupied by Attlee. The stakes in terms of power were like those between two parties in Parliament, each of which seeks to put its team in as the cabinet, but not to change the cabinet system. The Bennites, however—if one may use this or any singular term to identify the diffuse and fluctuating Left of recent years—also seek radically to change and indeed to diminish the basis of authority which they would win for him and, judging by what he says, so too does he.

The consequences of the reforms would be major; indeed so great is their potential for change that no one can say with any precision what their effects would be.[19] Individually and in sum, however, it is clear that they would greatly reduce the power of the leader. Mandatory reselection might well in some cases give local militants more

18. *ibid.*, p. 53.
19. For discussion of the proposed reforms at the 1979 conference, see debate on resolutions 18, 19, 25, 32 and 33.

leverage over MPs and so strengthen the Left, but hardly in sufficient numbers nor with sufficient solidarity to put into power an authoritative leader from the Left. In any case, the more the MP is forced to cultivate local support the less reliable he will be as a tool of the whips. To make the party leader the choice of an electoral college creates the chance, if not the likelihood, that he will not be the choice of the parliamentary party which he would then try to lead. To take from him his present large and usually dominant role in writing the manifesto diminishes his authority in the party and deprives him of a means of imposing his views on a future Government.

By the same token, if Benn—or any other left-winger—were to become Leader, he would find it difficult to carry out any mandate from those who had supported his election. To be sure, if some influential and tightly disciplined organization had manipulated his choice, it might be supposed to have the power to mobilize the main elements of the parliamentary and extraparliamentary parties in support of its chosen head or figurehead. In its hey-day the Communist party had been able to bring about such results within front organizations it had infiltrated. But a crucial distinction of leftwing politics today from then is precisely its hopeless fragmentation. The proposed reforms of the power structure do not fit into any credible scenario culminating in authoritarian control by the far left.

The Left/Right struggle of recent years has involved not only the familiar conflict between a more or a less socialist stance on policy and program, but also a conflict between two conceptions of how the party and indeed the country are to be governed. The three organizational reforms at issue are presented as measures of democratization and, whatever their origin or the intent of their various advocates, demonstrate by their wide acceptance the spread of the populist outlook in the Labour movement. In this conflict over constitutional values one may be tempted to find a reason for the exceptional hostility that has envenomed the Left/Right controversy of recent years. The change in tone and temper of intraparty debate surely demands explanation. For in the attacks on the Labour movement and its leaders launched by members of the Left at party conferences from the later 1970s, the rhetoric has reached a level of rancor that finds no comparison even at the height of the Bevanite struggles of the 1950s, as I recall them and they are recorded in the conference reports.

The conflict over unilateralism at Scarborough in 1960s—the occasion for Gaitskell's desperate "fight, fight, and fight again" speech[20]—is remembered as a time of bitterness. When one goes back and reads the verbatim report, however, the language, although impassioned, is gentlemanly compared with common usage at the conferences of 1976, 1979, or 1980. At one point during the Scarborough debate, for example, a rank-and-file opponent of the H-bomb demanded rhetorically: "When in Hell are we supposed to change our programme if we do not change it between elections." He quickly added however: "I hope you will pardon the strong language, but even that is not strong language compared with what I could use."[21] Moreover, on virtually all other items of policy—pensions, South Africa, rents, housing, fuel, and power—all was harmony. At the 1976 conference by contrast the attacks on the party leaders, who were at the same time members of a Labour Government, ranged across the board on policy and compared with the 1950s were launched from a totally different semiotic world: "horror and incredulity," "horror," "barbaric," "Neanderthal," "bankrupt," "reactionary" give a taste of the words that were routinely hurled at the leadership.

As the unrestrained rhetoric suggests, the attack on authority is, moreover, embodied in face-to-face behavior. In that change an astute observer finds the essential difference of the present dispute from those of the past. The "key to the understanding of the dispute," wrote the *Observer* correspondent, Alan Watkins, at the time of the 1979 conference, "is that there is a greater equality between the leaders and the led." He sees this difference displayed during the time for socializing. In the old days, twenty years or so ago, "the mass of the party knew their place, kept their distance. . . . [T]here were two conferences: the one revolving round the big hotels and expensive restaurants, the other round the boarding houses and fringe meetings. It is not quite like this any more. The delegates, jostling at the bar of the Grand, think they are as good as their leaders." Picking up language much used by James Callaghan, at that time still leader of the party, he finds one reason for the change in "the

20. *Report of Annual Conference,* Labour Party, 1960, p. 201.
21. *ibid.,* 192.

decline of deference.'' In this change of attitude he also finds the
reason for what in the light of the older behavior is a ''paradox'':

The big union leaders, we were told several times, were deeply distressed
by the week's goings-on. . . . And yet, how could the two resolutions on
constitutional reform . . . have been passed without the big union block
votes? The obvious conclusion is that the leaders are not in control of their
delegations. The decline of deference can have all kinds of results.[22]

Populism on the Right

As Watkins' *aperçu* suggests, however, the populist attitude was
not confined to the Labour Left—although it may well have exacerbated their incivility—but has affected all wings of the party. The
1980 conference voted to move the choice of the party leader from
the MPs alone to a wider electoral college also including trade unions
and local parties and to require sitting MPs to come before their
management committees for reselection before each election, and it
only narrowly defeated the proposal giving the NEC sole control
over the manifesto. Constituency delegates voted overwhelmingly—
probably as many as 90 percent—in favor of the reforms.[23] As we
have seen, delegates of the Militant Tendency were only a very small
fraction of this total. Many of the affirmative votes came from the
Tribune Left—now often called ''the legitimate Left''—which is by
no means friendly with the militants. Still others were cast by ''well-
meaning socialists of the traditional Labour Party sort.''[24] They were
traditional in the sense of being committed to basic democratic values, but now they demanded far-reaching changes in the authority
structure of the party in order to realize those values.

It is not only among local activists that the new populism has made
inroads. Among MPs, spokesmen of the Right have threatened to
hoist the Left on their own petard by advocating reforms of party

22. *Observer*, 9 October 1979.
23. The estimate of Roger Liddle, a delegate, who had been political adviser to
William Rodgers, minister of transport in the Callaghan government. Conversation of
October 7, 1980.
24. I owe this comment to Professor Peter Hall of Harvard who attended the conference.

organization that are even more consistently populist. On the eve of the party conference of 1980, for example, eleven MPs issued a warning to the party leadership reflecting such a stand. Opposing the use of the trade union block vote to return to "the good old days" when "the real business of running the Labour party" was "centralized in a very few hands," they declared that the "first priority" should be "to involve far more Labour voters in the workings of the party at every level." In a carefully constructed 2,500 word program they set forth their own six proposals for radically democratic constitutional reform. These would broaden the base of representation on the NEC, give individual members more weight in drawing up the manifesto, extend to all members the right to vote by postal vote for a party leader separate from the parliamentary leader, modify the dominant role of the unions in the party organization and give every party member and not just the management committees a vote in the election of local officers and conference delegates, and in the selection and reselection of parliamentary candidates.[25]

These proposals made no headway at the 1980 conference but that does not mean they had no future. The idea of one man-one vote for party leader was put forward—in vain—at the special party conference of January 24, 1981 at Wembley called to decide how that choice was to be made. Six of the eleven MPs joined the Social Democratic party which in framing its own organization took a similar radical democratic stance favoring a less centralized and more participatory model.

This conflict over party reform was not simply a replay of the time-honored battle in the Labour party over intraparty democracy. The premises of reform were quite different as were the proposals consequent upon them. In the days of Bevanism, for instance, the constitutional question at issue between Left and Right was the degree of control of conference over the actions of a future Labour government. The questions of how the Leader was to be chosen or whether MPs must face reselection did not arise. Both Left and Right in the parliamentary and extraparliamentary organization accepted the collectivist and therefore the solidary and centralist outlook of the socialist theory of representation.

25. *Times* (London), 22 September 1980.

So conceived, the Labour party in contrast to the Liberals was constituted not by the subjective fact of agreement among like-minded individuals, but by the objective fact of a unified and oriented working class.[26] As the comprehensive political organization of this class, the party set up branches, screened their members by its "proscribed list," disciplined MPs by its parliamentary party and central organs, and occasionally permitted reselection under close central supervision. It was wholeheartedly democratic, but the democracy to which it adhered in theory and practice was not participatory, but deferential, representative, indirect, and centralized. Populism was as foreign to it as localism and individualism.

The constraints upon participation in the Labour party in its collectivist period were not structural. One should not imagine that the spirit of populism had always flourished among Labour party activists, struggling against organizational barriers. The structure of the Labour party—and indeed of the Conservative party also—would have permitted far greater participation by party voters—if they had wanted it. The individual adherent could have acquired formal party membership for a pittance, and something very much like American primary elections could have been forced by the rank and file.

Under the traditional structure, a person wishing to be nominated could have asked party members—whose numbers his solicitation had possibly enlarged—to elect his supporters to the ward committees which in turn would have chosen the members of the management committee vested with the power of nomination. That is how it had been done before the days of the direct primary in the United States, when rivals within the same party competed for support in the "primary assemblies" that chose the first rank of the delegate convention structure. It would have been logical for similar practices to arise in British party organizations which had been modeled on the structures developed by Jacksonian democracy. If my own experience is any guide, the amazing fact that such competitive participation has not arisen is one of the first puzzles confronting the American who turns to the study of British politics.[27]

26. See "Party Government: Socialist Version" in *Modern British Politics*, pp. 79–91.
27. In one of the first things I wrote about British politics, I reflected this transatlantic contrast. "Few features," I said, "are more remarkable to an American than

A few starts in that direction were made in the late nineteenth century. And in more recent times, on a very few occasions something like a primary competition did break out in both the Labour and Conservative parties. But attitudes and sometimes formal rules have blocked the way. Over the years, in conversation with people in politics at all levels, when I have suggested such participation, I have met with, first, incomprehension and, secondly, repugnance. "But that would be a packed meeting," rejoined one agent, after I had with great difficulty got across the idea of candidates for a nomination soliciting votes for supporters at the election of a ward committee. A prominent MP put the point in positive terms: "It is much better that the party elders make the choice of the candidate." Yet if the spirit of rebellion had been present, it is hard to believe that suitably combative aspirants and adherents could not have got their way. At the most fundamental level of behavior, the deferential democracy of the civic culture was an effortless, but powerful reality.

The Labour party is a long way from the direct primary in the selection of its MPs or its Leader.[28] On the most favorable count individual membership was only 370,000 in 1980. Under present arrangements, moreover, reselection will be conducted not directly by these members, but by the local representative bodies, the management committees. The Leader will be chosen by the total membership acting through an electoral college constituted by MPs, local parties, and trade unions. The great bulk of this membership, recorded as nearly seven million, is accounted for by the trade unions who still quite effectively muffle participation in the control of their block votes. This is a far cry indeed from the more than thirty million who took a direct part in choosing the two main candidates in American presidential primaries in 1980. To their relief the British may be

---

this absence of what one might call the Jacksonian attitude underlying the American primary, viz., that it is for the mass of the voters to nominate the candidate as well as choose between them." "Great Britain: From Governing Elite to Organized Mass Parties" in Sigmund Neumann, ed., *Modern Political Parties: Approaches to Comparative Politics* (Chicago, 1956), p. 56.

28. Proposals for a direct primary for MPs have been put forward. See *Report on Electoral Reform* (Hansard Society Commission, 1976) and Peter Paterson, *The Selectorate* (London, 1967). These proposals are discussed in S.E. Finer, *The Changing British Party System 1945–1979* (Washington, D.C., 1980) pp. 213–214.

informed that the Americanization of their politics is still far from
complete.

Yet the loosening up and opening up of the collectivist system
continues. We can better see its full significance if we consider these
inroads of populism on the extraparliamentary organization in connection with the decline of unity and rise of rebellion within the
parliamentary party during the previous decade. This topic, however, can best be taken up when we also consider similar developments on the Conservative side under the general rubric of "the rise
of parliament."

THE WANING OF TORYISM

The emphasis up to this point on events in the Labour movement
does not imply that the new populism was uniquely the creation of
socialist intellectuals or that its impact was confined to the Left. On
the contrary, as we have observed when recording the decline of the
civic culture, the change in values arose in and affected all sectors
of political opinion. Like the counterculture from which it sprang,
the new populism has been pervasive. One reason for devoting so
much space to Labour is that the party was in power for most of the
period being reviewed in this essay. This reversal of the Conservative predominance that had been marked in the earlier postwar years
and indeed since the third Reform Act, is itself an indication of the
shift in political values. When, during the 1979 campaign, I asked
Anthony King, professor of politics at the University of Essex, what
changes had recently taken place in the party system, his first reply
was: "The collapse of deference toward the Conservatives. They are
no longer regarded as the party of competence." One can sense the
weight of this remark when, looking at the matter historically, one
recalls how the Tories have been regarded for generations as in a
special sense the seat of the governing class.

The impact of populism on the Conservatives can be examined
under the same three headings that were used in discussing the Labour
party: the decline of electoral support; the rise of new attitudes toward
policy; and the change in power relations within the party.

The effect of the decline of the civic culture on party support hardly
needs further elaboration. Dennis Kavanagh has spelled out what this

means in terms of the waning of "the old restraints of hierarchy and deference."[29] One result has been the withering away of that celebrated figure in British politics, the deferential working class Tory, who not long ago accounted for—depending on the stringency of the definition—a quarter to a half of the Conservative votes from the working class. Deference, however, was by no means confined to the working class. If one was looking for an attitude of trust in persons of superior social and political standing, one could hardly have asked for a richer display than that commonly exhibited by the middle class "representatives" toward their MPs and the platform at a Conservative conference. Whatever the reasons, the bonds linking middle class voters to the Conservative party have substantially weakened.

In the years 1964–1974 the proportion of middle class Conservatives steadily fell.[30] As the other side of this loosening of middle class political ties, the middle class vote for Labour has gradually, but persistently grown since the 1960s, a trend which, as we have seen, continued in the 1979 election.[31] In the increasingly instrumentalist mood of the electorate, dissatisfaction with the Conservatives' economic performance when in office and doubt of their competence to handle such problems as the trade unions were often the reasons for voters switching from the party.

Nor does one see this dissolution of old bonds and barriers only in the political realm. There was a decline also of the class/trade union nexus as well as the class/party nexus as more and more people in distinctively middle class occupations joined unions and took industrial action. Organized labor was "bourgeoisified" not only in the sense that it lost much of its old solidarity and was drawn into the group competition of the managed market of the collectivist polity, but also in the sense that, in Halsey's words, it "began to lose its class character, if not its class rhetoric." "Even the Association of First Division Civil Servants," he continues, "is now affiliated to the TUC."[32]

29. "Political Culture in Great Britain: the Decline of the Civic Culture," *loc. cit.,* p. 170.

30. Ivor Crewe *et al.,* "Partisan Dealignment in Britain 1964–1974," *loc. cit.,* p. 169. See Rows 1 and 2 of Table 20.

31. See above p. 117, Table 3.2.

32. A. H. Halsey, *Change in British Society* (Oxford, 1978) p. 76.

The ground for this new behavior was not that material differentiations between different occupations had ceased to exist. On the contrary, occupations in the growing service class carried attributes which in power and affluence set them off markedly from one another and from occupations in the intermediate and working classes. The reason people in these occupations behaved toward unions differently from middle class people of an earlier generation was that they put a different sort of value on union membership. They looked on it not as a badge of working class status which they must eschew for fear of derogation, but instrumentally as a means to personal goals of economic self-protection and betterment.

The Tory Remnant

The new populism is about policy as well as power. We have seen how in consequence it has complicated and envenomed the inner conflicts of the Labour party. A brief sampling will suggest its impact on Conservative thought. Again there is a conflict between two wings which has been exacerbated by the decline of the civic culture. One wing defends the main outlines of the welfare state and managed economy under a leadership representing the remnants of the Tory tradition, while the other adheres to the cause of economic liberalism and is at least cool toward the rule of the patricians. These two tendencies are sometimes called Left and Right respectively, although that usage belies the function of the terms "Tory" and "liberal" in the more distant past and obscures the complexity of the values at issue in the present.

Sir Ian Gilmour, bart., the tall spare former Guards officer; grandson of the duke of Buccleuch and Queensberry; educated at Eton and Balliol; author, editor and barrister; MP, and recently Lord Privy Seal and Defense spokesman in the Commons, is sometimes not strangely referred to as a High Tory. In his *Inside Right: A Study of Conservatism* (1977) he defends the postwar consensus, finds it in harmony with "Tory themes" and traces its origin to the measures adopted by Churchill's wartime coalition and interwar Conservatism rather than the program of Attlee's Government.[33] His argument is directed

33. References are to pages 34, 232, 196–199, 195, 210, and 209.

against neoliberals as well as socialists. As ever in the Tory tradition, doctrine, ideology, and system, with which he finds Dr Hayek and Enoch Powell alike afflicted, are rejected in favor of trust in history and pragmatic adaptation. In the present confusion of economic theories, "the wise Tory will be eclectic," feeling "no call to be either a card-carrying Keynesian or a card-carrying Friedmanite." What he calls "the Tory Party" upholds "private property" and "private enterprise," but "it is not a pressure group for capitalism" and will modify the free market as necessary. Most of what he says about style of government and substance of policy could have been written by Harold Macmillan, whom, indeed, he clearly admires and often cites.

In a passage already quoted, however, he sounds a very different note from Macmillan's hubristic tones of 1959.[34] He finds the constitution itself called into question by the loss of "legitimacy and authority" and the consequent inability of governments to "mobilize consent." His gloom is especially striking in contrast with his view expressed in a work published only a few years earlier. In both books he quoted de Gaulle's glowing tribute to British government in an address in Westminster Hall in April, 1960. There in a climactic sentence de Gaulle had asked rhetorically: "At the worst moments, who ever contested the legitimacy or the authority of the state?" In 1969, Sir Ian confirmed this tribute, adding, "In Britain legitimacy does not have to be sought; the system is impregnated with it."[35] In 1977, his comment was very different: "At the time those words seemed a generous but not unjustified tribute to the British constitution. Now they sound more like a funeral oration upon it."[36]

He found the fault largely in the crumbling of the party system that had resulted from Labour's swing to the Left. "For a two-party system to have any chance of working," he wrote, "the parties must be fairly close together; they must incline to the Centre rather than

---

34. On the crest of a spectacular boom in 1959 Macmillan led the Conservatives to their third consecutive victory under the party slogan "You're having it good. Have it better. Vote Conservative." Butler and Rose, *op. cit.,* p. 22. On the complicated question of whether Macmillan meant his warning of inflation to outweigh his boast when on previous occasions he used the more celebrated phrase "most of our people have never had it so good," see Anthony Sampson, *Macmillan: A Study in Ambiguity* (London, 1967) p. 167.

35. *The Body Politic* (London, 1967) p. 167.

36. *Inside Right,* p. 195.

to their outside wings; and they must have a deep respect for the constitution.'' He then went on to discuss a number of possible reforms that might prevent an extremist government from obliterating ''British freedoms.'' These included a stronger and partly elected upper chamber, use of the referendum on constitutional issues, a written constitution with a bill of rights, and electoral reform.

No American can have much quarrel with devices such as these. From the beginning it has been a pretty common opinion in the United States that the ''eternal vigilance'' which is ''the price of liberty'' must be directed against oppressive popular majorities, as well as overweening rulers, and embodied in mechanical restraints and written prohibitions. The British, on the other hand, have preferred to concentrate power and to trust for protection against abuse to a tradition—the civic culture in some form—and to the virtue and popularity of a governing class. ''Throughout the twentieth century,'' Dennis Kavanagh has observed, ''the [Conservative] party has been suffused with the values of upper-crust England, an 'Establishment' of wealth, exclusive London clubs, and the major expensive public schools. In little more than a decade that apparently secure ruling class has almost disappeared.''[37] The problem is not that people of breeding, education, and political virtue can no longer be found on Conservative benches, but that the party favored by them has lost its standing as ''the natural party of government.''

A thoughtful Tory of the younger generation reveals the impact of the new values in a more positive light. Impeccably aristocratic as the younger son of a twelfth earl; educated at Eton, Oxford, and Harvard; Fellow of All Souls, briefly political assistant to Prime Minister Heath, and recently elected MP from Bristol, William Waldegrave like Sir Ian looks to the past and in a bold and scholarly account published in 1978 consults ''the Conservative tradition'' for its relevance to the problems of the present day.[38] That relevance consists negatively in ''protection against the pathology of the forcible imposition of theory on people.'' Like a sensible man and a good Tory he argues that ''since no theory of organisation is complete, trust in this kind of theory should be abandoned.'' The warning strikes not only socialists, but also neoliberals whose ''political

37. Kavanagh, *loc. cit.*, p. 158.
38. *The Binding of Leviathan: Conservatism and the Future* (London, 1978). References are to pages 119, 39, 149, 124, 136, 125.

advice, derived from Liberal economic theory . . . leaves governors and its own adherents always frustrated at the distance between their model of the world and reality.''

But Waldegrave, although a defender of the welfare state, departs sharply from the Macmillan model in his hostility to the planned, centralized, corporatistic state. Indeed his vitriol matches that of the New Left, as do some of his ideas also. Today, in his view, ''increasingly powerless and increasingly desperate solitary citizens face the rambling structure of an ever-expanding state which can reach out and turn their lives upside down for the most trivial and unexpected reasons.'' As ''separate and contradictory factions'' push for ''a bigger role for the state,'' he sees ''a defunct constitution allowing the headless monster thus created to spread havoc amongst the patterns of living necessary for civilised society.'' He calls on Conservatives to ''bind'' this ''new Leviathan'' and direct the state toward the positive goal of the Conservative tradition, ''the tradition of community.''

For example, following ''an approach to society which is Conservative,'' trade union cooperation with a voluntary incomes policy would be sought by engaging them in a more formalized and widened process of ''discussion, education, and negotiation.'' While such a ''comprehensive community'' would function through a national forum, the ''natural communities'' that Conservative policy would foster would be mainly small and local: such as a city neighborhood or ''a properly organised place of work.'' In spite of Benn's ''ill-judged experiments,'' Waldegrave looks with favor on cooperatives. To be sure, in them ''every decision cannot be taken by the vote,'' but they would be ''self-regulating communities.'' The key is to release ''the natural tendency of men and women . . . to group themselves for mutual benefit.'' These ''natural communities'' are voluntary in their essence and, although indispensable to the individual for both ''happiness and survival,'' may not be imposed on him from without. They are not dictated by objective economic necessity. Even less are they Burke's ''little platoons'' based on fixed interests and embodied in traditional hierarchies. In their size, constitution and cultural function, they are no great distance from the humanistic communes of William Morris that were celebrated by the New Left.

Alien to the true Burkean model as Waldegrave's "natural communities" may be, one may still find in their smallness and decentralization an overlap with the tradition. What is startling, however,
in this scholarly and aware book on the Conservative tradition, is its
total silence on the question of hierarchy. The central thread—indeed
the veritable backbone and spinal column—uniting all the various
articulations of the Tory idea from Tudor days into the twentieth
century, through Bolinbroke, Burke, Disraeli and Randolph Churchill to Leopold Amery and R. A. Butler, is the commitment to
authoritative leadership as a permanent social necessity. According
to the Tory idea, whatever the economic or political order of the
nation, a governing class is necessary—as much in the age of democracy, mass parties, and the welfare state as in the age of monarchy
and aristocracy. Tory democracy was the adaptation of this basic
insight to the arrival of the universal franchise.[39] A discussion of the
Conservative tradition that did not take up this theme would truly be
Hamlet without the Prince of Denmark.

To be sure, as the franchise was widened and new demands arose
from the masses, the assertion of this principle was muted. Yet as
late as 1957 the Conservative party did not hesitate to publish a work
on *The Tory Tradition* which asserted forthrightly that "a class system, and a largely hereditary class system is morally right" since
any society needs a "governing class" with a "specialised prepara-
tory training" which will foster "generous self-confidence, not for-
getful of the lesson of *noblesse oblige*."[40] As an item of political
theory the Tory idea is by no means absurd and deserves serious
examination. Yet on this question the two contemporary Tories, William Waldegrave and Ian Gilmour, choose to say nothing. One could
hardly ask for a more convincing index of the collapse of deference.

Neoliberalism

There is nothing unusual about business interests being championed by Conservatives. In the late nineteenth century, financial,
industrial, and commercial wealth moved strongly to the party and

39. *Modern British Politics*, pp. 92–93.
40. Sir Geoffrey Butler, *The Tory Tradition* (London, 1914). Republished by the
Conservative Political Centre, with a preface by R. A. Butler, pp. 67–71.

businessmen increasingly appeared on its side of the House. "They were to have," in the words of two Tory Democrats of a later generation, "a profound effect on the party, purging it of most of its Tory philosophy and indoctrinating it with that peculiar blend of whiggery and laissez faire Liberalism which still colors the speeches of some of its leaders."[41] In that period of "Conservative inertia" between Disraelian Toryism and the reassertion of state power during the interwar years, ideological tones sometimes could be heard on the Conservative benches. But it would be hard to find then or at any time in the Conservative past a leading figure who cut himself off from the Tory tradition as systematically and conclusively as some of the neoliberal spokesmen of the past decade or so have done.

The brilliant and imaginative Enoch Powell led the way and set the example. He claims the name "Tory" and surely justifies it in his veneration for the institutions of the country—Parliament with its sovereignty, and monarchy with its symbolism of nationality. But in elaborating and applying his central belief in laissez faire, free-market capitalism his speeches and writings are not merely "colored" by liberalism; they display a rigor and consistency—not to say passion—that is quite untypical of Conservative thought. To appreciate the contrast one need only compare his intellectual style with that of Sir Ian Gilmour, who indeed terms Powell "the nearest thing the Tory party has, or rather had, to an ideologue."[42]

Since he was not only an ideologue, but also a demagogue, we need to take note of what he did as well as what he said. Rising from lower middle class origins, a precocious scholar and ardent imperialist, Powell distinguished himself in academic and military life before entering politics after the war. A moderate Butlerite in the days of Butskellism, he displayed his fears of excessive public spending in his resignation of 1958, but went on to serve in the cabinet under the interventionist Macmillan. He was seen to be on the losing side when in the elevation of Home in 1963 "the traditional party elites [sought] to block the growing influence of grammarschool educated Tories like Powell."[43]

41. *Modern British Politics*, p. 273, quoting Ray Lewis and Angus Mande.
42. *Inside Right*, p. 133.
43. Douglas Shoen, *Enoch Powell and the Powellites* (New York, 1977) p. 7. In the following discussion I have depended heavily on Schoen's excellent study.

His breach with Toryism, however, did not come until the mid-1960s. After the Conservative defeat in 1964 he began his wholesale attacks on the Butlerite consensus and the consequent acceptance of the mixed economy in postwar Conservative policy. He made these attacks, moreover, in the context of brilliant advocacy of the merits of the free market, which had great influence upon the rising neo-liberalism being cultivated by Edward Heath. It was, however, only when he turned to the immigration issue in his notorious Birmingham speech of April 20, 1968—"Like the Roman, I seem to see 'the River Tiber foaming with much blood,' "—that he broke with Heath and began his portentous rise in public opinion. In the 1970s Powell turned his passionate utterance against British membership in the EEC and again found a sympathetic echo from the public. In the Parliament of 1970 he was the principal leader of the dissidents that harassed Heath from the back-benches. Breaking with the party over the Common Market, he became an Ulster Unionist, but his uncertain position on devolution cooled his relations with his new associates.

In two ways Powell contributed to the waning of Toryism. First, his neoliberalism in style and substance cut him off from the diverse and adaptable heritage of the party. Secondly his very successful attempt to cultivate, independently of party and indeed against party, a wide personal following was unusual if not unprecedented in British politics. In his own eyes, writes Douglas Shoen, Powell "saw himself as a populist politician" not in the sense that he thought it his task merely to reflect the opinions of the majority, but in the sense that he believed "that politics had to voice the peoples' feelings, *especially* if they ran contrary to fashionable opinion or the élite consensus."[44] When he did this on immigration he was a demagogue, a role that fits ill with parliamentary sovereignty or with the rule of a responsible governing class.

Enoch Powell was to the Conservatives what the New Left was to Labour. In this party of tendencies rather than factions—to use Richard Rose's distinction—the subversion of orthodoxy was instigated by a personality rather than an organization. Powell did not try to organize a following in Parliament or the country. But in the years

44. Schoen, *op. cit.*, p. 273.

of his greatest popularity from the late 1960s into the mid-1970s he was, writes Shoen, "one of the three leading politicians in the eyes of the British electorate" and in 1973, according to the *Economist* it was "a rare Tory M.P." who did not have "a Powell group of some real consequence in his association." Like the New Left his greatest influence, however, appeared in the spread of his ideas in his party in the 1970s. His brand of neoliberalism came to be championed by a number of leading Conservatives, including in less rigorous, but no less willful form, Mrs. Thatcher. The principal figure in this group was Sir Keith Joseph, who had overall responsibility for Conservative party policy and research during the years in Opposition and whom Mrs. Thatcher made secretary of state for industry in May, 1979.

For our inquiry Sir Keith's career is of interest chiefly because of his "conversion" of 1974. From a background in business, he entered the House in 1955, held office as a minister under Macmillan and Home, and served in Heath's cabinet as the necessarily big spending secretary of state for social services. In his own words, however, "it was only in April 1974 that I was converted to Conservatism."[45] By that he meant the adoption of a single-minded neoliberalism which he then expounded in a series of speeches in the following years. These were collected in a volume entitled *Reversing The Trend* (1975). If Toryism may be understood, as I have understood it, as the belief in hierarchy, the organic society and the historical style, Sir Keith in this book was smiting Toryism hip and thigh.

His basic economic ideas were very much those of the Heath of Selsdon Park. A more competitive economy was the key to conquering inflation and achieving growth. So he would reduce intervention, cut spending, lighten the tax burden, and tolerate more unemployment. Like Powell he added to these ideas an ardent commitment to the rising school of monetarism. He repudiated the pure doctrine of laissez faire, aspiring rather to "a social market society," defined as "a market economy within a framework of humane laws and institutions." In damning "the collectivists" and the wrong way that

45. *Reversing the Trend: A Critical Reappraisal of Conservative Economic and Social Policies* (Chicester and London, 1975) p. 4. References are mainly to the last two addresses, "The Politics of Political Economy" and "Conservatives and the Market."

both parties had taken for thirty years, however, his originality lay not in these familiar ideas, but in the moral and political values with which he infused them.

When he declared in one of his first addresses after the "conversion," that "we have been eating the seed corn," he meant that Britons were consuming both "our physical capital and our moral capital." He praised the values of the Victorian middle class with their "willingness to defer gratification," and his style—earnest, explicit, sombre, unadorned, and humorless—accorded with his message. "Our objective is the good life," he said in a characteristically Victorian phrase. And he would see that objective realized by *"embourgeoisement*—in the sense of life-style, behavior pattern, and value-structure." He shared the Victorian liberals' vision of a classless society which could be achieved by such "a common value system." He deplored the fact that not only among workers, but also among the middle class, these values had declined in this era of inflation and pop culture.

Putting his finger on a crucial transformation of Victorian society, he regretted that "Britain never really internalized capitalist values." On the contrary, the rich man sought to get away from his background in trade and industry, giving his son an education "not in capitalist values, but against them, in favour of the older values of army, church, upper civil service, professions, and land-owning." Class struggle between the upper and middle strata was thereby avoided but at the price of mingling traditionalist with bourgeois values. This disdain for the bourgeois had much to do with the rise of socialism which "is not new at all. It is precapitalist, upperclass."

With his praise for liberal individualism and his rejection of Tory paternalism went an equally bold rejection of the patrician mode of rule. In contrast with the Tory view of the constitution, which makes the Government the central, energizing force, from which party derives its role, Sir Keith urged that "the party should never become an appendage of government or shadow government." On the contrary it should be "scouting out the ground, and marching ahead as skirmisher," if necessary bringing its influence to bear on ministers to prevent their being captured by the isolation of office. Overall in his political philosophy if not his economic theory, Sir Keith marks an even sharper break with the Tory tradition than Enoch Powell.

The problem for the Tory remnant is neoliberalism as a philosophy of politics and of policy. Neoliberalism, as practiced and preached by Powell and Joseph, challenges Tory élitism in party and Parliament. It also challenges the old values of the organic (though unequal) society which helped Tories to accept a degree of collectivism. And in its current mode of ideological thought and dogmatic action, it challenges Tory pragmatism.

By its attack on the civic culture, the romantic revolt made it easier for these challenges to be launched. It has also supported the rejection of the centralized bureaucratic state for which the neoliberals also call. Perhaps most important of all, populism shares with neoliberalism a fundamental individualism which on both the Conservative and Labour side undermines the premises of the collectivist polity.

The new attitudes that we have probed in the previous sampling of Conservative thought had a behavioral counterpart in striking changes in the power structure of the parliamentary party. Since similar changes have appeared on both sides of the House, we will consider how they have affected both Labour and Conservative behavior. These new patterns of action radically modify the operations of party government and indeed of the British constitution itself.

THE RISE OF PARLIAMENT

The decline of the civic culture played its part in bringing about party dealignment in the electorate. In Parliament also a marked and similar change greatly altered the power structure of both parties.

The Cross-Voting Explosion

From the mid-nineteenth century, party cohesion in the House of Commons had risen steadily, culminating in the early post war years when "it was so close to 100 percent that there was no longer any point in measuring it."[46] Only a few years after I wrote those words, it once again did become useful to measure cross-voting in the House. Philip Norton has chronicled[47] (and counted) the breakdown of that

---

46. *Modern British Politics,* p. 350.
47. Philip Norton, *Dissension in the House of Commons 1974–1979* (London, 1980). *Dissension in the House of Commons 1945–74* (London, 1975). *Conservative Dissidents* (London, 1978). *The Commons in Perspective* (New York, 1981).

"Prussian discipline"—my words—which characterized the parliamentary behavior of those "two bodies of freedom-loving Britons" and which was a leading feature of party government in the collectivist polity. Again, like the other discontinuities we have recorded, this break with previous behavior came fairly suddenly and dated from the turn of the decade into the 1970s. In the next ten years, more MPs rebelled than at any time since the latter part of the nineteenth century. They rebelled more frequently, in larger numbers, and over more important issues. It is indeed as if that malady of "desubordination"—to use Ralph Miliband's expressive neologism[48]—which simultaneously was spreading in industry had also infected the Palace of Westminster.

Nonpartisan and classless in character, the new behavior appeared on the Conservative as well as the Labour side of the House. To see this long-run contrast in Conservative behavior one may compare the decade immediately after the war with the 1970s. In 1945–55, there were dissenting Conservative votes in forty divisions; in 1959–70, in 162 divisions.[49] Indeed the new level of dissent first showed itself in sharpest form on the Conservative back benches when in 1970–74 a great wave of cross-voting, which had taken place on only forty-one divisions in the previous four years, rose to 204 divisions in the subsequent quadrennium. In the postwar parliaments before the 1970s, Governments enjoying an overall majority in the House—and they all did—had suffered no defeats on the floor of the House because of cross-voting by fellow partisans. In the Parliament elected in 1970 the Heath Government was defeated in this manner six times between April 1972 and February 1974. The issues varied in importance. The first in April 1972 concerned which local authorities should have the power to dispose of—as well as collect—garbage. In November of that year, probably the most important of the defeats occurred when the Government was defeated on its proposed new rules for immigration. Of the six defeats, three were on three-line whips. Yet Heath sought to reverse only one and that was done in the Lords. Nor did he call for a vote of confidence in consequence of any of them, but rather accepted the modifications imposed by the House.

48. "A State of Desubordination," *British Journal of Sociology*. Special Issue: Contemporary Britain: Aspects and Approaches. 29, no. 14 (Dec. 1978).
49. Table 1, "Conclusions," *Dissension in the House of Commons 1974–1979*. The following discussion is based on this work except where otherwise indicated.

The election of Mrs. Thatcher as party leader in 1975 after the Conservatives had gone into opposition was itself the result of back-bench rebellion. That broke no precedent; Conservatives are notably ruthless toward leaders who fail. The manner in which the revolt was conducted, however, carried a step further the departure from Tory practice in 1965 when election supplanted "emergence" as the method of choosing a leader—and this time the new approach had an even more unexpected outcome. When Heath refused even to discuss the leadership issue, the back-benchers by changing the rules forced an election, in which, as sometimes happens when elections are not rigged, a "dark horse" topped the poll. If there had still been a "magic circle" and it had been in control, Mrs. Thatcher would not have been the party's choice.[50]

Aware of the source of her authority, Mrs. Thatcher, in contrast to Mr. Heath, took care to involve the back benches in discussions of policy. Dissent, however, although less virulent in tone, increased in volume. Even more members were now willing to vote against their own side and to do so on more occasions. Important issues on which cross-voting took place included devolution for Scotland and Wales, direct elections to the European Assembly, Rhodesian sanctions, and incomes policy.

In these same years between the general elections of 1974 and 1979, dissent within the Labour party also reached new heights. Its minority position at the start and then again toward the end of its time in power accounted for a number of defeats. But also the factional discord, of which we have already taken note, ravaged the parliamentary party and cross-voting, strong among left-wingers, mounted in all sectors of the party.[51] On important questions related to government spending, taxation, devolution, and incomes policy, Labour MPs helped defeat their Government. In three cases of defeat, the Government felt the need to repair its standing by taking a successful vote of confidence, without, however, seeking to reverse the damaging vote itself. The comparison with previous behavior can be brought out by using Lowell's index of party voting. In the early

50. Butler and Kavanagh, *op. cit.,* pp. 61–64.
51. John E. Schwartz, "Exploring a New Role in Policy Making: The British House of Commons in the 1970s," *American Political Science Review,* 74, no. 1 (March, 1980) p. 30.

postwar years, as we have seen, there was almost no cross-voting by Labour back benches and the party voting score was virtually 100 percent.[52] By contrast in the five sessions from 1974 to 1979, according to Philip Norton, the scores were respectively 92, 92, 86, 86, and 69 percent.[53] To find a similar level of disunity one must go back to the early years of this century when, as in the sessions of 1906 and 1908, Labour's index of party voting was respectively 88.4 and 87.2 percent.[54]

As of this writing it is too early to assess the parliamentary fortunes of the Conservative Government that took office after the election of May 1979. During Mrs. Thatcher's first year in office, she suffered not a single defeat in the Commons.[55] Cross-voting continued, however, and pressure from back-benchers influenced the Government, as in obliging it to reverse itself on the question of increasing the pay of MPs and on the disposition of the fourth television channel. A clear prospect of defeat arising from resistance throughout the House also obliged the Government to back down on the form of sanctions against Iran which the foreign secretary had agreed with the other EEC countries.[56]

In the second session, the Government added to its legislative program announced in the Queen's speech a promise to repeal the "sus" law—relating to arrests by the police—in response to the threat of a select committee that if the Government did not do so, the committee itself would attempt repeal. When the chancellor opened his budget in March, 1981, a revolt by Conservative back-benchers against a proposed change in taxation reduced Mrs. Thatcher's majority to only fourteen from its usual level of around sixty. Some thirty—that is, about one in eleven—of all Conservative MPs defied a three-line whip either by abstaining (twenty-two) or by voting against (eight) the proposed change. "How the chancellor of the exchequer must long for the days when the annual budget was a rallying cry for the party faithful," commented the *Economist*.[57]

52. *Modern British Politics*, pp. 184–185.
53. Norton, "Conclusions," note 42.
54. *Modern British Politics*, p. 123.
55. *Economist*, 9 August 1980.
56. *ibid.*, May 24, 1980.
57. *ibid.*, March 21 and April 11, 1981.

Philip Norton put the new pattern of behavior in perspective:

The "habit," as George Cunningham terms it, of greater voting freedom acquired in the 1970s is not likely to be discarded. As Members have conceded, there can be no going back to the quiescence of the 1950s and early 1960s; "The old days of party discipline," according to one MP [Eric Heffer], are "dead and buried," a point that would appear to be borne out by the experience of the current Parliament.[58]

The Decline of Deference

When one tries to account for this abrupt and radical discontinuity in the behavior of MPs, one is forced to go back to the reasons for the extraordinary record of partisanship from which it was a break. And that phenomenon, the partisan behavior of MPs, cannot be explained without considering crucial features of cabinet government under the British constitution. To follow this explanation through to these levels of analysis is not a digression from our inquiry, but demonstrates rather the depth of the changes that are taking place in the British political system.

As anyone knows who has ever tried to explain party unity in the House of Commons to an American audience, the reasons for this behavior are not easily adduced. The mechanical explanations citing the threat of dissolution, the disciplinary power of the whips, the possibility of expulsion, the leadership's control over political advancement, pressure from constituency parties, and the like have never seemed more than partial explanations. After considering them in an informed and cogent analysis in 1967, Leon Epstein put his finger on the main point: "members of a majority parliamentary party share in the partisan desire to maintain their leaders in office." If, therefore, they refrain from cross-voting it is because they want to keep their party in and the Opposition out. "To avoid this ultimate catastrophe [i.e., putting the Opposition in power], not just to avoid dissolution," concluded Epstein, "is what provides the motivation for majority party cohesion."[59] From the same premises, it also follows, although not so strongly, that the party in opposition will hang together against the Government. Even when they cannot hope to

58. *The Commons in Perspective,* p. 248.
59. *Political Parties in Western Democracies* (New York, 1967), p. 167.

force a change of Government, they can forward that ultimate goal by displaying in the eyes of the Government, the public, and themselves their distinctiveness, self-assurance, and credibility.

Since party commitment is the main variable, cohesion will fluctuate with degree of party commitment. But for any given degree of party commitment, the behavior of a Government back-bencher—to leave aside for the moment the Opposition MP—will also vary with whether he believes that what he is doing threatens the life of the Government. This other variable in determining cohesion arises from the fact that he is operating under a parliamentary system. The incontestable and defining convention of this system in Britain has been that the Government must have the confidence of the House. Party commitment is never total and the policies of a Government and the political beliefs of its MPs will never be perfectly congruent. Whether the MP will deviate from party therefore depends on the two variables: (1) The less he is committed to party, the more willing he will be to run the risk of dissolution. But also (2) the less he thinks the risk, the more willing he will be to deviate from party. It is the parliamentary convention, i.e., the belief that the Government must have the confidence of the House, that creates and defines that risk.

The parliamentary convention was expressed in a classic formula in a vote of confidence moved by Sir Robert Peel in 1841. A Whig Government had been in office since 1834 during which time it had been defeated fifty-nine times in the House of Commons, without feeling impelled to resign or dissolve. As leader of the Conservative opposition, Peel moved:

That Her Majesty's Ministers do not sufficiently possess the confidence of the House of Commons to enable them to carry through the House measures which they deem of essential importance to the public welfare, and that their continuance in office, under such circumstances, is at variance with the Spirit of the Constitution.

Again defeated, although by only one vote, the Government responded with a dissolution.[60] During the preceding debate, Peel claimed that the "system of Parliamentary government," which "implies that the Ministers of the Crown shall have the confidence of the House of Commons," had prevailed since "the accession of

60. For this debate see 58 *Parliamentary Debates* (3rd ser.) cols. 667–1299 (1841).

the House of Hanover.''[61] As a matter of fact, in the "balanced constitution" of the Old Whig period, the responsibility of ministers not only to the House of Commons but also to the Lords and the King was incompatible with parliamentary government in the later sense. As Anthony Birch has shown, the convention of collective responsibility of ministers to the House of Commons was developed between 1780 and 1832, the first clear statement of it dating only from two years before Peel's motion, although even then the crucial word "confidence" was not used.[62]

The clear statement of the convention as in Peel's motion and by later authoritative spokesmen, however, did not end all ambiguity. How does one operationalize the principle of "confidence"? By what specific acts and words does the House make known its lack of confidence? Obviously, confidence is lost if the House refuses to authorize measures necessary for the performance of executive duties. The case is also clear when the word "confidence" or its equivalent, as in a motion of "censure," is used, or when the Government indicates explicitly that whatever the terms of the motion may be—perhaps only to adjourn the House—the Government will resign or dissolve if it loses. But these commonplaces leave a great deal of blank canvas in those areas of British political culture that determine the operational meaning of "confidence."

Peel indicated one source of ambiguity when he qualified the term "confidence" by relating it to measures which the Government deemed "of essential importance to the public welfare." One might infer from this proposition that a Government should resign or dissolve if defeated on a measure of "essential importance" even though the question of confidence had not been explicitly put. Governments have sometimes done so. But the efforts to operationalize the notion of "importance" in specific rules with general validity—for instance, by tying it to supply motions—have foundered on exceptions in practice. Indeed, at least one Government resigned after having suffered a defeat on a minor matter which was accomplished by a trick on the part of the Opposition whips and which would normally have been

61. *loc. cit.*, col. 805.
62. *Representative and Responsible Government: An Essay on the British Constitution* (London, 1964) pp. 132–133.

disregarded.[63] In the end, one must agree with Jennings that it rests
primarily with the Government to decide what is of "sufficient
importance."[64] Such ambiguity leaves Governments much leeway,
of which they have taken advantage by acting on a variety of rules
not all of which are consistent with one another.

The 100 Percent Rule

The parliamentary convention is given different operational meanings from time to time. These more specific rules may stabilize for
periods and so give the back-bencher more precise guidance as to
how far he can indulge his deviant wishes without endangering the
life of the Government more than he is willing to do. One such operational rule was embodied in a belief which, according to Norton,
was widespread among MPs and observers in the years before the
explosion of the 1970s. This was "the opinion . . . that a government must respond to a defeat by reversing it (if possible) or else
seeking a vote of confidence or resigning."[65] We may call the rule
embodied in this belief "the 100 percent rule," since, with only
slight qualifications added by some observers, such as the presence
of a three-line whip, it meant that any and every defeat for a Government was virtually a matter of confidence. As we have seen, any
such belief was challenged and proved false by the dissidence that
broke out against Heath. As further defeats confirmed this precedent,
further rebellion, as Norton says, was encouraged. The successful
exercise of that independence by MPs must have contributed to the
transformation of "the atmosphere of the House," which by the end
of the decade was generally recognized. The impact of these events
can be understood only within the larger context of the changing
political culture.

One of the most interesting things about the belief in the 100 percent rule is the light it throws on the norms of the collectivist polity

63. 34 *Parliamentary Debates* (4th ser.) cols. 1685–1748 (1895).

64. Sir Ivor Jennings, *Cabinet Government*. 3rd ed. (Cambridge, Eng., 1958) p.
495.

65. Philip Norton, "Government Defeats in the House of Commons: Myth and
Reality," *Public Law* (Winter 1978) p. 360.

and the distinctive conditions that made those norms possible. The 100 percent rule is intrinsically implausible. It means that a Government will seek to reverse any defeat by putting the question of confidence not merely in general terms but in relation to that issue on which it has already been defeated. It means, moreover, that the Government will take the consequent risk of dissolution, regardless of how unimportant the issue may be, no matter what stage the Government has reached in carrying out its program and, perhaps most crucial, whether or not it believes the time for an election is propitious. One could hold these beliefs as back-bencher, minister, or observer, only if they were never put to the test. Writing in 1937 Jennings showed in his authoritative treatise on parliamentary practice and norms that Governments had not acted on any such rule and that the then prevailing beliefs of politicians or observers did not include it.[66]

Belief in the rule could arise only under the distinctive conditions created by the hold that party government came to have on the House in the culminating years of the collectivist polity.[67] In his study of four sessions between 1947 and 1965 John E. Schwartz finds only four defeats for any Government on the floor of the House—and none of them, as we have seen, arose from cross-voting. During that period, as he concludes, "the House of Commons . . . was almost entirely deferential to the government."[68] Given such deference and such nearly perfect cohesion, ministers and whips might well say things that encouraged the belief that they would act on the 100 percent rule; they might even come to entertain it themselves. It was the enormous commitment to party among MPs in this period of British political development that made it possible for the 100 percent rule to gain such credence as it enjoyed.

Accordingly, the variable accounting for the outburst of cross-voting in the 1970s was a decline in that party commitment rather than, as Norton suggests, new information about the probable behavior of Governments revealed by the explosion against Heath. Cross-voting had been on the rise before Heath took office and among both Government and Opposition members. With regard to anti-Govern-

---

66. *Cabinet Government*. 1st ed. (Cambridge, Eng., 1937), esp. pp. 379–382.
67. *Modern British Politics*, pp. 122–123, 184–185, 257 and 262–263.
68. *loc. cit.*, p. 25.

ment votes, Schwartz has identified the turningpoint. Looking at defeats not only on the floor, but also in standing committee, he has detected an outburst of standing committee defeats beginning in that fateful year, 1968.[69] From the late 1960s, in short, a rising tide of dissidence on back benches on both sides of the House was radically changing the conditions of party government in the collectivist polity. The decline of party commitment in the House was undermining the conditions that had made it possible seriously to entertain the 100 percent rule.

Party Dealignment in Parliament

The decline of party in the House of Commons took place at a time when, as we have seen, other processes of disintegration were taking place in the polity—the decline of the civic culture, the rise of pluralistic stagnation, the decomposition of class, and party dealignment. We can suggest the connection of these broader changes with what was happening in Parliament by saying that in the House as in the country a process of party dealignment set in in the sixties and continued through the seventies.

In both arenas party identification remained high, but declined in strength and character. One might even say that in the House as in the country those years saw "the decline of the party stalwart." Already in the mid-1960s the perceptive Crossman, then Leader of the House, recorded the change in partisanship and "the need" it created "for a new kind of parliamentary leadership" which would no longer be content with "merely giving orders, adding up the score of the division records and punishing those who did badly," but which would "organize constructive criticism on the back benches and get our back-benchers participating in policy-making with the leadership."[70]

Crossman attributed the new attitude to the "new intake" of middle class MPs who were "much less reliable than trade unionists."

69. *loc. cit.,* p. 29 and Table 4. His data show "that the marked increase in the number of defeats that occurred during the sessions from 1974 to 1978 followed a trend of increasing defeats that began even under governments with majorities as far back as the latter 1960s" (p. 29).
70. Crossman, *op. cit.,* vol. I, p. 493.

Attempts to link cross-voting in the 1970s with a "new generation," however, do not check out either for Labour or the Conservatives.[71] A change in attitude took place, but it was pervasive. Quite generally in the House, as Norton remarks, the old notion that "the Government knows best" had waned and MPs were showing themselves to be more willing to act on their own instincts and even their own information in challenging the front bench on either side.

In a recent conversation, one of the "new intake" of 1979 among the Conservatives confirmed and filled out reports of the new attitude among MPs. Echoing the views of many of his fellow freshmen in the Commons, this new MP was quite positive about the rise of "bloodimindedness" on the Conservative back benches. They would never, he said to me, go back to the 1950s and 1960s when you did whatever the whips told you to do. They want to make a career of politics. How do they mean to do that? "They want to legislate." For him that was the key term: "legislate." And accordingly in the new select committee system he and his like-minded colleagues see a career opening up which genuinely rivals the attractions of the usual ladder controlled by the whips and party leaders. In the terms of *The Civic Culture* their attitude has shifted from "deferential" to "participant."

Such an attitude departs from the norm of party government as conceived in the collectivist theory of representation in either its socialist or Tory version.[72] Moreover, this shift from a deferential toward a participant role for MPs and Parliament raises the possibility that an even more profound change in the British constitution is taking place. It would seem that the parliamentary convention itself is being transformed: in other words, that the change in political culture is not only weakening the 100 percent rule, an historically limited specification of the parliamentary convention, but also the basic conception of the proper relation of parliament and Government expressed in the modern British idea of the parliamentary regime.

A form of parliamentary government is conceivable in which the members of the legislature take an active part along with ministers in introducing and making laws, levying taxes, deciding how to spend

71. Schwartz, *loc. cit.*, p. 32.
72. *Modern British Politics*, pp. 69–71.

money and so forth. In trying to imagine how such a regime would operate, one could start from the model of British local government, as some British socialists have done. The Webbs, for instance, explicitly modelled the structure of the Social Parliament, in their proposed constitution for a socialist commonwealth of Britain, upon the London County Council with its many specialized committees.[73] One need not go as far as the Webbs in their neglect of the need for an agency of central direction and coordination. Committees with special responsibilities, however, would be a principal means for establishing partnership between House and Government.

Needless to say, this model is not the one that emerged as the parliamentary monarchy of medieval times was gradually transformed over the centuries into an instrument of popular government. On the contrary, a triumph of British constitutional development was the transfer of the premodern concept of a monarch who governed into the concept of a Government which governed. As L. S. Amery observed a generation ago, the British constitution had always had two elements: an initiating, directing, energizing element—formerly the monarchy and latterly the Government—and a checking, criticizing element—formerly Parliament as a whole, and latterly especially the Opposition.[74] This bipolar concept of authority, arising in the earliest centuries of the polity, survived into modern times as a force shaping the relations of ministers and Parliament.

In historical terms, as Sir Courtenay Ilbert put it, in the eighteenth century "the executive authority of the King was put in commission and it was arranged that the commissioners should be members of the legislative body to whom they are responsible."[75] In sociological terms, one might make the point by saying that the monarchic role was assumed by the Government. This meant that ministers not only did the work of administration, but also, acting as the Government, monopolized decision-making in finance, most legislation, and generally those "matters of state" which in Tudor times had been

73. I have discussed this in my introduction to Sidney and Beatrice Webb, *A Constitution for the Socialist Commonwealth of Great Britain* (Cambridge, Eng., 1975) p. xxviii.

74. *Thoughts on the Constitution* (London, 1947), Chapter 2. Discussed in *Modern British Politics*, "The British Constitution: Tory View," pp. 94–98.

75. Introduction to Josef Redlich, *The Procedure of the House of Commons* (London, 1908).

reserved primarily for the monarch.[76] The House could question the Government; it could criticize the Government; in the last analysis it could get rid of the Government by forcing its resignation. But it could not itself do the work of the Government, but only put another Government in the place of the one thrown out. Confidence could be transferred from one team of ministers to another. But throughout "the Government" enjoyed confidence, trust, deference.

The word "confidence" drew together the various filaments in this deferential concept of the allocation of power. The term had been used by the Foxite Whigs in their struggle with George III in the 1780s.[77] But it is especially fitting that Peel, that exemplar of Tory statesmanship, should have moved the motion which came to be the classic source expressing the principle that "confidence" was a necessary condition for holding office in conformity with "the Spirit of the Constitution."

Select Committees

As our imaginary model suggests, the committee system of the House would provide the institutional means by which the legislature might move away from the old deferential, and toward a more participatory, concept of confidence. This would mean in essence that the House would not only be able to force the resignation of a Government, but also would routinely share with it in initiating and amending legislation, taxation, spending, and other "matters of state." During the 1970s there was much experimentation with select committees, culminating in a major reform put into effect by the Thatcher Government. The Conservative Leader of the House, Norman St.John-Stevas, who introduced the new system in 1979, described it as "one of the most important parliamentary reforms of the century" marking "a decisive shift of power from Whitehall to Westminster."[78] By 1981 there were fourteen of the new commit-

76. *Modern British Politics*, p. 6–7.
77. See motions by Fox of March 1 and March 8, 1784. *Parliamentary History*, vol. 24, pp. 677 and 736.
78. Alastair Hetherington, "Parliamentary Select Committees," *Listener*, 14 August 1980.

tees, each shadowing a government department.[79] Their task was "oversight"—the British called them "watchdogs." They had the power to request the presence of civil servants and ministers along with relevant papers for questioning by the committees which were assisted by research staffs and outside experts. As of this writing, they could not yet compel attendance nor had they yet acquired a role in reviewing proposed legislation, although efforts to give them both sorts of power were being made.

The committees had, nonetheless, made a considerable impact on ministers, the House, and the interested public. We have already taken note of how the home affairs committee, which was acting on its own investigation of the "sus" law, by threatening to introduce its own bill obliged the Government to promise repeal. The most assertive committee has been the one charged with overseeing the most vital area of government policy, financial and economic affairs. Under the chairmanship of Edward du Cann, himself a financier, the Treasury committee has been a center of severe and expert criticism of Government policy. A major example was the highly critical and unanimous report on the Government's monetary policy published in February 1981. Taking evidence from ministers, civil officials, academics, and central bankers and other practitioners, British and foreign, the committee produced four volumes of evidence and a report which concluded among other negative judgments that the Government's financial strategy "was not soundly based"[80] and which, moreover, took a modest step or two toward putting forward its own suggestions.[81]

How much further the committee structure will move toward the participatory model remains to be seen. But these mechanical reforms must be understood in the larger context of the changed "atmosphere" of the House and its new pattern of dissident behavior. The "new habits" of MPs make it possible for them to win a greater role in administration and legislation in step with the opportunities pre-

79. Listed with members, staff, and reports in "Select Committee Inquiries and Reports," *The House Magazine,* January 23, 1981.

80. Treasury and Civil Service Committee. Session 1980–81. Monetary Policy. vol. I, *Report.* H.C. 162–1, p. xcvii.

81. *Economist,* 20 December 1980, p. 56.

sented by a developing committee system. If committees gain the power to examine ministers, civil servants, and outside experts not only with regard to policy and administration, but also pending legislation, to which the committee may propose amendments, informed alternatives to Government policy will be presented as vehicles for cross-voting. "What the Select Committees can do," one observer has commented, ". . . is to explore and set out the range of choice for a government in its next move. It can secure an informed debate on the alternatives."[82] Conceivably the committees could also present opportunities not only for informed debate, but also informed voting on alternatives to Government policy.

We may, of course, feel that this is too much to expect of the ancient deferential British system. Yet so much that was unexpected has already taken place that we must at least consider the possibility.

NEORADICALISM

My neglect of the Liberals in the previous pages of this essay may seem inexcusable. I can perhaps put that neglect in a better light by saying that in a real sense my main theme has been the revival of liberalism. The most powerful idea in British politics in the past twenty years has been the idea of radical democracy embodied in the new populism. It has been my argument that this idea, exaggerated by the romantic revolt, in its negative aspect shaped the decline of the civic culture. Looked at historically it displays its positive aspect as the tradition descending from the failed democratic revolution of the seventeenth century, the Commonwealth. Often submerged, but never extinguished, that tradition won its victories against the old hierarchic and corporate order. As the doctrine of a party, it inspired the Liberals in the generation from the later Gladstone to Lloyd George.[83] In those years it too had its moments of excess. I doubt if any populist attack on Toryism in recent times can match the rhetorical violence of Lloyd George's Limehouse speech of 1909. A brief narrative will show how the radical tradition has survived, adapted, and in recent years informed the Liberal revival and the emergence of the Social Democratic party.

82. Alastair Hetherington, *loc. cit.*
83. *Modern British Politics,* Chapter II, "Liberal and Radical Politics."

In the radical phase of the party various Liberal thinkers, notably
L. T. Hobhouse, had put forward justifications for positive government and, in the years just before World War I, Liberal Governments
spelled out the new connotation with specific measures of social
reform. In the notable debate of 1923 on "The Failure of the Capitalist System," which at the instigation of Labour posed "a clear
issue of Individualism and Socialism," Lloyd George and his followers displayed the meaning of this advanced liberalism. While taking issue with the Labour party by refusing to overturn "the present
basis of society," which they took to be "the individualist system,"
they called for "far reaching measures of social redress" and the
removal of "the evil effects of monopoly and waste."[84] During the
following years, although their electoral fortunes declined, the Liberals continued to be the party of ideas as Keynes and Beveridge
developed the intellectual basis for an advanced liberalism that would
cope with the economic and social problems of an industrial nation.

The ideas of Keynes and Beveridge were utilized widely by the
people who framed the programs of the collectivist polity during the
postwar years. But Keynesian and Beveridgean thought did not itself
require or imply the centralized, planned, corporatistic state which
was produced by the 1940s and 1950s and which was accepted by
both Gaitskell and Macmillan. Although a center party, the Liberals
did not accept the consensus that emerged in these years. They clung
to their heritage of advanced liberalism, seeking to provide social
security in a market-oriented capitalist system. Their manifestoes
repetitiously called for "full employment in a free society," and
supported the social services, but also proposed co-ownership in lieu
of nationalization, criticized big government spending, favored
devolution for Scotland and Wales, damned the big parties for keep-
ing up the class struggle, and perhaps above all demanded electoral
reform. In that era of class politics and collectivist policy, the Liberals seemed to have no electoral future and in 1951 they won only
2.6 percent of the vote and returned only six MPs. Hard put to explain
even this tenuous survival, observers impatiently awaited the party's
final demise. Commenting on the 1951 election even the sympathetic
Manchester Guardian felt obliged to conclude: "It marks, it is hardly

84. *Modern British Politics*, p. 142.

too much to venture, the end of an independent Liberal Party as a force in the electoral field.''[85]

In the early 1960s, however, under the charismatic and intellectual Jo Grimond, the Liberals made a remarkable and unexpected recovery in both electoral fortunes and programmatic relevance. The electoral success was short-lived, but the ideas had vitality. The important point for our inquiry was their continuity with the party's past. In a quite fundamental sense the Grimond revival was, as Arthur Cyr has skillfully shown in *Liberal Politics in Britain,* a restatement of the radical tradition in relation to current problems. If a radical individualism was the first nature of Liberals, an attack upon the centralized bureaucratic state was second nature and entirely effortless, visited by none of the heart-searching agonies that afflicted the Labour party as it was invaded by the new populism. Grimond toyed with the modernization theme. He reasserted the old faith in free competition. But his main emphasis was on ''participation.'' In the 1960s the romantic revolt entered the Liberal party through a long opened door.

The populist impulse gained force as the ''Red Guards'' brought the raucous voice and disruptive behavior of the counterculture into Liberal gatherings. But the same impulse also brought new programmatic ideas and new political methods. In 1970 ''community politics'' was adopted by the party assembly as a major strategy. ''Community politics'' was—in Michael Steed's words—''a radical, popular democratic movement against the British political establishment embodied in the two major parties.'' It meant that the party would deal directly with people, emphasizing ''democracy and the concern with people in communities rather than as classes or sections.''[86]

As young activists surged into the party, Liberals turned their attention with increasing success to local government. Liverpool—it will not surprise the readers of the previous chapter to learn—was the arena of some of their more impressive victories. (Among my political mementoes I have a sticker that reads: ''Love Liverpool. Vote Liberal.'' On the back is a song, ''In our Liverpool Home,'' denouncing the ruin brought on the city by ''Planners,'' both Labour

85. Quoted in Arthur Cyr, *Liberal Politics in Britain,* with an Introduction by Michael Steed (London, 1977) p. 86.
86. Cyr, *op. cit.,* pp. 16, 20.

and Tory, but promising that "The Liberals took power/They've made a fresh start/The bad days are over,/The City's got a heart.'') There was a good deal of brave talk. I recall how at the 1973 conference one Liverpudlian declaimed, "We are the system breakers," when urging support for the parliamentary resolution entitled "Power to the People." And indeed the range of that resolution was immodest: demanding proportional representation, devolution, election of a European parliament, an elected second chamber based on regions, and reform of the House of Commons to include specialist committees, reduced power for the whips, and a five-year fixed term. In 1976 the Liberals became the first major British party to shift the election of its Leader from MPs to the party membership, to a great extent because, according to Steed, the new activists "were determined to apply within the party, the sort of participatory democracy that they were preaching in government and industry.''[87]

Trend to the Liberals

During the 1979 general election, in what the *Economist* called "strikingly the best election manifesto," the Liberals set forth a detailed and comprehensive program based on years of work.[88] In contrast with the approach of the other parties, its most significant feature was its emphasis upon the political in the broadest sense of that word. Fully aware of the crucial economic problems, the Liberals in the terms of my analysis made the restoration of legitimacy the first priority, calling political and constitutional reform "the starting point" and demanding "a democratic electoral system" in order "to generate the popular consent which is essential to support a long-term programme of economic and social reform."

When the manifesto moved into the economic sphere, here too the rationale of its approach was political. While rejecting the Conservatives' recent commitment to neoliberalism, the Liberals also spurned planning, big spending, and nationalization, identifying "the primary aim of government intervention in industry" as "the promotion of viable market enterprises." The key to that viability and "to reversing Britain's economic decline" was industrial democracy in

87. *ibid.*, p. 32.
88. *The Real Fight is For Britain. The Liberal Manifesto.*

a variety of forms. Their emphasis was redistributive, but the thrust was less toward a redistribution of wealth than toward a redistribution of power by participation and decentralization. Against this background they approached the burning question of inflation, their main proposal being a statutory prices and incomes policy supported by measures to ensure social equity. Throughout, in giving primacy to the political problem of the distribution of power, the Liberals of 1979 were true to the radical tradition. Indeed, the advocacy of devolution, the attack on the House of Lords and the defense of parish councils take one back to the spirit and almost the very words of the great Newcastle Programme of 1891.[89] By adapting their tradition to contemporary conditions, these descendants of the original radical democrats effortlessly echoed what for the other parties had been the new political doctrines of the sixties.

As an echo the Liberals offered a choice. Many voters made that choice: at the peak of their fortunes in the election of 1974, the party got six million votes, as compared with nearly twelve million for each of the other two parties. But did this choice by the voters signify merely a protest against the two great contenders, representing another stage in the process of party dealignment, or did it signify a preference for an alternative and Liberal kind of policy, government, and society? Some observers have said that the Liberal vote was only "an anti-party party vote." I should say that like the broad change in political culture which we have been tracing and which was in harmony with their outlook, the vote for the Liberals was both a protest and an affirmation.

There is much to be said for the view that for some time the Liberal vote has been essentially a protest vote, specifically a protest by people who have voted to put in office a Conservative Government, have changed their minds after it has been there for a while, but cannot go all the way to Labour, and so, as in 1973–74, a move over to the Liberals, only to find, as in 1977–78, that after Labour comes in they like that alternative even less, and so switch back to the Conservatives. From the sixties, however, along with this cyclical pattern, the Liberal vote has shown an overall upward trend. Liberal support did slump badly in the polls during the later years of the

89. *Modern British Politics*, pp. 56–58.

Labour Government. But during the 1979 campaign the party made
a sharp recovery, finally winning 13.8 percent of the vote. If one
looks at the percent of the vote received by Liberals where they put
up candidates, the figure was higher than at any election between
1945 and 1970. Reviewing the results a few months later, Ivor Crewe
concluded that "in spite of their reverses, the Liberals are in a better
position from which to make a comeback than at any time since the
war."[90] Over the two years following the election, their performance in the polls made good this opportunity, rising to 18 percent
in early 1981. These were much higher figures than those they had
scored during the first two years of the previous Conservative administration of Mr. Heath. By May 1981 David Steel, their leader, could
claim that if an election were held at that time, the party would win
25 percent of the seats in the House.[91]

Not only did the recent gains of the Liberals signify wider support
for postcollectivist ideas. In its lack of class identification that support also departed from the collectivist model and in a sense epito-
mized the social convergence of party politics generally in the 1970s.
In the nineteenth century, the Liberals were a distinctly middle class
party with a significant aristocratic component. They were also genuinely moved by their vision of a classless society, a conception that
lived on and was broadened when in their radical phase they claimed
to represent, and sought the support of, no particular class, but rather
"the people." Still, even though they were ready to champion social
reform and guarantee trade union rights on behalf of their working
class allies, middle- and upper-class predominance in the party, I have
argued, was a main reason why the working class of those years,
then in its phase of composition, felt obliged to form its own separate
organization if it was to achieve power in the state.[92]

In recent years, the activists of the party in terms of occupation, if
not self-image, were markedly middle class. Yet in attitude surveys
these same activists rejected, often with passion, the very idea of
class, not only refusing to believe that a voter ought to follow his
class identity when voting, but even refusing to use the concept when

90. "Prospects for Party Realignment: An Anglo-American Comparison," *Comparative Politics*, 12, no. 4 (July, 1980) p. 393.
91. *The Observer*, May 17, 1981.
92. *Modern British Politics*, pp. 146–149.

TABLE 5.1
Sources of Party Support
(in percentages)

	ALL	CONSERVATIVE	LABOUR	LIBERAL
ABC1	35	45	22	37
C2	34	31	36	35
DE	32	24	41	29

SOURCE: MORI, *British Public Opinion: the General Election of 1979*, Final Report (London, 1979) p. 12.

analyzing or explaining political behavior.[93] Reflecting these attitudes, the party continued to proclaim itself classless and to denounce its rivals as class-based and sectional. Many who voted for the Liberals did so in response to this appeal, preferring them because they were less divisive. And in the electoral outcome, Liberal voters were more representative of the occupational differentiation of the society as a whole than the voters of either of the other two parties. In this age of class decomposition, the Liberals have been able to draw support indiscriminately from all classes. (See table 5.1)

The Social Democrats

It is hard to find a time in the history of the Labour party when there was not a rift between a Left and a Right. Accordingly, the expectation that this rift would lead to a split waxed and waned over the decades with such regularity that it became an axiom of insiders that the split would never happen. Finally, on March 26, 1981, it did happen. At a press conference in London, four leading members of the Labour party announced the formation of a breakaway group, the Social Democratic Party (SDP), issued a document stating its "Twelve Tasks," said they would contest by-elections and the next general election, and called for members.

From the start it was not an effort to belittle. Of the "Gang of Four," the senior in age and service was Roy Jenkins, who had been an MP since 1950 and had served in the cabinets of both Wilson Governments, resigning from the second to become president of the

93. Cyr, *op. cit.*, pp. 234–250.

European Economic Commission. The other three, Shirley Williams, William Rodgers, and David Owen, had been junior ministers in the first Wilson Government who had advanced to cabinet status in the second. In addition to the two last named, who were MPs at the time of the launch, twelve other Labour MPs and one Conservative MP joined the new party. Outside the House of Commons the SDP split off an impressive block of support from the Labour party, consisting of Labour peers, former ministers, local councilors, and prominent academics. The public opinion polls immediately confirmed their previous indications that an alliance of such a party with the Liberals would have the support of two-fifths of the electorate.

The first electoral test further heightened the promise of the new party. At a by-election on July 17 at Warrington, in working class Lancashire, Roy Jenkins, the SDP candidate, although defeated, made a powerful showing well beyond what most observers had expected and the opinion polls had indicated. Table 5.2 gives the results in comparison with those of the general election of 1979.

In a turnout almost as high as that at the general election, the SDP in alliance with the Liberals nearly won this traditionally solid Labour seat. As expected the SDP drew from the Conservatives, but so greatly as almost to wipe them out. More interesting was its demonstrated ability to pull votes from Labour. No victory in his long political career, remarked Mr. Jenkins after the vote was announced, gave him such pleasure as this defeat.

In one sense the Social Democrats are simply another party of protest. As Anthony King has observed, "the two old electoral ice-

TABLE 5.2
Warrington By-election
(in percentages)

	1979	1981
Labour	61.7%	48.4%
Conservatives	28.8	7.1
Liberals	9.0	—
SDP	—	42.4
Other	.5	2.1
	100.0	100.0

bergs are melting—even breaking up." "As late as 1964, fully forty percent of British voters regarded themselves as 'very strong' or 'fairly strong' supporters of one or the other major party. In May 1979, only twenty percent did so."[94] While party dealignment in fits and starts reduces the strength of the two big parties, the Liberals inherit protesters on an upward curve. Now the secession of the Social Democrats breaks off another chunk and another party of protest appears. Like the big parties, protest itself is losing its cohesion.

Party dealignment, one might say, began with the voters, made its way into Parliament, infecting MPs, and now has finally reached the leadership echelon. Surely alienation from the present party system could hardly be more strongly expressed than by the founders of the new party. "We offer not only a new party," said Roy Jenkins when opening the press conference on March 26, "but a new approach to politics: we want to get away from the politics of outdated dogmatism and class confrontation . . . to release the energies of the people who are fed up with the old slanging match."

It is a curious party of protest, however, that stands for so much that is continuous with the past and widely received in the present. "Most of the policies which they put forward in their twelve-point programme yesterday," said the London *Times,* when welcoming the new party, "are ones which we as a newspaper have long supported. They are in favor of NATO and the EEC. They want to continue with the mixed economy and to introduce proportional representation." Moreover, their main economic and social proposals had a familiar ring. This "new beginning," the *Times* continued, turned out on closer inspection to be "a modern version of Butskellism," which at a time when the two main parties had "broken away in different directions from the postwar consensus" was "seeking essentially to bring that consensus up to date."[95]

Unlike the neoliberals or neosocialists, the Social Democrats sought not to depart drastically from that consensus, but rather to enlighten it with what had been learned from the hard experience of the 1960s and 1970s. In their eyes, that meant among other things rejecting hubristic Keynesianism, recognizing the importance of controlling the money supply, and strenuously pursuing an incomes policy. Both

94. *Observer,* 22 March 1981.
95. "The Gang Becomes a Party," *Times* (London) March 27, 1981.

Conservative and Labour Governments had been led, or driven, to a middle ground by their U-turns in the 1970s. The Social Democrats took their stand to the left of its center. Specifically, their stance on economic and social affairs was continuous with the policies of the Callaghan/Healey regime, of which the new party's four founders had been members. There was, as the *Times* observed, "no major policy propounded by the Social Democrats now which was not at least attempted by the Callaghan Government."

To seek that middle ground made good sense. But as the Callaghan Government learned at the moment when it seemed at last to have conquered pluralistic stagnation, mobilizing the consent to hold that ground is hardly any easier than mobilizing the consent to advance toward a "drastic choice." The Government's failure to cope with this essentially political problem brought about its downfall, and it was in their political approach that the Social Democrats had something new and different to say—different at any rate from the approach of their former rightwing colleagues in the Labour Government.

The Social Democrats' protest against the existing system expressed not simply alienation, but a theory of politics that pervaded their whole program. Among the twelve tasks[96] set forth in their inaugural declaration some were specifically economic—such as the use of oil wealth for new investment—or social—such as equal pay for women or protection of the environment. But throughout, the political stress dominated. The statement led off with a general plea for "breaking the mould," which meant liberation from the discontinuities, extremism, and class antagonism of the existing party system. It then went on to its first specific demand, proportional representation. Even in the paragraph concerned nominally with economic policy the innovations called for were "consistency" and "flexibility." Apart from a halt to nationalization and denationalization, the "mixed economy" meant "democracy at work" with trade unions that are "representative" and management that is "responsive." The welfare state should be "less bureaucratic," all races should be guaranteed equal opportunity, and, abroad, "Britain should cooperate with the world and not retreat into sour isolation." Particular political reforms included decentralization of administration, devolution

96. "Twelve Tasks for Social Democrats," *Times* (London) 27 March 1981, p. 2.

to the regions and nations of Britain, more parliamentary control of departments, and more open government.

In their emphasis upon political reform and upon the political aspect of social and economic reform, the Social Democrats were at one with the Liberals. Their theory of politics, moreover, also like that of the Liberals, reflected the radical tradition. Early policy statements could not match the detail of the Liberal program, but books by individual leaders filled out the first broad sketch. Published in the spring of 1981, *Politics is for People* by Shirley Williams— "Britain's most popular individual politician"[97]—was regarded as an authoritative guide to how the leaders of the new party saw Britain's problems and to what they proposed to do about them. It was comprehensive and specific, covering a wide range of policy areas and often getting into considerable technical detail. Far from being a miscellany, however, it was unified by a rationale we will readily recognize: quality of life, participation, and decentralization.

This rationale is suggested by the titles of the book and of some of its more important chapters: "Less Concentration: Industry," "More Participation: Trade Unions," "The Social Services: Involving People." But, what cannot be given too much emphasis, these themes were not mere rhetorical adornment, but the operational models, the "social science," of a sober, expert and carefully reasoned analysis. Repeatedly Mrs. Williams brings the discussion back to the recognition that the welfare state has entered an era of relative scarcity. The achievements of the postwar years depended on an unprecedented rate of economic growth. For various reasons, not least the disappearance of cheap energy, that prospect has been decisively dimmed. She sees clearly, therefore, the hard new necessities. In the same vision, so to speak, she shows how these necessities can be met so as to enhance the quality of life. New technologies, which can at best restore only a modest growth, will also free industry and communication from the constraints of location, revive the home and the community, and make the economic system serve "the requirements of the whole human being." Her lines of basic reform are decentralization and participation. Nothing new in that. Her strength lies in the detailed and factual way in which she works these familiar

97. George Brock in the *Observer,* 29 March 1981.

ideas into the grain of her argument in each of the problem areas. Indeed, she takes so much pains to face the facts and to consult the best research that one may wonder how she can succeed in politics. Still, if a lack of trust is what ails British politics, the blazing integrity of Shirley Williams might prove to be charismatic.

In this synthesis of a humane romanticism with scholarly expertise this Social Democratic champion joined other influential writers of the later 1970s. Her rhetoric and the ideas inspiring it had been made familiar not only by the utterance of politicians, but also by the work of serious students of society. The best-known statement of their outlook was surely E. F. Schumacher's *Small is Beautiful: Economics As If People Mattered*. Based on lectures and articles dating from the 1960s and first published in 1973, the book became a classic of the radical democratic critique.[98] Similar ideas had been developed by others, such as Barbara Ward, Evan Luard, and Fred Hirsh. Shirley Williams' *Politics is for People* was a culminating formulation for political use of the "full radical democratic critique" of British society which had been maturing during the 1970s.

Once we grasp the importance to the Social Democrats of their neoradical politics, it becomes easier to understand their rupture with the Labour party. As joint heirs of the collectivist consensus with the Callaghan/Healey wing, the Social Democrats would seem to have had good reason to stay in the party and fight for that inheritance. Some of their trade union friends had bungled tactics badly, but on balance the movement was not extremist. As the next general election approached and the chance of winning power loomed, the block vote could surely have been counted on to deal with the wilder spirits on the Left. That would have been in accord with the way things had been done in the days of Attlee, Gaitskell, and the early Harold Wilson.

If one read what the Social Democrats said, however, their objection to this sensible calculation was clear: they didn't want to win that way. In an earlier discussion of the need for a new party, Roy

---

98. I cannot resist recording the heights reached by the "small is beautiful" idea. When Prince Charles visited William and Mary College in May 1981 he told the students: "We need to rediscover the importance of the small and vulnerable as opposed to the materially vast and physically great." Not long ago his predecessors asked for the "land of hope and glory" that "wider, wider and wider may its bounds be set."

Jenkins had squarely faced the option.[99] Seeking a "relieving force" within the party against the constant "internecine war" instigated by the Left, Jenkins had identified the only source as "the money and power of the trade unions' leadership." He then rejected this option, not because it would not work but because "that would not be a healthy form of relief. It would obviously and inevitably increase the political power of the unions by making the Labour Party more and not less of a trade union party." When the Social Democrats broke with the party after the Wembley conference of January, 1981, they echoed this preference, giving as their first reason the fact that as a result of the decisions of the conference, "a handful of trade union leaders can now dictate the choice of a future Prime Minister." Their second reason for their break was "the drift toward extremism in the Labour party." That drift had been a problem for the party from its earliest days. In their first reason the Social Democrats expressed their refusal to use the traditional means for coping with that old problem.

The Social Democrats had cut a curious figure in the Labour party. One might suggest its outlines by saying that Shirley Williams is a populistic Gaitskellite, as Tony Benn is a populistic Bevanite, each of these labels being a contradiction in terms. With the neoradical inclinations of the Bennite left, the Social Democrats had a good deal in common, however much they might have fought over the exploitation of those attitudes for factional advantage. At the Wembley conference they asked for an even more participatory method of choosing the party leader—a "one member-one vote system of election." Like the Bennites they said that they wanted to break away from the centralized and quasicorporatistic instruments that the right wing had used in managing the welfare state and mixed economy. Yet they could not accept Benn's "socialism" with its vast extension of the public sector and perhaps even more heartily than Labour right-wingers preferred a strong free market component in the mixed economy.

Agreeing and disagreeing in quite important ways with both left and right wings, the Social Democrats faced a difficult future in the Labour party. But was it that much more difficult than the future that

99. In his Dimbleby Lecture on the BBC in December, 1979.

had been faced by other factions in the past when the pendulum of influence had swung against the Left or Right or Center? I have argued that the Left does not have monolithic power within its grasp and I cannot believe that differences with the Right could not have been compromised. In trying to understand why this split, so improbable in the light of previous party history, took place when it did, one must, I believe, consider the new climate of opinion which conditioned it. As in the case of those MPs who began to defy the whips, party had ceased to command the enormous loyalty of the previous generations. To break from your party was no longer that violation of inner norms and outer expectations that it had so long been. The values that had supported the collectivist age had been gravely weakened by the new populism.

The individualism of the SDP separated them from collectivism both as a concept of politics and as a concept of policy.[100] The Social Democrats no longer shared the attitudes that had shored up the massive power of party government in the previous generation. They also accepted a wide scope for the free market and a great degree of economic inequality as enduring features of the welfare state. What had happened was quite simple: the Labour party had been a socialist party. In recent years many of its adherents and leaders had ceased to believe in socialism. Therefore, they left Labour in order to take a stand for an advanced liberalism.

At this writing many observers are trying to calculate whether the SDP has a future outside the Labour party. The survey evidence is favorable when the Social Democrats are allied with the Liberals, unfavorable when they run as a separate party; the geographical distribution of political opinion is unfavorable; the effect of the electoral system is ambiguous; the likelihood that further leftwing victories at conference and in reselection fights will drive new refugees into the Social Democratic camp is considerable; the forecasts by advocates on all sides—and there are few forecasters who are not also advocates—are clearly exaggerated. I would be foolish to enter into this competition. But I must in an important sense take issue with the Social Democrats when they claim to be inaugurating a new phase in British politics. Needless to say I too believe that there is a new

100. See above pp. 10–12.

phase, but the whole thrust of the previous argument has been that it began years ago when populism undermined deference and the party system succumbed to pluralistic stagnation. The Social Democrats did not create, but were created by this new phase.

The question of interest to this inquiry is not the chances of the Social Democrats, but the chances of what they represent. As the Liberals represent the survival, the Social Democrats represent the revival, of the radical tradition. In its exaggerated populistic form in the 1960s that system of values undermined the civic culture and precipitated the paralysis of choice that afflicted government in the 1970s. In those same years, however, the positive values of radicalism were articulated, elaborated, adapted and carried into all sectors of opinion. The question is whether these positive values can be so embodied in institutions and practices as to restore legitimacy to the consensus and mobilize the consent to bear its burdens. The Social Democrats are only the most recent and striking embodiment of an affirmative answer to that question.

CONCLUSION:

The Radical Prospect

The study of history does not encourage the making of predictions. Looking backward, one may be able to detect some order in events. Usually this order is ambiguous, including patterns of action that point in different directions. A summary of the past will therefore suggest not one, but several probable futures. If one of them does materialize, our studies acquire an air of prescience. Even if none does, a grasp of what seemed to be the probabilities helps us more readily to perceive the unexpected when it comes. In this concluding summary, my primary interest in the past will be seconded by a kindred interest in the future.

The British political system, I have argued, has changed in quite fundamental ways over the past two decades. The most important change—most important in the analytic sense that it is the background condition that has precipitated the other changes—is the transformation of British political culture. We have looked at its two aspects: negatively, the decline of the civic culture; positively, the rise of the new populism.

The civic culture consisted of attitudes toward political behavior that were widely held at all levels of the polity. Embodying hierarchical and organic values, these attitudes strongly supported structures of action which mobilized consent for their respective goals among their constituents: the sovereign Parliament, the collectively responsible cabinet, the cohesive political party in and out of Parliament, the nationally organized functional body. The aggregative capacities of these structures enabled the system to cope exceptionally well with the pluralism inherent in any polity.

The decline of the civic culture greatly weakened these capacities for mobilizing consent and that change in turn released the tendencies to pluralistic stagnation. The pluralism was already there in the new group politics generated by the collectivist polity. This new pluralism had been kept in order, as it had been bred, by the robust regime of party government in the 1940s and 1950s. The fatal conjunction occurred when the new group politics, intensified by the period of consensual party competition, confronted from the mid 1960s a party regime with diminishing powers of aggregation. As parties lost cohesion, partisanship was exaggerated, but choices made by formal governmental decision often failed to elicit the cooperation needed to make them effective and sometimes met with outright resistance. In this way the change in the ideal foundation of the collectivist polity of the 1950s led to its self-defeating behavior in the 1970s.

Some might prefer to turn the argument around and say that the rise of a new and more powerful pluralism defeated the cultural and structural constraints of an older and milder order. No doubt in some categories the new groups had a much greater leverage on the processes of public choice than the actors in the old group politics had typically had. The latter, for example, had operated in an essentially private economy and their syndicalist power affected public choice only indirectly. But in the managed economy the new producer groups could directly slow down, divert or even halt the implementation of policy. To this reallocation of power we might plausibly attribute the defeat of deference and the disruption of class.

Given my own long-standing interest in pressure groups, my first inclination was precisely to look to these new structural conditions of collectivism as the source of the disorder. But the supposed cause simply did not add up to the observed effect. Greater power for individual groups is also greater power for a set of groups and is more reason, one would think, for those groups getting together to concert their demands rather than drawing apart into a self-defeating struggle of each against the others. The principal example of this puzzling behavior was the failure of the unions to use their massed syndicalist power for major reconstruction. But the counterproductive behavior of groups in the other scrambles also cannot be understood if one simply starts from structural change. Class and party solidarities could have been maintained if people had wanted, as in the past, to maintain them.

Public choice theory helps one make the transition from a structural to a cultural analysis. On the one hand, it provides a model of self-defeating pluralism that lights up a common pattern in what at first sight may seem to be a behavioral hodge-podge. But this model rests upon a certain cultural foundation, viz., distrust. Conversely, it points to the restoration of trust as a condition that would halt the Hobbesian struggle and revive the aggregative capabilities of the system.

Public Choice, Legitimacy, and Trust

We may first sketch abstractly what needs to be done and then examine the empirical probabilities.

In the political forum, trust rests on a cultural foundation in which expectations and norms are mutually reinforcing. As expectation, trust is a calculation about the probable behavior of others. We may return to the model set forth when we first defined pluralistic stagnation. Let us suppose there is some rule of conduct which, if followed generally by the members of a society, will bring considerable benefits to each of them. Although I want those benefits for myself, I will not be willing to follow the rule unless I know that I can trust the others to do the same. Otherwise, if I alone follow it, while the others do not, the benefits will not be realized, yet I will have borne the cost of complying, while they will get such advantages as their deviation may have brought them. Thus, Peacock and Ricketts' taxpayer, doubtful that others are "playing the game," will also fiddle his income tax, even though he recognizes that the fiscal restraint of paying in full would benefit all, if followed generally. Likewise, the trade unionist who (as he informs the pollster) recognizes the benefit to himself from an incomes policy will tend to deviate from its provisions if he thinks other workers are trying to steal a march on him. In short, if people are to act together, even for gains which may be purely individual, they have to have reason to count on one another.

Yet trust in this sense of calculation about the behavior of others is not alone sufficient to enable people to count on one another. For if the individual is aiming at nothing but the gain to himself, he will be tempted to act as the "free rider" who gets some advantage for himself by not complying, while others are so acting as to realize the benefits for all. If trust as expectation is to bear fruit in common action, it must be reinforced by trust as a normative commitment.[1] Besides his calculations, the individual has also to be motivated by some feeling of "ought" (at least equal to the "free rider" temptation) which inclines him to comply with the common rule for its own sake.

This normative commitment, this feeling of "ought," has a two-fold character. It is a feeling that the common rule of conduct is legitimate in a substantive sense. The tax system, for instance, is felt to be not too outrageously unfair; the scheme of wage differentials is seen as a reasonably equitable balance. Hardly separable from this belief in substantive legitimacy is the acceptance of the common rule as legitimate in the procedural sense. In real life such rules normally issue from a fairly complex process of formulation. If the members of the relevant public—union, firm, party, or nation—feel that the process was normatively acceptable, they will have further cause to conform to the rule produced by it. Legitimacy in both senses, substantive and procedural, strengthens the capacity of common rules to win the consent of the members of the group for which they were designed.

"Political distrust," in Vivien Hart's analysis, is the "perception of a discrepancy between the ideals and realities of the political process."[2] Political trust, conversely, is the perceived correspondence between the way public choices are made and the normative standards prevailing among that public. These normative standards are variables that change with the developing political culture of a country; hence, the standards of trust of one age may at a later date meet

1. I owe the observation developed in this paragraph to Howard Margolis. He starts from the fact that conventional public choice theory cannot account for the existence of public goods, since it assumes that the individual acts only for purely individual gains. In opposition to this premise, Margolis argues that in fact the individual may also act for gains to others (and not to himself), even though this act may impose costs on him. What I have termed "trust as a normative commitment" is an example of such action for the common good. For Margolis's original and subtle argument, see his *Selfishness, Altruism and Rationality* (New York, 1982).

2. Hart, *op. cit.*, p. xi.

with distrust. "The medieval peasant or the deferential working class conservative in Britain," writes Hart, "had low expectancies of control—they were not distrustful because their political beliefs endorsed this humble position."[3] Deference and the sentiments associated with it in the civic culture constituted a powerful bond of trust within the polity and its decision-making components. The collapse of deference reduced the capacity of these agencies to aggregate preferences in broad views of the common interest and so released the self-destructive Hobbesian struggles of pluralistic stagnation.

The vice of distrust is that it blocks the emergence of inclusive preferences and instead diverts individual and group actors toward narrow choices which in the end frustrate the very interests being pursued. The virtue of trust is that it opens up the possibility of options for collective action embracing a wide spectrum of preferences. Trust depends upon belief in the legitimacy and effectiveness of the mechanism of public choice. Does our review of British politics during the past two decades suggest how trust might be restored? What are the probable futures that emerge from our look backward?

Probable Futures

The probable futures are the main patterns of the recent past. Looking back over these pages, I detect five. Two are collectivist: Toryism and socialism. Three are postcollectivist: neoliberalism, neosocialism and neoradicalism.

Toryism should never be underestimated. This phoenix of modern Western politics has repeatedly emerged from the ashes of revolution and reform. Today Tory collectivism lives on, not only in the admiration of Ian Gilmour for the paternalistic statecraft of Harold Macmillan, but also in the programs and institutions of the regime that Macmillan helped to create. In the light of enduring Tory values one can imagine how these patterns might survive and develop. The teleology would seem to be toward a corporatist economy managed by a technocratic elite, moderated by the traditional controls of party government and parliamentary democracy. Likewise building on the centralized, bureaucratic state, a Bevanite version of socialism would

3. *ibid.*, p. 28.

tend toward a planned economy with egalitarian social programs enjoying the support of a coherent trade union movement and a mass party of "workers by hand and brain."

Neither of these collectivist futures can be ruled out. Each has an extensive presence now which will not quickly vanish. The cloud over their future development is the same for both: they suffer from the contradictions of collectivism. Insofar as deference has collapsed, class has decomposed, and pluralism has paralyzed public choice, both the Tory and the socialist versions of collectivism have a dubious future. Even if one supposes that they adapt their economic policies to the lessons of the 1970s, the political difficulties would remain.

The other probable futures do face up to the political problem. Each has a strategy for escaping from the disorder that has afflicted the system of public choice. The neoliberals would seek to move very substantially the burdens of social choice from government and politics to the market. By reducing the number and complexity of questions that government has to decide, they could hope to enhance the coherence and legitimacy of its decisions. The neosocialists and neoradicals, on the other hand, would leave these tasks in the public sector, and would try by participatory reforms to revive the power of the political system to mobilize consent.

Since we have already considered the other options, Mrs. Thatcher's current effort deserves more extended treatment.

"Attempting to do too much, politicians have failed to do those things which *should* be done," read the Conservative manifesto in 1979, echoing in almost the same words the message of the white paper of 1970 that "government has been attempting too much" with which Edward Heath launched the first neoliberal effort.[4] Mrs. Thatcher made control of the money supply a primary goal, but otherwise her program resembled Mr. Heath's: lower taxes, less government spending, a reduced budget deficit, and withdrawal from intervention in the economy. As a departure from the surviving economic and social policies of the collectivist consensus, this strategy represented a "drastic move." In light of that goal, its success should be judged by whether inflation has been contained, economic growth

4. The Reorganisation of Central Government, Cmnd. 4506. par. 2.

resumed, and a reasonable level of employment maintained.

After rather more than two years, the economic results were dismal. By the summer of 1981, inflation, which had soared during the first months of the Thatcher administration, had finally fallen, but seemed stuck in double figures at about the level the Conservatives had inherited from Labour. Industrial production, far from recovering, had declined to an even lower level than it had been in the terrible year 1975. As the economy sagged, bankruptcies rose steeply and unemployment reached 2.94 million, or 10.9 percent of the labor force. This was twice what it had been when the Conservatives took office and approached the levels of the Great Depression of interwar years.

The economic strategy itself was very much to blame. The decision in 1979 to raise interest rates to record levels in order to fight inflation had added immensely to the costs of servicing the public debt and had depressed economic activity. Spending cuts in one area had the side effect of forcing up spending in other areas. The economic decline brought on by government policies forced up payments to the unemployed and eliminated the taxes that they would normally have paid. Similarly, public and private industry, hard hit by the slump, absorbed enormous increases in public lending and other support. Contrary to a fundamental goal, therefore, public expenditure did not fall, but as a proportion of gross domestic product rose from 11.5 percent to 11.5 percent in two years, a jump twice as large as that achieved throughout the whole five years of the previous Labour Government.[5]

Our concern, however, is with the political aspect of these economic failures: specifically, whether the Thatcher Government was able to cope with those "resistances" which Michael Stewart feels have prevented any lasting "drastic move" by British Governments over the past ten or fifteen years. Mrs. Thatcher herself insisted that "the lady's not for turning" and continued to fight for her antiinflation policy despite heavy economic, social, and political costs. Yet if we compare her performance with her original strategy, we see that with regard to most of its commitments the Government had executed not one but several U-turns. In a real sense, she had not

5. Gavyn Davies and David Piachaud, "Why Public Spending has Gone Through the Roof," *Times* (London) 8 July, 1981, p. 16.

been able to carry out that strategy, not only because of its internal
flaws, but also because of forces of resistance that can only be termed
political. These operated in her cabinet, the Whitehall machine, the
economy, and indeed the lower depths of British society which
exploded in the ugly riots of 1981.

Consider the crucial question of public spending. Repeatedly,
ministers in charge of the spending departments successfully resisted
in cabinet the efforts of the prime minister to curb their demands.
For some—whom Mrs. Thatcher christened "wets"[6]—this resistance reflected coolness toward neoliberalism itself, as we might
expect from adherents of the Tory tradition. We cannot believe,
however, that any ministers took office intending to repudiate their
firm and repeated election pledges to cut spending and reduce the
budget deficit. Obviously, this was not the case with Sir Keith Joseph,
who as secretary of state for industry proved to be the greatest over-
spender of all as he poured money into public enterprise in the form
of British Steel and British Leyland.

If we are to understand the collective action of Thatcher's ministers, we must consider not only their political attitudes but also the
situation in which they made their decisions. Reports of their behavior—and from this disunited and leaky cabinet they have been
numerous and circumstantial—remind us again of the centrifugal
pluralism of ministerial decision-making, as portrayed by inside
diarists such as Richard Crossman. Typically, the individual minister
is connected by a complex linkage with his department and its powerful dependents in the public and private sector. In the cabinet he
confronts other ministers similarly urging their valid claims to public
succor, not to say largesse. It was in response to "individual and
collective pressure," concluded the *Economist* in the spring of 1981,
that the Thatcher cabinet allowed spending and borrowing to rise,
the value of social benefits to be maintained, local councils to raise
rates, nationalized industries to be fed with loans and grants, with
the overall and unintended result that this neoliberal government
"spent countercyclically with greater munificence than any since the
war, including Labour Ones."[7]

6. "Wet" is a term used in public schools to refer to boys who shrink from rough
games, such as football.
7. *Economist,* 21 March 1981, p. 11.

The social depths from which such pressures could erupt were revealed by the riots that suddenly burst forth in the summer of 1981. Beginning in Liverpool early in July and sweeping through thirty cities and towns, arson, looting, and physical assaults caused $50 million worth of damage, injured at least 700 police officers and led to the arrest of more than 2,000 people. The blow to Britain's self-esteem was shattering. That ancient image of social peace and civility mirrored in Lowell's remark about Britain as a country of "law and order" and "contentment of the people" had already been clouded in recent years by a rising crime rate and urban disturbances. But nothing remotely on this scale had taken place for generations. "To Think This Is England!" exclaimed one headline.

Theories to explain this disaster proliferated in an intense public debate. It is hard to believe that unemployment, which in Liverpool, for instance, had reached nearly 40 percent, did not contribute powerfully. Yet, as Mrs. Thatcher was quick to point out, Britain had had higher unemployment for a far longer time during the interwar years, but saw no such outbreaks. Race was a new factor that was frequently brought forward as an explanation. In postwar Britain the number of black and brown people from Commonwealth countries had greatly increased, large concentrations forming in certain urban areas. From the Notting Hill Gate riots of 1958, confrontations between white and nonwhite groups had flared up from time to time. But the mobs of 1981 often included far more white than black and brown faces. Moreover, as one scans the reports of what the participants themselves said, their motivation was rarely racial. Nor indeed did unemployment and material deprivation figure largely in their complaints. The principal refrain was hostility to the police and the violence itself often took the form of pitched battles between rioters and the police.

No one can speak with confidence of the causes of these outbreaks. Nor can one say with precision how much justice there is in the complaints against the police. A good deal of inquiry, public and private, is going forward which may produce answers. For our analysis, however, the important fact is the break in popular attitudes marked by such massive hostility. Traditionally, the British police have enjoyed exceptional authority among all classes, as exemplified in their practice of carrying no firearms. In their original study Almond and Verba found that the British police occupied a pinnacle of respect, as compared with the forces of the other nations studied.[8]

From the early 1960s, however, criticism of the police increased. One response was the Police Act of 1978 which set up a board to provide an independent review of action taken as a result of complaints from the public. By the end of the decade, however, "there was disturbing evidence that the public confidence in the police had declined," especially among ethnic minorities.[9] It should be no surprise to learn that the crisis of authority which has undermined the civic culture in more exalted spheres is also affecting the most elemental relations of state power and the citizen.

The Political Task Ahead

The failure of Mrs. Thatcher's effort to mobilize consent for many of her principal measures, even within the leading echelons of the government and the economy, casts doubt on the chances of the neoliberal strategy to dominate the future. For the political task of that strategy is not simply to persist in a deflationary policy against all pressures. That could merely postpone and prepare the U-turn taken by a successor government. Nor is the political task of neoliberalism merely to win reelection for Mrs. Thatcher. It is rather to create a wide and sustained basis in public opinion for the neoliberal goal. That goal is a system of social choice which has been shifted markedly from public choice to market choice. But that goal itself must be achieved by a process of public choice which mobilizes for it a wide and lasting consent. This neoliberal option is still a possible future, but the political record of Mrs. Thatcher's Government during its first two years does not enhance the probabilities.

This political critique of neoliberalism also says something about

8. *The Civic Culture*, p. 109.

9. Max Beloff and Gillian Peele, *The Government of the United Kingdom: Political Authority in a Changing Society* (New York, 1980), p. 325. An *Observer*/National Opinion Polls survey made in October 1981 showed marked erosion of public confidence in the police, especially among the young. Only 45 percent of respondents said they had "a great deal of confidence" in the police, a figure that dropped to 27 percent among 18- to 24-year-olds. Twenty years earlier a similar survey had found that 83 percent of the public felt "great respect" for the police. *Observer*, 15 Nov. 1981, p. 1.

the chances of neosocialism. I have used that term to identify the new outlook that arose with the New Left in the 1960s and spread in the Labour party in the 1970s, its principal advocate being Tony Benn. For a sketch of the future it promises, we have consulted the 1976 party program and the recent speeches of Benn. Egalitarian in the socialist tradition, neosocialism departs sharply from Bevanite collectivism in its thrust toward a radical decentralization and democratization of the economy.

For the neosocialists as for the neoliberals, the task is not simply to win an election based on such promises. It is rather to mobilize a lasting consent in the major sectors of society. This consent must be wide and deep enough to enable such a Government to embody its promises in institutions and programs and sufficiently durable to protect them against reversal by an opposition at a future election. In short, political success would mean the establishment of a new consensus shifting the distribution of opinion radically and lastingly toward the neosocialist left. One can imagine some unprecedented crisis that might bring about this transformation. As we have observed, however, the fragmentation of the Labour left and the weakness of the political instruments it is constructing make it unlikely that the massive mobilization of consent for such a shift could be achieved.

The neoradicals include the Social Democrats and the Liberals and quite possibly a fair number who still call themselves Conservatives or Labourites. As we have seen, in economic and social policy they eschew a "drastic move" from the middle ground marked out by the U-turns of the big parties, taking their stand to the left of its center. In terms of my analysis this is to say that they accept an up-dated version of the consensus brought into existence by the system of party government that dominated public choice in the postwar years. Even more important, the neoradicals have adapted to the contradictions that have undermined that mechanism of public choice. They recognize and embody the revolution in political culture which has fatally weakened the old hierarchies and solidarities which formerly supported that mechanism. Thanks to these attitudes toward both policy and politics, their attempt to mobilize consent runs closer to the grain of political reality than the attempts of their rivals.

They confront a formidable task. The radical tradition from which they draw their strength has deep roots in British history. It has been the enemy of deference ever since the Cromwellian Regicides, in Carlyle's words, "did in effect strike a damp like death through the heart of Flunkyism universally in the world." But can that tradition muster the constructive power to make the British polity again an effective mechanism of social choice?

Index

Adorno, T. W., 109
Almond, Gabriel A., 1, 2, 6n, 112, 114, 115, 217–18
Alt, James, 39n, 46, 54, 81n, 114–45
Annan, Noel, 25n
Aron, Raymond, 134, 151
Arrow, Kenneth, 108n
Attlee government, 6, 7, 13
Authority, respect for: as tenet of Conservative party, 12; undermined by new populism, 4, 163; undermined in unions, 50, 55, 152–55, 165; needed for mobilization of consent, 108; its basis in deference, 114; undermined by romanticism, 128; undermined in Labour party, 133, 162–65; undermined in Parliament, 191–93; and the decline of police authority, 217–18; see also Deference; Hierarchy; Legitimacy

Babbit, Irving, 127
Bagehot, Walter, 113, 123
Baldwin, Stanley, 44
Balogh, Thomas, 51, 152
Beatles, 137–43
Beckett, Alan, 140
Beloff, Max, 218n
Benefits scramble, 30–47; defined, 30–31; fueled by party competi-

tion, 31–32, 39–40, 41; expanded by bureaucratic "repercussion," 33–34; the contribution of technocratic influence, 34; its scope, 35–37, 39–40; its basis in hubristic Keynesianism, 37–39, 42; fueled by voter expectations, 39–40, 43; and the dilemma of ministerial control, 42–45
Benn, A. W. (Tony), 15; and the subsidy scramble, 69, 70; his populist ideology, 156, 158–60; compared to Bevan, 158–62, 206; his proposed Labour party reforms, 162–63
Bevan, Aneurin: and Labour's Old Left, 32, 131, 158, 162, 163; compared to Benn, 156, 158–62
Beveridge, William, 11, 195
Bevin, Ernest, 52
Bićat, Anthony, 137n, 140–42
Birch, Anthony, 186
Blackburn, Robin, 151n
Bogdanor, Vernon, 137n
Bornstein, Stephen, 95–96
Bradley, Ian, 35
British political system: nonpolitical influences on, 3; its transformation from mastery to drift, 1–2; evaluation of, xi–xv, 1, 5–6
Brittan, Samuel, 43
Brock, George, 203n
Brown, Norman O., 136, 137

221